PRAISE FOR
THE BEER DRINKER'S GUIDE TO GOD

"This book is full of enough humor and heart to captivate even nonreaders. Everyone who picks it up will find it nearly impossible to put down. Father Bill's candid self-evaluation of his life and relationship with God are a pleasure to read and provide a great deal of food (or in this case, drink) for thought."

—Debbie Viguie, *New York Times* bestselling author of the Wicked series

"The well-schooled theologian or the purveyor of spirits will both savor *The Beer Drinker's Guide to God.*"

—Rt. Rev. C. Andrew Doyle, author of *Unabashedly Episcopalian* and Bishop of the Episcopal Diocese of Texas

"Bill Miller gives religion a good name. His book had me laughing out loud in parts and highlighting other sections for later reference. Buy this book, read it, then toast to spiritual transformation."

—Vince Poscente, *New York Times* bestselling author of *The Age of Speed*

"You may have had the experience of reading the book you were always hoping to write. This is especially tough when the one you are reading is better than anything you could have done. That is my experience with *The Beer Drinker's Guide to God.*"

—The Rt. Rev. Gregory H. Rickel Bishop of Olympia

"In *The Beer Drinker's Guide to God*, Father Bill Miller writes with eloquence and great humor—two qualities missing in much of Christian writing today—to remind us that Christianity is a religion of joy, celebration, and love. Father Miller's sermons are crafted like parables, and so is this wonderful, joyous, profound, inspiring, wise, and deeply funny book, which strikes the perfect note and doesn't miss a beat."

—William Broyles, screenwriter on the films *Cast Away, Apollo 13*, and *The Polar Express*

THE
BEER DRINKER'S GUIDE TO
God

The Whole and Holy Truth About
Lager, Loving, and Living

· WILLIAM B. MILLER ·

HOWARD BOOKS
A DIVISION OF SIMON & SCHUSTER, INC.
NEW YORK   NASHVILLE   LONDON   TORONTO   SYDNEY   NEW DELHI

Howard Books
A Division of Simon & Schuster, Inc.
1230 Avenue of the Americas
New York, NY 10020

First Howard Books trade paperback edition May 2014

HOWARD and colophon are trademarks of Simon & Schuster, Inc.

For information about special discounts for bulk purchases, please contact Simon &
Schuster Special Sales at 1-866-506-1949 or business@simonandschuster.com.

The Simon & Schuster Speakers Bureau can bring authors to your live event. For more
information or to book an event contact the Simon & Schuster Speakers Bureau at
1-866-248-3049 or visit our website at www.simonspeakers.com.

Interior design by Jaime Putorti

Manufactured in the United States of America

10 9 8 7 6 5 4 3 2 1

Library of Congress Cataloging-in-Publication Data is available.

ISBN 978-1-4767-3864-2
ISBN 978-1-4767-3868-0 (ebook)

Certain names and identifying characteristics have been changed.

For the bands, bartenders, dancers,

drinkers, investors, and partners

who made Padre's possible,

especially Doug, Paige, and David.

CONTENTS

PART 3

Song

"I should like a great lake of finest ale for the King of kings."

—ST. BRIDGET OF KILDARE

THE
BEER
DRINKER'S
GUIDE TO
God

FIRST IMPRESSION, PRELUDE, AND APERITIF

If one desires truth, tell of life as we experience it ourselves.

—VINCENT VAN GOGH, ARTIST, CLERGYMAN

I am not a Christian artist. I am an artist who is a Christian.

—JOHNNY CASH, ARTIST, CHRISTIAN

*I*n the movie *Walk the Line,* a young Johnny Cash asks his older brother Jack, who aspires to be a preacher, why he knows so many stories from the Bible. Jack tells little J.R., "If you want to help people, you've got to know which stories to tell them."

What follows are a few stories that I live to tell. I can tell of life only as I have experienced God's ongoing revelation for myself. Since God is not finished, I reserve the right to be wrong and the right to change my mind. Otherwise, I'm not sure that I can change anything, or that God can change me.

Many of my stories involve beer or some other high-octane beverage. And all of them reveal the presence of a more holy spirit.

This may sound unbelievable to a teetotaler who cannot imagine a "beer with Jesus," but people of Christian faith actually come from a long line of beverage aficionados. The Psalmist consistently celebrates God's gift of drink, and the "fruit of the vine" has become a most potent symbol of the presence of Christ in the holiest of sacraments. In his first miracle at a wedding reception in Cana, Jesus made his momma proud by turning water into wine. Had he been Messiah in Texas or Hawaii rather than Palestine, I'm sure he would have turned it into beer! The Apostle Paul admonished the young disciple Timothy that whenever church people were about to wear out his last nerve he should sip a little wine and all would be well—advice that I follow like a fundamentalist to this day. Some church historians insist that it was St. Patrick or some other Celtic saint who invented the distilling process for whiskey. And the best beer in the world is still brewed in Trappist monasteries in Europe by holy, and whole, men of true faith—and great taste!

Even beyond theological traditions and the spiritual insights offered by those who imbibe, I believe that beer can solve many of the most difficult ethical dilemmas of our time. In matters of discernment, in trying to decide if a person is righteous or whether they may be misguided, I suggest the simple and enlightening Beer Test. That is, if the person in question is one with whom you would like to share a beer, that individual must not be far from the Kingdom of God. And if the person offers to pick up the tab, you know that the Holier Spirit abides within. However, if the subject of inquiry is not one with whom you'd like have a drink, this lost soul does not speak for God. If there is not a desire to open a tap, then the other should shut his trap. Most of the time, this simple test will reveal a more profound truth—about truth.

As I survey the spiritual and religious landscape, I see three great heresies that have emerged:

1. Religious truth does not contain the whole truth.

2. God is not funny.

3. The spiritual life is a solo pursuit.

A heresy is simply half the truth parading as the whole, and a lot of what is advocated for on behalf of the Higher Power these days seems to be half-truth, not to mention half-cocked, if not half-assed. The more beer I consume, the more emboldened I am to challenge these half-truths.

First, for better or worse, I have tried to be honest, to tell the truth about God's presence and participation in the whole of life, including the parts other religious writers usually leave out. My hope is to keep it real, acknowledging that I am not a "Christian storyteller" as much as I am a storyteller who is a Christian. Even that statement is a stretch. When those who equate salvation with categorical certitude ask me if I've been saved, I admit, "not yet." When they ask if I am a Christian, I reply, "still working on it." And when they demand to know if I am "born again," I often tell them, "And again. And again. And again."

In telling the truth, I acknowledge that there will be occasions when my tongue is planted in my cheek, my foot is lodged in my mouth, and perhaps my head has entered into that realm of my anatomy where the sun does not shine. But even in making fun and having fun, I am paying attention, called to be a keen observer of life and to notice the revelation that never fails to unfold right before my eyes.

Every once in a while someone will label my truthful observations with the pejorative term *ogling*. I would suggest that there is an equally pejorative term for the person who does *not* notice, appreciate, and even focus intently upon the revelation of truth and beauty in all of its forms, especially the human form. That word is *dead*. To notice is to live. To appreciate is to live well. As St. Irenaeus said centuries ago, "The glory of God is the human being fully alive." I choose life. To glorify God is to be engaged and aware, even to ogle in awe at the wonders that God has wrought and brought into our lives.

Second, rarely does a contemporary religious work reveal anything funny about God. We are much too serious in our attempts to understand a God who is far more playful than those who claim to speak on his behalf. The truth is that serial solemnity and spiritual awareness have nothing in common. God is funny. God is the originator of irony, the progenitor of the punch line, the creator of comedy. You have to laugh— that is, if you are going to get God. As my favorite Jewish country-western singer and Texas gubernatorial candidate Kinky Friedman has said, "Humor has a lot to do with truth." I would add "and even more to do with God."

Third, we have compartmentalized our lives into neat, un-related categories and separated ourselves from each other in pursuit of the spiritual. But to become what God has ordained is to connect with all that God has created in the context of community.

Without my family of faith, I would be half the Christian, half the human, half the priest that I am today. Fellow Chris-tians may drive me crazy on occasion, but they also keep me honest, hold me accountable, and expand my knowledge. A parade and procession of pilgrims—praying, working, sharing, serving, learning, loving, growing, and giving together—keep me consistent, on track, and in the game. There is no such thing as lone-ranger spirituality. This is one game you cannot play by yourself. If you choose to do so, you will ultimately lose, or at least lose out.

Unfortunately, many of us are not only disconnected from our fellow travelers, we are far removed from life itself. We have dichotomized the divine and erected artificial barriers between complementary, interconnected, and overlapping parts of the whole. We have driven unnecessary wedges between spirituality and service, politics and piety, worship and work. We have drawn lines in the sand between the sacred and the secular, the profound and the profane. We have opted for either the baptismal font or the watering hole, for approaching the altar rail or bellying up to the bar. We assume we have to distill out the goofy to reveal what is godly. God makes no distinctions. God made it all, blesses it all, and uses it all to further God's loving purposes in the world.

Such separations and distinctions are sometimes even comical. I have seen people get particularly worked up over what they perceive to be styles of music that are set apart. Take for example that most patriotic anthem, "The Star-Spangled Banner." Do you know the source of that tune during which you place your hand over your heart, stand at attention, and salute the flag? It is an old English drinking song! Why not? And what about that most staid and standard good Christian hymn, "A Mighty Fortress Is Our God"? That melody was originally a German drinking song! Martin Luther may, in fact, be rolling over in his grave when we admit such origins, but only so that he might order another beer!

To help people, you have to know what stories to tell them, what songs to sing them, and even what beers to buy them. God works in all of these for good, with those who tell the truth, get the joke, and embrace the holy whole. There's another, even more profound spiritual image that motivates me in my quest to quench this deepest of desires. Just before Jesus acknowledged on the cross that he had actually accomplished the difficult task to which he had been called, right before he said, "It is finished," Jesus said something no one was expecting. He said simply, "I am thirsty." Where did that come from and what did he mean? As in all the expressions of truth in this life, there is more than one meaning in what Jesus said. On one level, here was a dying man attempting to catch his breath and desperately needed a drink. He was given a sponge on a stick dipped in inferior wine, and perhaps that helped him in some way. Maybe he was reminding us of his humanity and his human needs. But was that all he meant? I don't think so. I think Jesus was using a powerful image to describe his deepest desire and longing, a longing that offers us a kind of life for which we can eventually look back and say—mission accomplished. Indeed, it is *finished*. Although I may die, at least I know that I've lived. Jesus thirsted for life. He thirsted for relationship. He thirsted for love. He thirsted for the One who made him and sent him. He even thirsted for you and for me. This kind of thirst cannot be quenched by anything other than the most powerful spirit—far more potent than anything 200 proof.

—

Other than my ongoing desire to thirst for such "proof" with a kind of holistic passion that Jesus exhibited, and my deeply profound knowledge of grain-based beverages, who am I to write this book? Or, as my parishioners and exes are fond of putting it: *Just who the hell do you think you are?!*

I am a priest who owns a bar. I suppose such a rare vocational combination does qualify me to express some thoughts on the subject. It also drives me to drink on occasion.

I somehow escaped religious fundamentalism on my way to purgatory and ended up in seminary in Chicago. I've now been a priest for a while. I was a youth minister and then ordained at the tony Church of St. John the Divine in the fashionable River Oaks neighborhood of Houston about twenty years ago. My job interview there took place in the fanciest country club in town, where the sommelier was the beneficiary of the senior pastor's entertainment account. Those were five fun years that ended with three of my youth group kids choosing unwisely to follow me into the ranks of the ordained clergy. Their parents still hate me, I'm sure.

After Houston, I became the priest of a predominantly African-American parish, St. James, in funky Austin, but in a neighborhood that was more urban funk than hippie funky. My job interview took place in a French bistro with the bishop footing a wine bill that I am sure he is still paying off. In Austin I briefly pursued a career as an actor and a model. I made enough money doing those two things to feed a family of cats. And I'm talking fairly *large* cats here. I kept my day job but started writing and collaborating with creative people on out-of-the-box projects—like jazz festivals in churches, for example. I must have been a bass player in a previous life, or a bartender.

After St. James I thought I'd head to New York or Los Angeles, but they don't serve Lone Star, St. Arnold Ale, or Shiner Bock there, so I headed back to my hometown and became the priest of historic Trinity Church near downtown Houston. I can't remember where that job interview took place but I do remember that margaritas were involved. God bless Texas.

About seven years ago I was called to go and suffer for Jesus in Hawaii ("Here am I, Lord, send me—*please*!"). I have been the priest at St. Michael's Church on the island of Kauai for more than seven years. My job interview took place at the home of the man who made the best mai tais on the island. Tell *me* there is no God!

I've been a priest for over twenty years. I've been a bar owner for four. I had a vision of owning a bar for a long time, especially whenever the bishop would call me into his office and ask me, *"Just who the hell do you think you are?!"*

I don't know exactly where this vision originated. I love music, stiff drinks, and soft people. I like places where one can move and groove and dance. I enjoy the occasional uninhibited expression of the self. I also realize that there can be abuses of alcohol and various addictive behaviors, and those are never good things. But like all good things that the Creator has entrusted to each of us—such as work, sex, food, and even religion—different people have different struggles. These things can be inherently good as long as we don't abuse them. We shouldn't necessarily throw the beer out with the baptismal water.

So my business partners (mostly Episcopalians and musicians) found a hundred-year-old adobe building that had been a funeral home in the very cool West Texas high desert arts town of Marfa. Marfa was recently called, on a *60 Minutes* episode, the "Capital of Quirkiness," and it most assuredly is. Since this whole thing was my idea, my business partners let me name the bar Padre's.

It's been a wild ride, with some memorable moments and interesting characters. In that way, being a bar owner is not unlike being a parish priest. There are lots of similarities, actually: great music, joyful movement, an atmosphere of acceptance, potent sacramental beverages, an occasional brawl, all mixed in with moments of transcendence, confession, penitence, love, and loss.

I can tell you this: if you want to get rich, don't open a bar in a tiny town in the high desert of West Texas. It's not about the money. It's about the adventure. It's about bringing people together and even, on some level, bringing people into an awareness of the good gifts of a loving God. We've nearly gone broke with Padre's in just four years of operation. But come to think of it, I'm not exactly cashing in with my priestly calling, either.

The truth is that I am richer because I'm a priest. And I am richer for owning a bar. And grateful. And still thirsty. And hope I will be until the day I can declare that it is finished, that my particular and unique work on earth is done.

In the "unfinished" meantime, grab a cold beer and enjoy the stories that follow. I've grouped them into three sections because, well, as unorthodox as I try to be, my Trinitarian tendencies still get the best of me. These three sections represent, in some ways, my three greatest passions in life, my thirst-quenching quest to live life to its fullest. I suppose you could call these three sections Drinking, Dating, and Dancing, or even Laughing, Loving, and Listening. Or perhaps, in keeping with the less than solemn theme that informs the whole, let's just call them Wine, Women, and Song. And that takes us right back to the Bible, that great source of drinking stories.

One of my favorite Sunday school stories is about the teacher who was testing her students on the story of the Prodigal Son. The Sunday school teacher began by asking her students, "Now, children, who was the prodigal son in the Gospel According to St. Luke?"

One little boy raised his hand, jumped up, and enthused, "I know! I know! That was the guy who spent half his inheritance on wine, women, and song. And the other half he just wasted!"

We are blessed, having inherited grace upon grace. Let us not waste all that God has so graciously given.

PART ONE

Wine

You cause the grass to grow for the cattle,
and plants for people to use,
to bring forth food from the earth,
and wine to gladden the heart.

—PSALMS 104:14,15A

1

BEER GOGGLES

The beauty of the virtue in doing penance for excess,
Beautiful too that God shall save me.
The beauty of a companion who does not deny me his company,
Beautiful too the drinking horn's society.

—"THE LOVES OF TALIESIN," WELSH, THIRTEENTH CENTURY

*L*ouis "Dynamite" Johnson is the best gay, black, liberal, conservative, antiwar, pro-life, eleventh-grade American history teacher I ever had. In fact, Louis Johnson is the best teacher I ever had.

I will never forget my first day in Johnson's class. As a self-conscious adolescent introvert, I had not intended to draw attention to the debut of my "so geeky it's hip" eyewear. My gigantic, tortoiseshell glasses made me look like a mutant horsefly wearing antique aviator goggles. It never occurred to me that I could be singled out as a living object lesson for the chapter on Charles Lindbergh and American aviation history.

I planned to blend in with my back-row desk, maintaining my eleven-year streak of nonparticipation in class discussion.

However, Johnson ruined my plan by pausing in the midst of a series of inane student responses to a thought-provoking question. Apparently he assumed that, as high school juniors, we might be capable of a deep conviction, critical analysis, or original thought. What Kinky Friedman wrote about American historical figures was also applicable to our student body: "You can lead a politician to water, but you can't make him think!"

Johnson's pedagogical method caught us off guard. We were used to ingesting data and regurgitating it in the form of multiple-choice tests. Our former history teachers, football coaches whose biceps dwarfed their worldview, were uninterested in historical inquiry and their ethos was encapsulated in the adage "The best offense is a good defense." As far as they were concerned, that pretty much summed up the past, present, and future of American influence in the world.

Dynamite took great delight in lobbing explosives into our heretofore unchallenged understanding of the world and America's preeminent place therein. He encouraged us to do independent research so that when we came together in class, we could engage in informed discourse and even debate the merits of various ideas. Johnson wanted us to look at the deeper issues of causality, telling us that the removal of our red, white, and blue–tinted glasses might help us to become better patriots, and a stronger nation.

On that fateful first day of class, our American history teacher grew more exasperated with every inarticulate utterance my classmates made. Finally, Johnson looked right at me and my studious-looking spectacles. Hoping that I was seeing through the lens of illumination, he pointed at my most noticeable accessory. He shouted, as if I might be the great, wise hope, "*You,* the intelligent-looking young man in the back row, what do *you* think?"

I have no idea what came out of my mouth that day. It must have been in English, reasonably articulate, and somewhat morally sound, because I remember Mr. Johnson affirming my brilliant point by pounding his podium with the force of a Baptist preacher. To this day I could swear he gave me an "Amen."

Talk about a setup. From that day forward, I made a concerted effort to live into Louis Johnson's perception of me. Maybe he had seen something that really was there, or maybe he just needed glasses.

Because of his insight, I made some profound discoveries that semester. Prior to Dynamite's influence, I had no idea that there was a large, quiet room on the premises of our school that was filled with books that could be "borrowed" by students. I always assumed that room was the assistant principal's dungeon. Furthermore, there was a lady who lived in that room called Library Ann. She helped you find things that could make you smarter.

As an added bonus, I discovered that girls often hung out there, and they didn't seem to mind guys with geeky glasses as long as there was a brain behind them. It was in that library, early one morning, as I was investigating LBJ's Great Society, that the homecoming queen began to snoop around my table. After hearing a preliminary report on my findings, she proceeded to ask me out on a date. As there is only so much one can learn from books, I was too stupid to say "Yes!"

But something happened to me in Louis Johnson's American history class. I got smart.

I had failed a geometry class the year before. An F brings a GPA to a point of almost no return, but I made so many A's after the "Johnson Mandate" that I was inducted into the National Honor Society just before graduation. What's more, Johnson challenged me to integrate my philosophical and theological convictions into my political and historical worldview. He was the teacher who convinced me that George Bernard Shaw was right: those who cannot change their minds, cannot change anything. I would never look at anything uncritically again, and I would never see the world in the same way.

Just as events in American history were not always black-and-white, issues in Johnson's class were not always clear-cut. During one discussion, no one could provide a reason why we should care about what happened to non-Americans. Johnson turned to me, pointed, and boomed, "Bill!" I boomed right back, "Because they are human beings!" "Because they are human beings" became the class mantra for the rest of the semester. During another discussion, he attempted to help us understand that other cultures, even those we have sometimes labeled "primitive," were also innovative and intelligent. American know-how was not the only knowledge out there. While Johnson was unsuccessfully trying to coax "crossbow" out of us as the invention of Native Americans, I had a momentary relapse and got in touch with my inner idiot. "Flaming arrows," I offered. I must not have been wearing my glasses that day. Johnson seemed to relish pointing out to me that fire had been invented several years prior. I'm sure even Einstein had an off day.

Sometimes the work of challenging accepted attitudes and ideals made us downright uncomfortable. Once, defending the Palestinian cause and criticizing America's unwavering support for Israel, Johnson got a classmate so worked up he stormed out of class, accusing Johnson of being "anti-Semitic." Another time, a majority of students and faculty were outraged when Johnson openly challenged a Vietnam War hero over his interpretation of the rationale and success of the war. "That's just disrespectful," my fellow classmate intoned. Later he would marry an army recruiter. Later still, they both became Lutheran pastors and liberal Democrats. Hey, if you can't change your mind.

I still change my mind, and I still recall that initial explosive force that started to knock the scales from my eyes and open me up to alternative realities. Years later, I still attempt to see myself as "that intelligent-looking young man," although these days I am forced to admit that one out of three ain't bad.

—

There is an optical phenomenon, mostly among males who imbibe, that we have come to call "beer goggles." After the consumption of an indeterminate number of beers, the brew begins to travel directly from the stomach to the brain, then through the optic nerve, filling the vitreous and aqueous humors with material that is funny only to oneself, and perhaps to the eventual focus of the goggles.

As this eye-opening phenomenon develops, the visual axis is completely inverted. The retinal blood vessels become amber-colored and a white foam begins to coat the entire cornea, distorting one's vision, but in a most positive way. The lens of the eye begins to focus intently on a previously undesirable object of affection. Right before one's beer-goggle-covered eyes, this person grows in wisdom, stature, and beauty. Though a temporary condition, the beer goggles may be removed only by a good friend in possession of your car keys. Such lenses also tend to dissipate in the morning light.

As far as I am aware, I have suffered only one serious case of this visual disorder. I was on Sixth Street in Austin, in a very crowded club, when I became incredibly attracted to a striking young woman who was there with her sister. She was obviously seeing her own date through beer goggles, a loser (that is, "not me") upon whom she was far too fixated. Initially unimpressed with her sibling, I downed an entire case of Mexican beer and began to view the sister with a south-of-the-border version of beer goggles called "Cervezavision." Through Cervezavision, I began to see the sister as a virtual twin to the true object of my desire. The sister was not a twin. In fact, not nearly a twin. In fact, according to my wingman for the evening, it is conceivable that she was actually her brother. Still, since my brain was filled with an oxygen-depleting liquid, my "better judgment" decided it was time for a siesta and I made a bold move.

Although I have a friend whose nightlife philosophy can be summarized as "Go ugly early," I have never subscribed to this theory. Fortunately, my good friend and wingman assumed the role of another helpful winged creature, pulled me away from locking lips with the non-twin, and gave me a lecture on optical illusions. Thank God I was not drinking alone.

Once, a normally insightful friend of mine came down with an acute case of this condition. He and I were hanging out at a funky little pub in Hong Kong where I was completely smitten with my exotically beautiful Nepalese server. I was off in my own private Kathmandu when I finally returned to the table and found my friend had somehow made space for two Norwegian women. In fact, he made a lot of space. I have traveled to Norway, and I can attest to the incredibly attractive people in this Nordic wonderland. These specimens, however, were not.

As I gazed upon the Norwegians, the defensive line of the 1986 Super Bowl Champion Chicago Bears came to mind. These ladies made William "Refrigerator" Perry look not only small, but also highly desirable. My friend leaned in to me and said, "Dude, these chicks are hot." I leaned back to him and said, "Dude, these chicks are not. You are now going to get up from this table and follow me back to the hotel. No, you may not have another beer. Trust me on this one. Tomorrow morning you will thank me for this."

And he did.

Another friend with what one might also call "Alternavision" is the Reverend James Douglas Hunter. Jimmy Hunter is an African-American Missionary Baptist pastor in Texas. He is my most stylish friend. His shoes have Italian names and are crafted from the hides of the world's most exotic animals. When he wears his full-length black leather coat, he comes across as smooth as the silk shirt underneath. When we are out on the town together, people often stop and stare at us as if we are famous. Let me rephrase that. When we are out on the town together, people often stop and stare at him as if *he* is famous.

What's really fun about the Reverend Hunter is that if he suspects there might be a Baptist lurking nearby, he will order his margaritas in a coffee cup. Adjacent tables are always astounded that so much caffeine can put a man to sleep.

I met Jimmy Hunter at a funeral in East Austin. I had accepted a call to a predominantly African-American parish

where the local custom was for all ministers who had any relation to any relation of the deceased to participate. This was
not only my first funeral, it was my first public appearance in
the neighborhood. With some trepidation, I walked into the
David Chapel Missionary Baptist Church to participate in
the funeral for someone I did not know, among ministers I
did not know, according to a religious tradition with which I
was completely unfamiliar. They were all wearing ties. I was
wearing a clerical collar. They were all carrying Bibles. I was
carrying my Episcopal Book of Common Prayer. They were
all men of color. I am more pale than ale. They were all professionals when it comes to extemporaneous speaking. I am
an Episcopalian, so I read my prayers verbatim. They've memorized half the Bible. I've read some of it. Their services go on
for days. My services are done in one hour. They mostly don't
drink. I needed a beer.

As soon as I walked in the door, I spotted the reverend. He
was smiling and nodding at me as if he had spotted a long-lost
friend. He walked over and greeted me: "Welcome. We're so
glad you're here." He told me to follow him and do what he
did. I almost sat in his lap, I was so comforted by his presence.
I managed to look pious for two and a half hours, and, as we
began to process out, the senior pastor nudged me and said,
"Pastor, won't you share some scripture?" The prayer book
comes in handy from time to time. After the service, the Reverend Hunter told me that if he hadn't known otherwise, he'd
have sworn I was a Missionary Baptist. He was lying, but in a
nice way. We've been friends ever since.

We've come a long way since that initial nerve-racking encounter. Our time together is now much livelier. We've had a
good-natured, tongue-in-cheek contest going on for many

years as to which one of us is "the Greatest in the Kingdom of God." Our opinions differ on that. We've debated facetiously over the years regarding the superiority of our respective preaching styles, intellectual prowess, spiritual depth, biblical knowledge, congregational growth, teaching ability, motivating force, musical preferences, and impact on the world at large. Each of us is always pointing out how God has most recently revealed his overwhelming preference for one at the expense of the other. I was ahead in the count and just couldn't leave well enough alone.

One evening I was feeling filled with the Holy Spirit as our conversation turned toward a hero to both of us: the Reverend Dr. Martin Luther King Jr. We admired King's ability to integrate theological understanding with decisive and life-changing action. Some people talk the talk. Some people walk the walk. King did both. Despite Dr. King's preoccupation with selfless service as the core of Christian faith, I decided to use him as another stepping-stone on the way to my rightful place at the right hand of God.

"You know, Jimmy," I reasoned, "it is obvious to me that, just as God chose Dr. King to be a great prophet in *his* time, so God has chosen me as the greatest prophet of *our* generation, far greater than *you* anyway. I make this observation because King's birthday, as you know, is January fifteenth. But what you don't know, my dear Reverend Hunter, is that January sixteenth, the very next day, is *my* birthday. It is readily apparent that this is the sign we have been seeking to determine, once and for all, who is greatest among us. When it comes to you and me, my lesser brother, you are Howard Cosell to my Muhammad Ali. *I am the greatest in God's kingdom!*"

The Reverend Hunter looked at me as though shocked and deeply disturbed, as if he had just lost a great and final battle. Then the twinkle in his eye became a knowing if not superior smile.

"Just so I am clear," he began. "You assume that you are the greatest in God's kingdom because the great prophet, Martin Luther King, was born on January fifteenth and you were born on January sixteenth?"

"That is correct, 'O Ye of Smaller Stature,'" I replied.

Nodding his head as if to affirm my logic, he stood up and towered over me, bellowing the prophetic question, "And do you know when my birthday is?" I was about to offer the day after Groundhog Day as a possibility when he thundered forth, as only a surefire Baptist preacher can do, "*December twenty-sixth!*"

Okay, so I am the second greatest in God's kingdom.

As enlightening as that revelatory moment was, the Prophet James was not finished opening my eyes to greater realities. I fondly remember visiting him just after he had accepted a call to a Missionary Baptist Church in Port Arthur, Texas. "It's the silk-stocking congregation," he told me, still in competitive mode even after he had handily won the birthday contest.

Port Arthur is part of the so-called Golden Triangle of Southeast Texas, with the cities of Beaumont and Orange completing the polygon. Neither obtuse nor acute, this triangle is more of the oblique variety. That is, you have to tilt your head a bit to find the proper viewing angle and look a little harder to find the gleam. Over the years, the gold has lost some of its luster. Port Arthur is a town that has endured white flight, polluting petrochemical plants, territorial tension after an influx of Vietnamese shrimp boats, a vacated downtown, corrupt politicians, and economic downturn. But it's still a pretty interesting place. It is no longer the confining and conforming place it was fifty years ago. These days you can take one part Cajun-spiced alligator, mix in some swampy blues and urban hip-hop, throw in a pinch of cowpoke and Texas football, and you get Port Arthur. It is a town that has given the world the painter Robert Rauschenberg, football coach Jimmy Johnson, and the legendary singer Janis Joplin. Driving around the ramshackle streets of Port Arthur, you begin to understand how a little white girl could wail the blues with conviction and how Rauschenberg's *Combines* of trash and found objects made artistic sense, and also why Jimmy Johnson now lives in Miami.

The Reverend Hunter drove me over Rainbow Bridge and eventually to what's left of Pleasure Island. Years ago it resembled Coney Island with a big amusement park and an Olympic-sized swimming pool. Now there are a few lonely sailboats, some scraggly fields, and a crumbling parking lot.

We drove to the top of the bridge to get a view of the city below upon our return. There was a barge or two in the distance, a meandering, all-but-forgotten waterway, and a neighborhood of coastal houses that seemed to be standing on stilts just to be noticed. I was about to say something stupid regarding the depressing ugliness of the landscape when the Reverend Hunter took his hand off the steering wheel and waved it over the scene ahead and below.

"Isn't it beautiful?" he asked. "From up here, it looks just like a postcard."

I looked again. Blinked my eyes. Tilted my head. Refocused my gaze. The water was glistening with the first hint of a setting sun. The houses below were painted the most vibrant colors. The swampland appeared as a patchwork quilt of alligator green and golden brown. And the Reverend Hunter was looking as stylish as ever.

Perhaps that is why they call the prophets seers. They see things most of us miss. They view that which is in front of them through a lens that transforms reality right before their eyes into images of radiance. Mere eyesight becomes rare insight.

I wonder what the world would look like if it didn't require beer goggles to behold such sights, if we no longer saw dimly a distorted reality, but clearly focused on God's great vision for all creation. I wonder what perspective might appear if each day I removed the scales of skepticism from my eyes and looked through the lens of a more loving and appreciative Alternavision.

Dynamite, I'll bet. And beautiful, too.

Too beautiful.

2

BREWED OVER ME
AND DISTILL ME, O LORD

Everybody wants me to go to heaven, but nobody wants me to die.

—RAPPER SCARFACE

Being Irish, he had an abiding sense of tragedy, which sustained
him through temporary periods of joy.

—WILLIAM BUTLER YEATS

There is nothing quite like discerning God's will to ruin an otherwise lovely day.

It was a scene rivaling a panel from the Sistine Chapel ceiling. On my final afternoon in the Holy Land, just before the sun began to set over the Old City of Jerusalem, I climbed toward the top of the Mount of Olives and planted myself under an ancient olive grove. It could have been the very site of the Garden of Gethsemane in Jesus's time.

I would soon be graduating from McCormick Theological Seminary in Chicago. I had spent the last six weeks studying in the Holy Land, at St. George's College in Jerusalem, and when I got back, I would embark on a new life of ministry and service to the real world. But beyond that general sense of calling, I had no clue what I was supposed to do and where I was supposed to do it. My plan was to spend these final hours in a state of peaceful tranquillity and meditative supplication, praying for guidance and an overt revelation of God's plan and purpose for my life.

I prided myself on my openness to God's will for my life. Career-wise, I was utterly available for the Supervising Potter to mold me from a lump of wholly subordinate clay. Whatever career path God had chosen for me, I was ready, willing, and able to heed that call. Well, there were two exceptions, actually: minor details for a God who worked within the context of his subject's particular gifts and interests. Apart from these two quite understandable conditions, I was totally, completely, 100 percent wide open to whatever God had in store.

The first stipulation was about squandering my intellectual prowess on unworthy specimens. In graduate school I had done well academically, which is often what happens when one is too poor to party. Academia can be downright stimulating, even scintillating, for those with no other options. The library became for me what a gentleman's club is to an NBA all-star—a garden of forbidden fruits beckoning the player to "come hither," only in this case seductively whispered in Greek and Hebrew with an occasional Latin phrase thrown in lest I become bored. Fashioning myself a spiritual smarty-pants, I decided that my theological genius would be wasted on adolescents. My brilliant elucidations would be beyond the grasp of a group of not-yet humans who assume transubstantiation can happen at Taco Bell, or that the ultimate sacerdotal paradox occurs when an altar boy farts while lighting Eucharistic candles. While the cheesarito may, in fact, be proof of the Incarnation, I had bigger burritos to enlighten. No youth ministry for this brainiac.

Second, because of my passion for social justice and my commitment to the economically disadvantaged, I recognized that my thoroughly developed conscience would not allow me to serve in a wealthy parish. My particular prophetic passions would be wasted on the well-heeled. I had studied urban ministry extensively, and it is clear from reading urban ministry authorities that poor people are the only city dwellers who deserve our ministerial attention. Beyond that sociological reality, biblically speaking, God has an actual bias toward those with lower incomes. Thus the "haves" could fend for themselves without my noble services.

Other than youth ministry and work with an affluent parish, I was absolutely open to God's will and call upon my life. I couldn't wait to discover the path revealed by the Spirit on the edge of the world's most sacred city.

That afternoon on the Mount of Olives was the most conducive setting to spiritual enlightenment that I could possibly have imagined. The setting sun seemed to set apart the Church of the Holy Sepulchre, illumined for my personal viewing pleasure. The Dome of the Rock was enlivened with a radiating spiritual presence. The ancient city walls seemed to speak of the revelatory power of prayer, the real possibility of discerning one's purpose. Taking in the vast expanse of the place where many souls had been summoned by God for centuries before me, I began to focus on my own soon-to-be-revealed future in the Kingdom that has no end.

I took a deep breath and uttered my first "Dear Lord" when a rock sailed over my head, missing my skull by a centimeter. Not to be deterred by a mere chunk of limestone, I returned to a posture of holy petition. Then a second, larger stone flew within a sound wave of my right ear. "Okay," I thought, "whoever you are, you now have my attention."

I stood up and discovered that I was completely surrounded by a group of Palestinian teenagers, all grinning at me like they were ready to rumble, in a playfully threatening kind of way. I was on holy ground, all right, but it was their holy ground. I had chosen as my place of prayer the local teenage hangout, and they weren't going anywhere. I was, however. They began to remove ancient stones, revealing a stash of party paraphernalia. They were up to no good. My prayers were over, if not answered. I could not believe that God had allowed a group of impious adolescents to ruin my day, not to mention the revelation of my life to come.

God was trying to communicate to me that day, interrupting my plans while surrounding me with teenage troublemakers. The only job I was offered upon my return to the United States was that of youth minister. Not content to reject just one perfectly reasonable demand, the Dear Lord took great delight in making sure that that one job offer was at the wealthiest church in the entire state of Texas! So began my ministry. Interrupted. Surrounded by teenage troublemakers up to no good. Teenagers with trust funds.

It wasn't easy. I had a serious learning curve. At one point I think I killed the existing youth group, which turned out to be exactly what needed to happen. Eventually, over time, too long a time for some, things began to turn around and even flourish beyond our wildest dreams and expectations. Those five years as a youth minister at an affluent parish turned out to be five of the best years of my life.

Those kids taught me more about ministry and life than I had learned from three years hibernating in one of the world's foremost theological libraries. These hormonally challenged adolescents eventually formed, of their own initiative, a group called "Youth for Justice." They intended to tackle the world's problems from a systemic level rather than simply content themselves with service in the name of Christ, although they did that, too, building houses in Appalachia and Mexico and doing a host of good works in the most economically disadvantaged areas of their hometown. In the years to come they would become ordained clergy, teachers, counselors, social workers, pediatricians, attorneys, and musicians. I would hire one of them as my own youth minister in a congregation I later served.

They somehow managed to combine their adolescent worlds with God's ultimate concerns. They once picketed the local Taco Bell because management had removed the cheesarito from the menu. Television news cameras rolled while the group, holding placards that read "Give me the cheesarito or give me death!" chanted "Hell no, we won't go, till we get our cheesarito!" The cheesarito was returned to the menu immediately. These teenagers changed the world in ways none of us had anticipated.

Up there in the Garden of Gethsemane, among a pack of up-to-no-good kids, I first recognized the truth about God's will. One man's caveat may be one God's call. While praying, always duck and cover. The authentic spiritual pilgrimage may require that you walk all the way up a holy mountain, only to haul your ass right back down and still not have a clue where you were, are, or will be.

—

I remember the day I volunteered to work at our local brewery here on the island of Kauai. I wanted to learn about the brewing process, and I figured that the only way to learn about it was to engage in it. Having spent a major part of my life in tasting rooms, I assumed that I was well prepared for whatever I might find on the other side of the tap. Besides, I had already set a world record for distillery tours in Scotland by an ordained person, and I recalled how much I had thoroughly enjoyed learning about malting, milling, mashing, mixing, and maturation, a process that yielded the descriptive acronym MMMMM.

I also knew that many of the steps in the Scotch distilling process are the same as those in the beer brewing process, only more intense, which is why you end up with a smaller batch of liquid.

But most important, I remembered that each tour always ended with the liquid fruit of someone else's labor; and I figured, if a mere tour ended with a small sample, an actual workday would most assuredly conclude with a keg. I imagined myself skipping around the brewery all day, lifting only a right palm in a circular motion under my left nostril, breathing in a sacred scent, saying clever things like "You know I'm not happy if it's too hoppy," sampling the goods, several times just to be sure, and exclaiming to all passersby, "Don't bother me; I am *working* right now."

My real motivation for volunteering was the inherent romance of brewing. I figured guys who could use a line like "I distill single-malt Scotch" or "I brew beer" when asked "So, what do you do?" would garner the same level of respect as those who answered, "I am a spy for the United Nations," or "I am the Sultan of Brunei," or "I work for God." Plus, I assumed the only elbow grease I'd have to expend would be to raise a bottle toward my mouth.

Instead, my assumptions and attitudes got distilled, if not destroyed. I discovered that the more halfhearted the brewing, the more half hearty the beer, that there is a correlation between deluded and diluted. I worked my ass off, as well as several pounds of beer belly, and tasted nothing but my own sweat. I should have remembered that what is true in baptism is true in brewing—you've got to be washed up and reborn before you can belly up to the altar and put your lips on the chalice—or the bottle.

Filling my seventh giant plastic barrel with spent grain that would be recycled as feed for Kauai's most stress-free farm animals, I realized I had grossly miscalculated the work-to-pleasure ratio in the brewing process. Just the preparatory work of cleaning the equipment was grueling. I doubt that the average hospital operating room is so well sanitized.

My guide and taskmaster, Matt, informed me that about 75 percent of his total work time is spent "cleaning, sanitizing, and purifying" and that the brewing process always begins with the all-important very first step: "Give everything a good flush."

I noted over the course of the day that transformation occurs in ways that are not always pretty and never easy. Raw materials get broken down, heated, and mixed up. Grain gets toasted. Seeds get cracked, but "just enough so that they don't turn to mush." The barley gets baptized in a mash tun, where the protective husks get separated from the liquid. The protective husks, if they hang on, can turn things bitter. That preliminary beer liquid is called wort, not a very romantic term. Spice gets added by way of hops. Then someone turns up the heat. In a distillery, it gets so hot the liquid changes form and is then recaptured in a still. Here at the brewery, the wort gets spurged as hot water removes any lingering sugar. The fermentation tanks are sanitized yet again. Then there is constant maintenance and meticulous measuring.

Matt tells me that it's not all science, that there is still some art to the process. And that there is a lot of "testing" that goes along with it. Throw in some good old-fashioned trial and error and you might end up with something drinkable.

Whether we are brewing, distilling, discerning, or converting, change is part of the process. Things get crushed and broken down, purified and cleansed, heated and cooled, mixed and tested, infused and fermented. There may be some science, but there is also art. Trial and error is unavoidable. You can drink to the power of the process, but not till the hard work of transformation is done.

—

Leonard Cohen sings, "There is a crack in everything. That's how the light gets in." Perhaps that's what God was trying to tell me when I headed back down that holy mountain that day. Perhaps it was only after my prayer plans were not all they were cracked up to be that the Spirit could crack them open to *become* God's plan, in God's time. Jesus said, "Unless a grain of wheat falls into the earth and dies, it remains a single grain, but if it dies, it bears much fruit."

Maybe that's the point of giving up our preconceived plans and purposes, even allowing them to die, so that the fruit of God's labors might be revealed. Unless we're willing to let go of what we thought best, we cannot possess what God only knows is best. As we open up and offer ourselves completely to the Brewmaster, the Spirit transforms us into something different and more powerful. We are washed, crushed, and changed into something we had never foreseen or anticipated. Our best-laid plans are no substitute for those of a God who broods over us until a new creation is hatched. And in the process our most carefully protected shells get shattered. But we emerge reborn, better than we were before.

Much that is written for the spiritual seeker these days appeals to those who want to go to heaven, but don't want to die; for those who want to taste the fruits of someone else's labors, but don't want to plant, pick, or harvest; for those who show up at the tasting room to sample the goods, but wouldn't dare be distilled or brewed over themselves.

But there can be no nightclubs without distilleries. There can be no bars without breweries. There are tourists who expect to be told precisely where to go, but there are pilgrims who discern the way as the journey unfolds. The difference in these two approaches is the difference between the brewer and the drunk. One can appreciate the product because he has appreciated the process. The other can't appreciate either.

—

Some years ago an authority on children's ministry, having just attended her twelfth "Building Positive Self-Esteem" seminar, decided that the flesh-and-blood, down-and-dirty stories of the Bible were a little too difficult and demanding for impressionable young children. So for a children's story, she told a modern-day, warm and fuzzy, wholly-affirming, nonoffensive, nonthreatening, new-agey, inner-beauty-radiating, low-cost, no-demands, feel-good parable that exuded nothing but saccharine, syrupy sentimentality. At the end of her completely inoffensive and mostly uninteresting tale, she closed her book and asked, "Tell me, children, what does this story mean?" There was a prolonged, uncomfortable silence. Finally, a little boy in the back of the room raised his hand and shouted, "Nothing!"

Even in the spiritual realm, we get what we pay for. The potency of the beverage is in direct proportion to the process of transformation. Instant gratification is but a fleeting buzz; prepackaged energy drinks are all caffeine and sugar. But the sacrificial fruits of our labors of love can sustain for eternity. All in all, I'd rather have a beer, or at least some beverage that requires time, patience, care, cleansing, and effort.

In the Trinity College Library in Dublin there are a number of artistic, scientific, literary, and theological treasures. The best known is the Book of Kells, a stunning illuminated manuscript containing the Four Gospels, painstakingly painted and calligraphed by Celtic monks centuries ago. Some traditions attribute its creation to St. Columba himself, and it has been called Ireland's greatest national treasure.

However, I was more impressed by a subtly displayed copy of Louis Pasteur's groundbreaking scientific treatise *Studies in Fermentation: The Diseases of Beer, Their Causes, and the Means of Preventing Them*. It is a catchy title in its own right, but I prefer the original French, *Etudes sur la Biere*. Sounds more like a drinking song than a scientific undertaking. The million-dollar question that Pasteur tackled was how to brew a beer that was robust without being sour, how to culture the right microorganisms and remove the wrong ones, and how to tell the difference between something that adds flavor and something that adds bitterness. Pasteur figured it out for the breweries of his time. We're still working on it for the storehouses of the soul in our own day.

I suppose what happens in the holding tanks is not unlike what happens within ourselves when we are transformed. The secret is not to remove all of the unknown, potentially dangerous material, for that would make for a rather watered-down life.

The secret is how to blend it to create something rich and flavorful, without turning sour at the prospect that something is brewing deep within, that someone may even be distilling us into something completely different.

The tour may end at the tasting room.

The pilgrimage goes on forever.

3

CALL ME INTEMPERATE, OR IT'S NINE O'CLOCK SOMEWHERE

Doubtless, it is unnatural to be drunk. But then, in a real sense, it is
unnatural to be human. Doubtless, the intemperate workman wastes
his tissues in drinking; but no one knows how much the sober
workman wastes his tissues by working.

—G. K. CHESTERTON

These men are not drunk. . . . It's only nine o'clock!

—THE APOSTLE PETER, ON THE DAY OF PENTECOST

*I*n the illustrious annals of my mostly tragic dating history,
there was the brief interlude with the television news anchor-
woman. While stunning to behold, she possessed the passion
and personality of a teleprompter. My encounters with this particular anchor always left me with a certain sinking feeling, as if
a large pointy iron weight had been hoisted onto my vessel. She
was so uptight that she made Bill O'Reilly come across like Miss
Congeniality. I can speak about Miss Congeniality with some
sense of reference because I once actually had a lunch date with

a real Miss Congeniality. You would think that a woman who reports on the pressing issues of our time would have more to say than a baton-twirling pageant contestant. In this case, that would be an incorrect assumption.

On my first date with the news anchor, I swiftly realized I would need a drink, and I steered our conversation to wine. (Little did I know there would be *none* at our table.) Her aversion to wine, she said, was not a moral thing. She simply did not like it, in the same way that she did not like broccoli. This comparison baffled me, as if she had said she did not like cockfighting in the same way that she did not like ballet. She steered our conversation from dinner wine to Communion wine, asking me if I typically partook *before* each service.

"Why would you ask that?" I wondered out loud to her.

She replied, "Because during the service, you act like you have."

Although Miss Contemptuality was unaware of it, she had paid me a handsome compliment. From the very inception of that lively, unpredictable religious institution known as the church, outsiders and onlookers have wondered the very same thing: did you get into the Communion wine before it was time? On the Day of Pentecost in Jerusalem, the Holy Spirit blew through the words and actions of the apostles like a Pat O'Brien's hurricane. It made people wonder, "Did these guys get into the Communion wine?" The Apostle Peter stood up and eloquently delivered the very first sermon of the newly founded church. The sermon began with the following disclaimer: "We are not drunk. It is only nine o'clock."

And people think I begin my sermons strangely.

How fitting that the very first sermon began with a sobriety test and that Peter had to defend himself against a PWI—Preaching While Intoxicated! Peter went on to point out that when the Spirit is present, one might confuse such presence with some other spirits. For when the Almighty appears, things will get interesting at the least, and often out of control and over the top. The intoxicating presence of God seems to have that effect, whether one has dipped into the Communion wine or not.

Call me intemperate.

I have witnessed firsthand the extremes to which God will go to renew, resurrect, enflame, and empower. There is nothing mild or moderate about grace, an extravagant and extreme gesture that knows no limits and has no bounds. When God shows up, the party is elevated from mere lampshade helmets to dancing tongues of fire, from a place where "shaken or stirred" ventures far beyond the martini glass and inhabits the human vessel. God's motto seems to be: Moderation in nothing.

Once, when Jesus was having dinner with his disciples, a woman, who apparently worked the night shift and knew something about appetite and excess, approached him. She held an alabaster jar filled with a very costly perfume. It was the rarest of scented ointments, valued at the equivalent of an entire year's salary. As the woman came closer to Jesus, she held nothing back. She poured out the contents, not only of her fragrant gift, but also the contents of her very self—her soul, her adoration, her love. She wept profusely, bathing Jesus's tired and dirty feet with her own tears. She gathered her long, beautiful hair in her hands and used it as a towel to delicately dry Jesus's feet. Then she took the entire contents of the jar and poured it all out—extravagantly, intemperately, unconditionally—on his head and on his feet, until the entire house was filled with the fragrance of perfume.

There are slightly different versions of this story in the gospels, but in every version the disciples are portrayed as moderate pragmatists, cautiously prudent, careful in their allocation, consumption, and enjoyment. Judas, the conservative keeper of the purse strings, gets particularly worked up over this squandering of a precious commodity that could have been utilized for something far more important, like feeding the poor. The disciples, in fact, scold the woman for her extravagant and wasteful deed, telling her to get her priorities straight, to be more reasonable in her rationing of untempered religious fervor.

But Jesus scolds the disciples and tells them to get *their* priorities straight. To be good sometimes demands a squandering of goods. Jesus says that he is honored by the beautiful, costly, lavish gift and over-the-top act of love and passion. In fact, Jesus says, her act is so good and so meaningful that her story will be told for all eternity to all those who desire to draw intimately near the heart of God. One wasteful act, offered in love, may bring us closer to the heart of God than a thousand prudently measured deeds.

The wonder of love is often its extravagant compulsion. Its pursuits are not timid or hesitant. It is costly, over the top, and goes the extra mile. I was reminded of that at another dinner party.

Years ago, my father exhibited such immodest excess in his love for his only grandson, my nephew Chris, who as a very young boy was diagnosed with a rare metabolic disorder. He was a finicky eater, but it wasn't because he wanted to be difficult; it was the result of his body's terrible time metabolizing proteins and fats. Over time, we discovered that Chris had only one favorite food that he could truly savor and enjoy— green beans dipped in ketchup! But not any bean would do. Chris had a definite and distinct taste for Kentucky Wonder beans. Now, I am no green bean authority. As long as my green beans are simmered in pork fat, slathered in butter, or drenched in cheese, I am happy to eat all of them in a healthy and nutritious manner. But Chris will eat only Kentucky Wonders, mountains of them at a time, accompanied by a bottle of that miracle condiment the Reagan administration labeled an actual vegetable.

One Thanksgiving, my father was preparing a feast for our family: smoked turkey, his world-famous corn-bread dressing with a hint of sage, sweet potatoes topped with pecans from his own trees, broccoli-and-rice casserole with real Cheez Whiz, and chocolate almond bar pie. One thing was missing.

Two days before Thanksgiving, very early in the morning, my father left for the local grocery store to purchase a bundle of Kentucky Wonder beans for his favorite and only grandson. Alas, no beans were to be had! He drove on to the next store. Same sad, beanless, nonwonderful situation. On he drove for the next twelve hours—to Randall's Flagship, Whole Foods, Kroger, Safeway, Sak-N-Sav, Minimax, HEB, Farmer's Market, Produce Haven, Harvest Time, Food City, Food Land, Food-a-Rama, Food Lion, Food Giant, Food Midget, Vegetarian Temple, Bean World, Nothing But Beans, Beans R Us, Kentucky Fried Chicken, the Jack Daniel's Distillery. You name it; he traveled there in search of Kentucky Wonders. Finally, he found them at the Fiesta Mart right down the street from his house! Will wonders never cease?

As he shared the story of his heroic search, we wondered about his extreme perseverance, not to mention his obsessive-compulsive behavior and produce-section addiction. We wondered about the wisdom of depleting an entire tank of gas and half a day, all for beans. But at the Thanksgiving table, my father peered over the wonderful red and green precipice that towered over Chris's plate and proclaimed, "It was worth it. After all, I have only one grandson. Why, I would've driven all the way to Kentucky to get those beans."

My mother's favorite cousin was a man by the name of Jerry Ray. He lived in Austin, Texas, and his claim to fame was that he owned a bowling alley called the Dart Bowl. The Dart Bowl's claim to fame had nothing to do with strikes, spares, or turkeys. It was known for serving the best cheese enchiladas in all of central Texas. The Grill at the Dart Bowl was run by a bunch of old hippies, and no one does cheese enchiladas better than a bunch of old hippies. The portions were so generous and satisfying that eating them was not unlike a religious experience. In fact, they were served with the same sense of abundance with which Jerry lived his life.

Jerry was one of those rare people who always pick up the tab and would do anything for you, even if they hardly know you. He adored my grandmother, so he treated us like royalty any time we were with him. Every time I saw Jerry, he related to me the same story that initiated the intense, unrestrained love he had for my grandma, his aunt Viv. Jerry was a little boy during the scarcity of the Great Depression. Times were hard and even the smallest luxuries nonexistent. Basic needs could not even be met. But one day Jerry's aunt Viv showed up at his house with a special gift for him, something delicious and opulent and unexpected during those times of trouble. She gifted this little boy with an entire carton of Juicy Fruit.

When Jerry tells the story, he says, "Not a stick, for which I'd have been eternally grateful, not a package, which would have seemed like an endless supply, but *an entire carton*! To this day I have no idea how she got it, but it was one of the most treasured gifts of my entire life."

There is more to Jerry's story that reveals why he was so grateful for such an imprudent gesture. One day, many years ago, my grandmother's sister and her husband, a young Disciples of Christ minister from Brady, Texas, walked into an orphanage in Fort Worth. They entered a room that was completely filled with tiny infants in their cribs. For some unknown reason, Jerry says, that young couple walked over to a particular crib, reached down and picked up one baby boy, and took him home to be their new son.

When Jerry reflects back on that day, he will tell you, tearfully and gratefully, with full emphasis on the grandeur of that unanticipated gift, "I do not know what happened to those other infants who were in that room with me that day. But I just pray, every day, that their lives have been as blessed as mine. Some people ask me, 'Jerry, don't you want to know who your *real* parents are?' and I always tell them—Oh, I know who my *real* parents are. They're the ones who did not hold back, but reached into my crib that day and chose me to be their own." One extravagant, undeserved gesture can make a lifetime of difference. One tiny sip of intoxicating grace can send us stumbling toward a lifetime of sharing.

Holding back will only hold us back, whether it is the moderate pronouncement, the timid overture, the careful strategy, the cautious prayer, the balanced approach, or the cards held close to the vest. None of these characteristics will ever be confused with the full-throttle, high-octane energy of the seemingly intoxicated preacher on Pentecost. Like a fragrant, overpowering wind that fills an entire space comes the holy pronouncement that can make all the difference: Moderation in nothing.

The immodest and immeasurable reveals the holy presence. That has been my experience, from the spa massage table to the Sunday school class, confirmed by a variety of personalities who have dared cross the lines of proper propriety in the name of a more profuse passion.

I recall the out-of-control burly massage therapist at the Hotel Gellert who, after a tiring pilgrimage from Prague to Budapest, slapped me around between belches of beer, even massaging the foam into my tired joints. The experience was so sloppy and surreal I had no choice but to relax.

I remember stories told with delight about a former bishop of Texas who had been a controversial parish priest in Kentucky. Back in the Bluegrass State he was apparently quite a wonder in his own right, opposing a formidable group of parish prohibitionists, inviting every saloonkeeper in town to come find a spiritual home in his congregation. His recurring motto was "The Church is for sinners, not for saints." He was also known to effuse with frequency, "Another bourbon, shall we?"

And I also remember little Garrett Taylor in his Lenten Sunday school class at Trinity Church. When asked what he was giving up for Lent, Garrett boldly stated, "My future!"

The other children quickly convinced him to change that to candy, but the former response, as extreme as it was, is much more appropriate if we are to play with the fire of the Spirit of God. We are called to go all in.

Moderation in nothing. As William Blake has said, "Prudence is an old maid courted by incapacity."

There's an old story about one of my favorite professional football players, the left-handed quarterback from Alabama, Kenny Stabler. After a long and lively career in Oakland as a Raider, he played for my former Houston Oilers for a few years. While living in Houston, he opened a country-western saloon. Never has a strip mall been the site of so much character. I hear things got occasionally, uh, rowdy over there. Stabler was nicknamed "the Snake," and I do not want to know why. Just the fact that he was called Snake gives me a reason to quote him. A reporter read to Stabler a credo that is attributed by some to Jack London, As the story goes, the reporter read the following to Stabler: "I would rather be ashes than dust! I would rather that my spark should burn out in a brilliant blaze than it should be stifled by dry rot. I would rather be a superb meteor, every atom of me in magnificent glow, than a sleepy and permanent planet. The proper function of man is to live, not to exist. I shall not waste my days in trying to prolong them. I shall use my time."

After letting these stirring words soak in for a moment, the reporter asked Kenny Stabler what they meant to him. The Snake slithered back in his chair for a moment, pondered the words, and spoke: "Well, seems to me he's sayin'—*always throw deep!*"

Always throw deep. And always drink deeply.

Call me intemperate, but it's nine o'clock somewhere.

4

THE CATHEDRALS OF DUBLIN

The vaults from one end of the cathedral to the other are made into
tippling houses for beer, wine, and tobacco.

—LETTER FROM 1633 DESCRIBING THE CRYPT OF CHRIST CHURCH, DUBLIN

Sometimes you want to go where everybody knows your name. . . .

—THEME SONG FROM *CHEERS*

As a priest and bar owner, I am always seeking confirmation that my dual identity has some sort of divine origin, that
the service provided by the celebrant and the bartender emerge
from similar spiritual roots, and that true community can be
formed by sharing a common cup, whether it is a Communion chalice or a beer mug. Thus, when my longtime travel
companion, drinking buddy, and prayer partner Michael
Soper and I arrived in Dublin for the beginning of a one-week
Celtic pilgrimage across the Emerald Isle, we were ecstatic to
discover that Dubliners proudly boast of having not just one
or even two, but *three* cathedrals: St. Patrick's Cathedral,
Christ Church Cathedral, and the Guinness Brewery.

This unlikely tippled trinity has slaked more than spiritual thirst over the centuries. There is still no saint that provokes more potent partying than Patrick. Should March 17 fall on a Friday, even the most devout Catholic will call in a pontifical pardon to observe the feast. In certain ecclesiastical circles, this "get out of fasting free" card is known as "the Corned-Beef Concession." The former dean of St. Patrick's Cathedral, the satirist Jonathan Swift, was said to rival the bawdiest bartender when engaged in theological banter, possessing a sense of humor the dark color of stout. He is rumored to have said during a sermon that he loved babies because they were so "delicious"! This tradition of irreverence has carried over to modern times. When I was touring St. Patrick's with the present dean, he stopped and motioned toward a tiny bust of a former archbishop, much smaller than the sculpted heads of other archbishops. The dean reasoned, "He was no beauty."

Just up Patrick Street from St. Patrick's is, according to its sign, "The Cathedral Church of the Holy Trinity Commonly Called Christ Church Dublin." The church's alternative identities—further confirmation of my own—are reflected not only in its names, but in its understanding of mission, purpose, and service to the world. During at least the sixteenth and seventeenth centuries, the outpoured sacramental wine from the sanctuary was supplemented by the outpouring ale taps at a pub in the cathedral crypt. That's right, Christ Church Cathedral was in the bar business! Holy Trinity! At TCCO-THTCCCCD, which sounds a bit like a drunken slur, while some pilgrims knelt at the altar above, others bellied up to the bar below. This undercroft arrangement reminds me of my seminary years in Chicago and my surprising discovery that the Lutheran seminarians operated a bar in the basement of their student housing. While I'm pretty sure they had nailed ninety-five beer labels to the unmarked door so we could find our way, I am absolutely positive that it was there I learned firsthand, according to Luther himself, "the power and efficacy of Indulgences."

While the third member of the urban Hibernian trinity, the Guinness Brewery, does not exude the same mystical ambience of the Anglican cathedrals, it is nonetheless a powerful place of pilgrimage for those in need of refreshment. Besides, Arthur Guinness was a man of true faith whom God smiled upon, as evidenced by the lease he signed at St. James Gate in 1759—forty-five pounds per year for nine thousand years!

The old brewery building has now been turned into a drinker's Disneyland called the Guinness Storehouse. Viewers ascend a building whose center resembles a giant pint glass while paying homage to the four primary sacramental substances of water, barley, hops, and yeast. There is a small altar dedicated to the worship of Arthur Guinness, an explanation of the transformative powers of the brewing process, and an exhibit dedicated to the alchemical prowess of the dean, also known as the brewmaster. There is also an Evangelism Center where one is bombarded with the history of advertising in the name of Irish stout. The converts are finally led heavenward toward the highlight of the tour—the top-floor Gravity Bar and the opportunity to turn in their alms token for a cold pint of the real deal. Even at the Guinness Storehouse, it is in the sacramental cup that one finds strength for the journey.

I would have been impressed with this cutting-edge marvel of technology and innovation had I not experienced the finest brewery tour in all the world just a few days earlier in Kilkenny. The Smithwick's (pronounced SMIT-icks) Brewery in Kilkenny, like many top-tier breweries in the world, began in a religious community. Smithwick's was originally brewed by monks at St. Francis Abbey, starting in the fourteenth century. It is Ireland's oldest operating brewery. What its tour lacks in marketing sophistication and technological innovation, it more than makes up for with intimate interpersonal connection, soulful authenticity, true community, and a miraculous ever-flowing tap.

As soon as Michael I arrived in Kilkenny, we made a beer line straight to St. Francis. We found an old, weathered sign hung on a green barnlike door that indicated "Tours begin here," but the silence and stillness of the scene resembled the most cloistered monastery. We wondered if the last tour had taken place some centuries before the Reformation. We wandered the grounds of the brewery in search of clues, or errant kegs, until we stumbled upon an old-fashioned booth inhabited by a portly security guard. He meandered out, looking about as menacing as Friar Tuck with a badge.

"Is there a brewery tour today?" we pilgrims inquired.

"Aye, lads," he said, smiling and patting each of our bellies in a gentle, nonthreatening way. "Yur not here fur the tur, yur here fur the BEER!"

I have been frisked on occasion by airport authorities, thoroughly interrogated by the border patrol, and been told to spread my legs by police officers, but never have I had my belly rubbed by a security guard, particularly one who had the prophetic power to ascertain my true motives.

"Wait yonder by the sign," he said. "And have one fur me!" he added, clutching his own quite impressive belly, no doubt made rounder by the consumption component of his compensation package.

The "tour" was even better than the guard's unexpected hospitality. It consisted of a teenage boy telling us to sit down on beat-up metal folding chairs in a room that reminded me of an old fraternal lodge in some tiny town that time forgot. The young man's introduction consisted entirely of this statement: "And now we'll watch the video." Tapping into his vast supply of budding beer knowledge, he inserted a tape into an ancient video player. This tape had all the production pizzazz of those "educational" human reproduction films we were tortured with back in seventh grade. It was so bad that it was delightfully entertaining, better even than the world's best collection of Super Bowl beer commercials.

At its conclusion, he paused before making this profound pronouncement: "And now we'll drink the beer." He was much more articulate behind the tap, telling the cheering hordes (all six of us), "I'll pour till you stop drinking." Over the next few hours our bellies grew so round that security had to be summoned on the suspicion we were smuggling beer babies. I love beer babies. They're delicious.

During the drinking portion of our brewery tour, Michael and I bonded with two guys from Los Angeles who, like us, were there for the educational component. As often happens during prolonged pourings of free beverages, we became best friends and shared the most intimate details of our lives. Such an exchange reminds me of the meaning of Communion, that it is simply a sharing of something significant with others in a setting that promotes intimate fellowship and honest rapport. Patting bellies. Sharing stories. Drinking beer. Sounds pretty sacramental to me.

Michael and I decided to forgo our planned castle tour and join our new friends on a pub crawl through Kilkenny. By this time we were, in fact, literally crawling, so we made it to exactly two pubs. As it turned out, that was one too many.

The Thostle Bar in Kilkenny is among my favorite bars in the world, along with La Kiva in Terlingua, Texas, and Padre's in Marfa. Like all sacred sites, it is a place made holy by a procession of pilgrims who go there to share some communion. As I took in this tiny place of pilgrimage, I sensed that the surfaces had been textured by decades of tears, sweat, blood, beer, and whiskey. Its diminutive size belied its prominent status in the lives of those who are known here—a place where I can imagine that profound losses were mourned, battles were waged, sins were forgiven, justice was demanded, and bonds were forged. Its authentic stained-glass windows commemorate not biblical scenes but prominent pints of Guinness, otherwise known around here as "the Holy Spirit." I asked the bartender how long the bar had been in operation. "More than two hundred years," he said, "but I've only been here for fifty!" The menu consisted of packages of peanuts and "heated sandwiches." Strategically placed around the bar were alms boxes that supported various missions, shrines, and ministries. The one to assist children with cancer was stuffed full of coins. Icons of saints and a lovely portrait of the Blessed Virgin Mary looked kindly upon any brokenhearted soul who might pause for a pint and a word of consolation. Here was a drinking establishment that took seriously the well-balanced grace said before meals or over a pint: one that not only includes a debt of gratitude for that which is about to be enjoyed, but also asks that one be made "mindful of the needs of others."

There were only a handful of customers, all men, but you got the sense that they were known around here. Each had a story, and all the others had some role to play. This was their community and sacred space. One of them read the newspaper. Another fed peanuts to the dachshund that sat patiently at his feet. Another watched with awe as Judge Judy dispensed her unique brand of justice on a tiny television above the bar. "We like the American shows," the bartender told me; his preference did not extend to American beer, however. Other than the religious motifs, the walls were mostly bare. No framed write-ups in the trendy Nightwatch section of the *Irish Times*. No "Pub of the Year" award or "Thostle Bar Bikini Team" calendars. No tapas to taste or "reserved" signs to navigate. The lone photo on the wall was a hurling team with staid expressions and a single word underneath: KILKENNY. Brevity and barrenness often convey the most profound beauty. I would like to have my ashes scattered in such a place.

Later that night, at the Californians' behest, we ended up at the most popular watering hole in town, at least for that month, a crowded club with all the mass-produced character of a restaurant chain. It was called "Paris Texas." These are two of my favorite places, but they were totally out of context in the land of Patrick. A mediocre band played Top 40 cover tunes with just enough Irish influence that it made you want to cry in your Guinness, or, in this case, Budweiser. So, the most frequented place in town was not an Irish pub, and the most requested beer was brewed in Missouri.

I once heard an anthropologist explain that we humans are really good at appreciating every culture but our own. Perhaps the same is true of our spiritual truth. If it is too close to home, or shared by those we know all too well, it is relegated to the place of the unenlightened. We would rather have nothing to do with it. When identity feels just too familiar to be divinely inspired, our surroundings too well known to be worthy of our love, we may be throwing the baby out with the bath—and the beer. Before meeting up with Michael in Ireland, I had embarked on a similar one-week Celtic pilgrimage in Scotland with my almost-fiancée Jennifer. Jennifer and I alternated between whiskey tastings and prayer on our trip, recognizing the elevated power of experiencing both in the presence of another person whom you love and care for. The whiskey tastings typically took place after pilgrimages to distilleries, while the prayers were uttered in ancient churches as well as in the privacy of our one-on-one time. I taught her the art of tasting so well that she pondered changing her legal name to "Single Malt Bonnie," while she taught me the power of prayer so well that I pondered becoming a priest.

One afternoon Jennifer and I wandered through the ruins of the magnificent Elgin Cathedral in Scotland. For me there is nothing more beautiful than towering Gothic remnants being rewoven into creation by the green caress of the plant world. The missing pieces now allow radiant shafts of sunlight to illumine the sacred stones in a new and different way. That late afternoon when Jennifer and I visited the grounds, the entire space seemed to come alive as if baptized and raised to new life by the light. Tiny, translucent flower blossoms were dancing in the setting sun. It was as if an old story were resurrected in an unlikely collaboration of creation, contemplation, and celebration. The stones seemed to sing that day.

The young man who waited patiently for us to come back to earth and exit the gate so he could lock up and go home and have a pint found out that I had lived in Austin, Texas. His face lit up as he told me that his favorite musician was the late Austin guitarist Stevie Ray Vaughan. He enthusiastically shared with me the details of his trip to Austin, where he went to Town Lake to pay homage to the Stevie Ray statue, and how he heard "real music" every night he was there. He informed us that Celtic music "sucks" and, waving a hand of dismissal toward the ruins behind him, he noted, "This here is crap." As inspiring as I find Stevie Ray Vaughan and much Texas music, I find Celtic music and the scene just beyond his outstretched hand just as inspiring.

"ZZ Top," he insisted, "now that's a real band." Again, one of my favorites, too. But the encounter became surreal as we gazed back at the awe-inducing cathedral and imagined the voices of the faithful and the presence of centuries of pilgrims while being serenaded by a Scottish skeptic singing ZZ Top's "Tube Snake Boogie."

I remember waiting for a friend near the entrance to the Village Vanguard in New York City. There is nothing quite like descending those fifteen well-worn stairs into that tiny triangular space upheld by the trinity of music, drinks, and history. Knowing that a pantheon of performance gods, from Miles Davis to John Coltrane, played on that stage is worth the price of admission.

On this night, a couple from out of town approached me and asked me the following question: "Excuse me, sir, but do you know any good places to hear jazz?"

When I realized that they were not kidding, I pointed to the Vanguard door. "It doesn't get any better than this place," I told them.

Glancing skeptically at the unmarked door, they asked once more, "Anyplace else?"

I suppose I value my pubs in the same way I value my temples. I am not all that impressed by sleek production values or catering to the masses. I am more moved by context, history, authenticity, and intimacy. I do not want to be herded through the latest techno-wonder and be fed the spiritual equivalent of high-fructose corn syrup or watered-down beverages. I would rather have my belly patted, my ass slapped, and my name known. I would like the branding on my drinking vessel to have stood the test of time. I like to worship and I like to drink in places hallowed by real pilgrims' tears—tears of anguish, triumph, sorrow, joy, desperation, and peace. And if, while there, I am made mindful of the needs of others, all the better.

—

I am frequently astounded by folks who proclaim their spiritual superiority by denouncing "organized religion." As one southern parish matriarch said innocently to a skeptical newcomer: "It's okay, honey, we're not all that organized around here!" Such a criticism would parallel opposition to the neighborhood pub on the grounds that it promotes "organized drinking." Yeah, those pubs are filled with hypocrites who don't buy nearly enough rounds for those in need. The pub's tenders just want your money. For me, solo spirituality makes about as much sense as preferring to drink alone.

Years ago when I was traveling through the Holy Land, I visited numerous sacred sites recorded in religious history and tradition. I realized there that two distinct sides to my personality had shown up: the archaeologist and the mystic. The archaeologist was determined to sift through the literal sands and get the facts straight, to unearth some tangible evidence, to dig deep for quantifiable proof. The archaeologist persistently wondered, "Is this where it actually happened?" or even "Did it really happen at all?"

The mystic, on the other hand, viewed those same sites through eyes of wonder and imagination. The connection was made more with the real people, the wandering pilgrims who dared to venture forth to an unknown place and had traveled to these same sites over many centuries, to pray, remember, and be renewed.

The two parts of my personality struggled over questions like: Was this land made holy because this is where "it really happened," or was this land made holy by a procession of saints, pilgrims, and partyers who'd come before me? What presence makes any place holy? How many kisses of the devoted bring a place to life and make it as real as it is transforming? Are we really in search of the actual Holy Grail? Or do we more profoundly seek a common cup called communion, where they know your name, and are glad you came?

I lean toward the latter, believing that the shared cup, consumed in common, more profoundly reveals the reality of the sacred presence. This ultimate revelation of community was reinforced some years ago when the Diocese of Texas had its annual convention in Longview, deep in the heart of East Texas, not far from the Louisiana border. There are two good reasons to attend the Diocesan Convention in Longview: (1) the pork ribs at the Country Tavern in nearby Kilgore, Texas, and (2) the casinos of Shreveport, Louisiana, just an hour away. On this night most of the delegates from our home church piled into the senior warden's car and we headed due east, all the way to Shreveport. We assumed that not only could we drink for free and tithe some blackjack winnings, but we would also find a quality restaurant, since it is the nature of casino hotels to offer fine cuisine. Sure enough, there was a highly rated steak house at our casino of choice. Our senior warden, Brad Beers, a take-charge kind of guy, approached the steak house hostess to request a table, but he was one step behind me. The hostess told us there would be a short wait and requested our names. At virtually the same time, with me just a millisecond ahead of him, we blurted out our last names.

To this day, we are known in Shreveport, Louisiana, as "the Miller Beers Party"!

Individually, I am just a Miller, and Brad is just a Beers. But put us together and we control 35 percent of the market.

The gathered community possesses a power beyond the sum of its individual parts. It is the power of true communion that transcends even the particulars of time and place.

I'll drink to that.

In a bar.

And even in a cathedral.

5

EXOTIC SUCCULENCE

O taste and see that the Lord is good.

—PSALMS 34:8

Life is a banquet, and most poor suckers are starving to death.

—AUNTIE MAME

I live on Kauai, a place known as "the Garden Isle" for good reason. Surrounded by flowering abundance and tropical beauty, not to mention hula girls, I awaken each morning to a brilliant, multihued sunrise over a canopy of coconut palms. My front lanai, or "porch" to those of you not from around here, faces a silhouette of Sleeping Giant mountain. A mere thirty-minute hike to the top reveals a sweeping panorama of paradise. My back lanai overlooks my neighbor Bette Midler's agricultural land, a vast wide-open space with King Kong's mountainous profile rising up in the distance. Someday, I'll invite Bette over for a beer. We'll sing a few show tunes and enjoy the cooling ocean breeze while the occasional grazing cow will conjure up fond memories of Texas.

From my yard I can handpick papayas, mangos, avocados, lemons, and limes. One morning a giant pink pig sauntered right through my open gate. Had she stayed put, I could have lived off my land for a year without ever stopping at Safeway. Throw in a couple of bottles of rum and a coconut bra and I could have opened up my own private luau—Padre's Paradise.

I am unsure why God called me to Hawaii instead of sending me to Gary, Indiana, or Buffalo, New York, or Yuma, Arizona. Perhaps God confused me with some other William Miller. It's a fairly common name. It is possible that I am about to draw a "Go Directly to Hell, Do Not Pass Go" card, and this phase of my life is akin to a final requested meal on death row. Maybe this is God's way of compensating me for all those years I spent cheering for the Houston Oilers. Or it could be that the St. Michael's Church search committee was impressed that the most compelling question I posed to them during the interview process pertained not to theological formation, indigenous spirituality, or congregational development. I wondered sincerely, "Who among you makes the best mai tai?" I felt that it was important to know. Apparently, so did they.

My Hawaii driver's license is as lovely as the state it represents. Its most prominent feature is a colorful rainbow that stretches nearly its entire length. It starts at my smiling face and reaches all the way through my height, weight, hair color, date of issue, class, and restrictions, terminating at "Organ Donor." The rainbow continues off the edge of the card, as if its beginning and ending cannot be contained.

One of the things I've noticed about rainbows, now that I live in Hawaii, is that it is rare to see a well-defined, ground-touching, full-spectrum, clearly delineated bow. It's often impossible to pinpoint precisely where the rainbow originates and where it terminates. Furthermore, I've also observed that if you are traveling near one, just when you think you've arrived at its points of origin, it moves! It's still there, it seems, just not exactly where you thought it was. It's on ahead, beyond, away. Or maybe it's actually behind, whence you have come. Or perhaps it's right where you are and you just can't see it. It's like the refracted rays of religious illumination—you could be standing on the pot of gold and still be looking for it. It can be anywhere and everywhere, if we're paying attention and willing to taste and see all along the way.

When I travel now with my rainbow-themed Hawaiian driver's license, people are downright incredulous that I am visiting wherever it is I am visiting. Whether it's Prague or Peoria, Oslo or Ohio, the most commonly asked question is "What are you doing *here*?" It is as if living in Hawaii means that there is no reason to venture forth, nothing of any interest or inspiration that I could possibly discover on a distant shore. But a rainbow's reach does not end at any horizon. In fact, it doesn't end at all. The spectrum seems to go beyond wherever we are and may lead us to perceive beauty, goodness, and abundance in the most unexpected places.

—

When first my nephew, and then my niece, graduated from college, I offered each of them the opportunity to travel with me. I will never forget the day of my nephew Chris's graduation from the University of Texas. After the commencement ceremony, the extended family gathered at County Line barbecue to offer gifts and congratulations to the chemical engineering grad. After a multitude of Longhorn-themed presents had been opened, I turned to my nephew and said, "Chris, I want you to think about this decision very carefully because this is my gift to you. If you could travel anywhere in the United States with me for a vacation, absolutely anywhere, what destination would you pick? Choose wisely, my man. And take your time."

Approximately 1.2 seconds elapsed before he blurted out a vacation destination that surprised everyone.

"Cleveland, Ohio," he said.

Amid shouts of protest and gasps of disbelief, Chris reiterated in a case-closed tone of voice that is generally reserved for the most unflinching fundamentalist, "Yes, Cleveland, Ohio," and returned to his ribs.

Our trip to Cleveland remains one of the fondest travel memories of my life.

While there, we cheered the Indians on to victory at Jacobs Field and enjoyed a pig sandwich at the Hard Rock Cafe. We visited the pro football temple in Canton and worshipped a variety of guitar gods at the Rock and Roll Hall of Fame. For Chris, a classic rock buff, this was his Mecca. We made a quick detour to another less-traveled vacation spot, Pittsburgh, to watch the Pirates lose at PNC Park. There is some justice in a bad team having the best baseball stadium, another lesson in the equalizing effects of karma and cosmos. My nephew afforded me the guilty pleasure of a pregame visit to the Andy Warhol Museum, my fifteen minutes of pop culture.

"You call that art?" he asked, pointing at the paintings.

"You call that baseball?" I asked, pointing at the Pirates.

We ate pretzels and hot dogs, drank beer (me) and Dr Pepper (him), watched giant pierogi race around the field, and admired guitar art sculpture all the way to Lake Erie. While some have referred to Cleveland as "the mistake by the lake," I now think of it as "the graduation cake by the lake." Abundance appears in the most unlikely places—if we keep our eyes, minds, and mouths open to the possibility.

My niece Jennifer, on the other hand, takes a more traditional approach to travel. For months she debated between Miami's South Beach, the Big Apple, and Las Vegas, but when she figured out that increased airfare would be offset by free lodging, she packed her grass skirt and hightailed it to Hawaii.

Jennifer and I have always shared common areas of interest. When she was a little girl, for example, the two of us were the only family members who enjoyed roller coasters and country music. Once I took her to the local theme park, Astro World, for a concert, and we ended up riding the Texas Cyclone coaster with Tanya Tucker. Other than "Jesus Loves Me," the first song lyrics I ever memorized were those to Tucker's classic "Delta Dawn." Later in life I would come to appreciate a couple of other timely Tucker tunes such as "What's Your Mama's Name, Child?" (best line: "Has she ever mentioned a man named Buford Wilson?") and my personal favorite, "The Man That Turned My Mama On" (best line: "I wish I'd known the man a little better that turned my mama on"). But I can still wail from memory that mournful tune about a faded rose from days gone by and feel an eschatological fervor rise up within me as I wonder about the meeting that will "take her to that mansion in the sky."

Jennifer is also a bit more of a partyer than the rest of her family, although she parties in moderation. I had warned her before her visit that Kauai has absolutely no nightlife. Here people are early to bed, early to rise, and prefer an active lifestyle that is oriented toward the outdoors—hiking, swimming, surfing, kayaking—pursuits that Jennifer has no interest in whatsoever. Somehow while here, Jennifer and her friend Caroline managed to discover every nightspot on the entire island, all twenty-three of them! One night Jennifer called me from Rob's Good Times Grill, way past my bedtime, to tell me that the hula girls from the luau we had attended earlier had descended on the place. Knowing me well, she said, "I just thought you might want to know."

There have been phases in my life where such news would have roused me from the deepest slumber. After three hundred push-ups and a shower, I would have been at Rob's within a matter of minutes, buying Lava Flows for every dancer in the show. That night, I rolled over and went back to my dreams about the *kalua* pig at the luau buffet. So, my priorities have changed a bit over the years.

However, if you had gone through the buffet line at the luau that night, you would have sympathy for my choice. A luau, though a bit too tikified these days, still combines some of the best elements of paradise: a garden setting, free-flowing mai tais, all-you-can-eat Polynesian delicacies, and lovely Tahitian dancers. That night I had used my *kama'aina* (local) discount to get us into the Smith's Tropical Paradise, Garden Luau, and International Show. We had been instructed to get there early and stroll through paradise at our leisure. So we did, at a pace probably a little too laid-back for the girls. We chased peacocks through the Japanese Garden Island, the Hibiscus Garden, the Bamboo Rain Forest, the Filipino Village, the Fruit Forest, the Polynesian Village, the Ginger Section, and past the Lagoon Theater to the Luau House, where we discovered that the bar did not open until after the Imu Ceremony.

We suddenly had a keen interest in the Imu Ceremony, particularly its conclusion. In Hawaii, the Imu Ceremony is akin to setting the altar table and bringing up the elements for Holy Communion. For it is here that the buffet star is unveiled. After a day underground, the *kalua* pig is removed with great fanfare from the earthen oven (*imu*) but only after it has been, according to our detailed program guide, "steam-roasted to an exotic succulence."

There are many similarities between Texans and Hawaiians. Other than a crazed obsession with high school football, the foremost is perhaps that we all like to eat our favorite local foods. Although I have yet to develop much of a taste for poi, a pasty purple dip made from the taro root, I have found that deep-fried taro chips dipped in ranch dressing (another ancient Polynesian delicacy) are to die for. A good Kauai friend also creates a local dish called *lau lau*—chunks of tender pork wrapped in taro leaves, then covered with ti leaves and steamed. Put a little Louisiana hot sauce on that concoction, and it'll make you wanna slap your *kapuna*! While fresh ahi is hard to beat, I would have to say that *kalua* pork is my absolute favorite Hawaiian food. It must be its otherworldly "exotic succulence." Or it could be that succulence abounds for those would-be suckers who refuse to starve to death at the banquet of life, those who taste and see God's goodness at all times, in all places, even those we do not suspect. I had such an unexpected "succulent" experience at a favorite monastery near Santa Barbara, California, when one evening all was serenely quiet on the Pacific western front. I was already in bed, alternately reading selected passages from a number of spiritually demanding books, including *Fasting for the Gourmet, Flagellation for the Faint of Heart,* and *Self-Denial for the Self-Absorbed.*

I knew that I would be up in a matter of hours to join the brothers in prayer at their predawn service. The monastery is a favorite place for me because of its rhythm and routine. Silence is observed from just after dinner all the way through breakfast the next morning. Not having to talk to anyone is pretty damn close to paradise for an introvert like me! Also, I tend to lose a few pounds at the monastery, always a good thing. There are lengthy hiking trails along mountain streams and through canyons just outside the monastery gate. The meals, though thoughtfully prepared, are simple and usually meatless. *Kalua* pig is rarely on the menu. A ripe piece of fruit is about as close as one gets to culinary decadence. Of course, a ripe piece of fruit is pretty decadent if you really taste it.

On this particular night there was a gentle knock at my cell door. It was one of the brothers extending an invitation. "Would you like to join us?" he whispered. "We're going in to town to have some dessert." We all piled into the monk-mobile, a beat-up compact car, and drove down to the city below, where we each ordered something sinfully rich. We charged it to the monk credit card.

"How often do you do this?" I asked.

"Just often enough," replied one of the more astute brothers, winking at me, as if I might get the subtle nuance of the relationship between moderation, appreciation, and the unexpected. Like James Thurber once noted, "One martini is all right. Two are too many, and three are not enough." I thought about ordering a beer with my cheesecake but did not want to push it. However, the sugar went straight to my head as I raised a tasty morsel and toasted, "If this is poverty, give me chastity!" I'm sure the brothers have never heard that one before. Being gracious men, they laughed anyway.

Life is a banquet. From the monastery to the luau. From Kauai to Cleveland. Paradise is less about place, and more about perspective, less about exotic locales and more about paying attention wherever you are, less about overindulgence, and more about appreciating the gifts already given.

Wherever you are: taste and see that the Lord is good.

6

A DINGLE IN MY WINGLE

Let us go on. . . .

—JESUS

Jesus just left Chicago, and he's bound for New Orleans. . . .
Ah, take me with you Jesus.

—ZZ TOP

*D*uring my spiritual pilgrimage/beer drinking excursion to Ireland with my occasionally wayward wayfaring friend Michael Soper, wherever we went we repeatedly encountered that most enduring expression of Celtic Christianity—the distinctive Celtic knot. This recognizable symbol expresses the interlacing of God and humanity, heaven and earth, the sacred with the secular. The pattern is without beginning or end, beautifully reflecting the ongoing process and never-ending, nonsegmented pilgrimage that is the discovery of faith and encounter with the divine. The Celtic knot intersects, backtracks, detours, connects, weaves in and out, and always keeps moving. It represents well the spiritual journey, not as a frantic flailing about, but as a purposeful pilgrimage discerning the divine directive.

In Ireland our purposeful pilgrimage frequently led us in search of beer, and our encounters with the locals further refined our itinerary. At a bar in the lovely Irish town of Dingle, an even lovelier Irish lass approached me and asked me a question that caused me to completely reevaluate my lifestyle, values, itinerary . . . and hairstyle. Seductively sidling my way, she said, "My friend wants to know if you're a hairdresser?"

Not recognizing a compliment when I heard one, I replied matter-of-factly, "No, I'm a priest."

Such a revelation left my admirer speechless and sent her scurrying back to her seat. I took this encounter as a sign that I needed to expand my baseball cap collection and as a reminder that I was not in Ireland merely as a tourist on the prowl, but as a pilgrim on a journey. I returned to my beer and my conversation with Michael.

I have traveled the world with Michael. When we travel together I am frequently reminded why Jesus sent the disciples out into the world in pairs. It is difficult to bail yourself out of jail.

Michael and I complement each other. Our individual strengths compensate for one another's weaknesses, and as a duo, we are able to engage larger groups of girls. I am the type who plans ahead, plots an itinerary, and navigates a course. Michael likes to show up, fly by the seat of his pants, and frequently ask, "Now where are we?" I prefer some spiritual dimension along the way, an educational component, or even some time for solitude and reflection. Michael likes to dance on tables in taverns, party like a rock star, and even run for public office wherever we might be. In Budapest, I swear he was almost elected mayor of both Buda and Pest in a single night. This was the same evening we had asked our favorite Hungarian hottie, Susannah, to recommend the bar that had the best view. She responded with the rather obvious metaphysical follow-up, "What do you want to see?"

We've discovered that sometimes Michael and I are looking for love, meaning, and happiness in very different places. I am the type who likes to learn about indigenous cultures and even master a few phrases in the local dialect. Michael likes to speak Spanish, loudly and poorly, to any native within earshot, even if we are in Lithuania. While his behavior borders on the obnoxious, he is often surprisingly cautious and wary, taking a step back to evaluate the situation before making a rash decision, and asking "Is this safe?" I can be more of a carpe diem kind of traveler. Caution is not in my travel vocabulary. If an opportunity arises, I will seize it first and ponder its implications later.

We once traveled from Bulgaria to Istanbul by bus with a cast of characters that made the local Greyhound station look like high tea at the Junior League, at a rate of speed easily surpassed by that of a box turtle. I struck up a conversation at the border crossing with an older, eccentric Scot who was traveling with a younger, tougher-looking Turk. We were stopped at the Turkish border, where the border guards had us remove every piece of luggage and display it on the pavement for no apparent reason, while they took naps, played cards, watched TV, drank whiskey, and smoked entire cartons of cigarettes. The odd couple was in a panic because they were traveling to Istanbul to see a soccer game between the premier teams from Scotland and Turkey. Before you could say "Attaturkey," we commandeered a cabdriver to drive the four of us all the way to Istanbul. Even a border guard understands the universal language and imperative of soccer, so they let us grab our luggage and pass right on through.

We piled into Akbar's cab, and after a brief beer stop, with Middle Eastern tunes blaring, we hightailed it to Istanbul in time for kickoff. Michael waited until he had knelt down and kissed the *H* in the entry mat of the Hilton hotel and had given the bellman a big bear hug before he asked me, "What the hell did you just get me into?" We immediately went to the rooftop bar to celebrate not only our arrival, but our survival. Sometimes you have to get off the tour bus, heed the available opportunities, commandeer alternative modes of transport, and travel with unusual suspects to get to where you need to be.

Back in Dingle, after Michael analyzed every conceivable dimension of the "hairdresser" comment and its manifold reflections on my emasculated sense of self, we honestly shared our travel priorities for Ireland. Since the girl's comment had slapped me straight back into a state of spiritual awareness, I told Michael, in no uncertain terms, that there were only two things I absolutely had to experience while in Ireland.

One, I wanted to take a boat out to Skellig Michael, or Michael's Rock: an isolated, hard-to-reach, austere precipice in the middle of nautical nowhere, the site of a sixth-century monastery, a significant place of pilgrimage and prayer even today. Such sites were called "thin places" by the ancient Celtic Christians. In these places, the veil between heaven and earth, the space between the temporal and the eternal, was so sheer, so thin, that one could almost reach across to the other side and touch the holy. Skellig Michael was an absolute on my spiritual itinerary.

Second, I told Michael that I wanted to climb St. Patrick's Mountain near Westport, another place of pilgrimage, penitence, and prayer for countless Christians over the centuries. A formidable trail leads to the top, where Patrick spent his last Lent and offered many prayers on Ireland's behalf. I told Michael, clearly and unequivocally, that if I did not make my pilgrimage to Skellig Michael and climb St. Patrick's Mountain, my trip to Ireland would have been in vain.

Michael responded just as clearly and unequivocally about his own itinerary priorities. "Much like you," he pointed out, "there are two most important spiritual tasks in which I must engage while on this holy isle. There are two priorities that fully encapsulate my passion and purpose on my Irish pilgrimage. While here in Patrick's land, following in that great procession of saints and scholars, I simply must do two things: one: play a lot of golf, and two: drink a lot of beer. If I do not play a lot of golf and drink a lot of beer, then my journey here shall have been in vain."

Our respective journeys were not in vain.

After finding out that the very few boats traveling from Portmagee to Skellig Michael were all full, I dropped Michael off at the country club and drove to Portmagee anyway. I had discovered through prior experience that perseverance and persistence were integral components of true pilgrimage. When I arrived at the dock, I was greeted warmly by a ruddy, red-headed sailor who happened to be the captain of the ship. His kind eyes, one of which seemed to be perpetually focused on the distant sea, assured me that I would get on board. He said it was a sure sign that I was to be there that day, because his father's name was William and his middle name was William and my name was William. I also had sixty euro in cash, so I got the last seat on the boat.

When I think about pilgrimage, I am reminded of one definition of faith—it is the direction our feet start moving when we find that we are loved. Of course, a pilgrimage could take us in any number of directions. Perhaps the key is movement; we walk, rather than just talk, our prayers. Such faith operates more in the realm of the unknown than the known. It is most at home when it is away from home, immersed in mystery and surprise, and occasionally in need of a cab.

Monks were drawn to such thin places as Skellig Michael, as we are still, because faith is most meaningful when experienced on the edge, hammered out at the literal and figurative margins of our lives and our world. The spiritual journey places us on the threshold of encounter, awareness, and discovery, when we step away from what we think we already know or wander off the course we have mapped out and isolated on the GPS. The thin places in our lives are often hard to get to, little known, and not for the faint of heart or soul.

As the mist cleared, the towering 750-feet-tall face of the *skellig* greeted us with both a welcoming and a wary eye, and I was moved to silence and awe. As often happens at these moments when we glance at the face of the divine, wonder and awe were followed by gratitude. I was grateful that God, and William's son, had made a way for me to get there. I was grateful to be propelled by a faith that keeps showing up, even when we don't know the way, or if a way will be made for us.

After a long hike to the top, I arrived at the monastery ruins and eavesdropped on a group of tourists who seemed more interested in circling prey in search of a pickup than risking transformation by way of an interconnecting knot with an unknown beginning and end. Their cluelessness reminded me of a comment I had heard in New Orleans years before. A young partyer in search of Jell-O shots and mindless karaoke paused at Preservation Hall, the birthplace of jazz. Observing the long line of music pilgrims patiently awaiting a chance to enter the holy of Dixieland holies, she turned to her friend and said, "Huh, must be some kind of club."

Yes, and Skellig Michael is some kind of rock. And pilgrimage must be some kind of journey. And prayer must be some kind of conversation. And God must be some kind of upper-management-level employee.

At the monastery ruins on the mountaintop, three guides were attempting to impart some semblance of knowledge about this unusual place, coming at it from three very different perspectives. The first was a young man wearing a beer shirt adorned with Irish brews. He spent the better part of his commentary finding humor in the monastic lifestyle, understanding monks and monasteries to be great repositories of comic material. It was irreverent but inoffensive, at least to a real monk, who had to have something of a sense of humor to spend a lifetime on a *skellig*.

The second guide, a young woman, talked incessantly of puffins—their mating, eating, and nesting habits. Their survival depended on finding a home here on such *skellig*s, she said. Her pilgrimage was understood in terms of a wildlife sanctuary, the sacredness of the site related to the stewardship of creation and the conservation of our feathered friends.

The third guide, an older, scholarly looking woman, knew all about monks, prayer, sacrifice, faithful fringes, marginal lives, and the thick as revealed in the thin. She spoke of heroic deeds, Viking raids, creative processes, the value of beauty, and the perception that the *skellig* was on the cutting edge of spiritual battle, and not an isolated opportunity for retreat and withdrawal.

The three guides all took the same path to the top, but somehow arrived in very different places. The revelation that came to me that day was that the solemn sister, my personal favorite, was not any closer to the kingdom than the irreverent jokester or the wildlife conservationist. Humor and steward-ship reveal the sacred in our lives just as the daily offices and austere lifestyle revealed the sacred in the lives of the monks. This thought brings me back to golf and beer, reconsidered.

That night, over an Irish ale, Michael described his unfor-gettable golf outing to me, stating in pilgrim fashion that "walking that ancient course was like walking with God." Per-haps the common thread linking all illuminating experiences is that, whether we are climbing a narrow footpath on a *skellig* or walking eighteen holes, we become keenly aware of the bless-ing of our context. We move forward into something new and other, into a reality that we can readily appreciate with new eyes and ears, new hearts and souls. This motion forces me to consider the unlikely possibility that perhaps I am called to be something I am not now, something I could not imagine being, such as a hairdresser, for example.

—

As the chief liturgist and priest in charge of Trinity Church Houston, whenever I officiated in my fanciest liturgical duds at the worship services, I would often face the brass cross tow-ering over the high altar in the neo-Gothic space. The cross was dedicated to the memory of Trinity's third rector, who served in the early 1900s after moving from his home in Jackson, Mississippi: the Reverend Robert E. Lee Craig. I must confess that when I would glance up at his name on the cross, I would think about Atticus Finch's observation in *To Kill a Mockingbird* that "naming people after confederate generals made for slow steady drinkers" even though that was apparently not the case with Father Craig. It was always such a blessed irony to proceed from that space to a jazz service in a chapel where a painting of the Resurrection by the eminent African-American artist Kermit Oliver towered over the altar. Father Craig was an avid traveler and a big baseball fan and was frequently spotted at Houston Buffalo games. He was a bachelor for the first seven years of his ministry until he married the governor of Mississippi's granddaughter. And he was apparently used to getting his way.

Before he came to Trinity, while he served St. Andrew's Church, now Cathedral, in Jackson, the temperance movement was gaining steam and popular opinion rallied to close the saloons. The members of the leadership board at St. Andrew's, most of whom were community leaders, were also the "citadel of saloon power" in town. (Episcopalians have not changed much over the years.) In 1897, the St. Andrew's vestry petitioned for an election to allow the saloons to remain open. While I think the vestry's action was incredibly heroic, a true testimony to their commitment to social justice, Father Craig thought otherwise. He reprimanded the vestry from the pulpit. The vestry censured Father Craig. The congregation voted. The vestry lost, and a new temperamental, temperance-minded vestry was elected. I am so glad I never had to host a Christmas party for that vestry!

In the earliest decade of the 1900s, Trinity Church, a little wooden chapel, was located on an obscure, almost invisible, dead-end street. The Reverend Craig said he would move to Houston and become their priest on one condition: they must move! God called God's people, Father Craig told them, to "face the world more prominently." Moved by Father Craig's demand, they moved!

At Father Craig's initiative, the little wooden chapel was loaded onto a long wagon and pulled by a team of mules all the way to Main Street. Neighborhood children gathered around and formed a parade alongside the now-portable sacred space. Upon arrival, the contractors split the building in half and expanded the little church to accommodate many more people. I am glad the early members of my former parish did not tell the Reverend Craig to go home to Mississippi, that they were staying put, that their church was not moving anywhere. Instead, in the immortal words of theologian Tom Waits, they concluded: You gotta get behind a mule. And move.

And when they moved, God moved among them.

The good southerner's call toward movement calls to mind another earlier saint who was described as God's gypsy, with a wagon that contained his altar. St. David of Wales liked to pray standing in the ocean, allowing the great movement of the waves to sweep over him like the great movement of God in his life. I have often thought that an appropriate dismissal for a Celtic liturgy on David's feast day might go something like this: Saddle up, pilgrims. Wagons, ho! Or perhaps: Surfs up—paddle out!

From the Celtic lands to Texas, a recurring theme about faith is our willingness to move with God. There is a story told about a Sunday school student, a budding young physicist who had recently pondered the theory that the presence of matter indicates motion. The young seeker also had some clue about a theology that says motion matters.

He asked his teacher how fast Jesus was traveling when he ascended toward heaven. The teacher thought about the Ascension story for a moment and responded that it had to have been slower than the speed of sound because Jesus spoke words of blessing on his way. The young scientist's eyes grew wide as he shared with the class his own scientific and spiritual observation—that, if that's the case, Jesus is not there yet! Jesus is still moving!

For those who call themselves followers, this observation has some demanding implications.

—

From Dingle, Michael and I traveled to Westport, where, over another ale, he surprised me by telling me that rather than spend the next day on the golf course or at a pub, he wanted to see, and possibly even climb, a portion of St. Patrick's Mountain. "I don't need to get all the way to the top," he said, "but I'll join you for the first leg of the journey."

At the beginning of the trek, we walked silently, in awe of pilgrims who trod barefoot, their bloodied feet evidence of their intentional penitence and prayerfulness. A very old, frail woman, her face determined and kind, was slowly making her way to the top, helped by a younger man. A mysterious woman in black, shimmering in sweat and gold jewelry, passed us like a woman on a serious mission. Much later, back at the base of the mountain, I would watch her get into a black Lamborghini, where her boyfriend waited at the wheel.

Halfway up, after Michael had discovered that shouting "Beer man!" was not going to make one materialize, even in this place of the miraculous, he told me to go on ahead. He had had enough pilgrimage for one day. We agreed to meet down below. Almost to the top, my face set like flint toward the summit, my penitential mood was broken by a scantily clad lass asking if I had a light and holding a cigarette seductively in her lips. Not wanting to confuse a pilgrimage with a pickup opportunity, I looked away and said, "Sorry," which I was. For what, I was not exactly certain.

Upon reaching the top, I beheld a disappointing place where pop tops, worn socks, donation boxes, and padlocks reflected nothing but gloom. I debated in my mind whether the careless tourists or the crass religious institution had done more harm to the site. The tourists' scattered trash dishonored the saint, while the church's halfhearted attempt to extract treasure dishonored the seeker—both were equally unenlightened and unenlightening. The question started to haunt me: Do you have a light? Someone? Anyone? The best part of the summit was the misty cloud that obscured any sort of view, and the rocks, all original. Slippery, hard, weathered rocks. I heard a lone sheep bleating in the distance. I heard the smoker's mother lecture her on the importance of being prepared. I think she was alluding to light, perhaps.

I headed back down St. Patrick's Mountain, wondering if Michael had found a beer man down below. Suddenly I saw the light. Bright, radiant, revelatory light. It was on Michael's face as he climbed toward me.

"Bet you didn't think you'd see me up here, did ya?" said the tourist turned pilgrim. I walked back up the final ascent of the mountain, this time part of a pair, the favorite formation of Jesus's disciples. We stood together on the top of Patrick's Mountain—or is it now known as Michael's rock?

"I get the thin place thing," Michael said. "I feel Patrick's presence." Now fully in touch with his inner pietist, Michael suggested, "I think we should pray, or something." So I prayed, or something, out loud, holding hands with Michael, awkwardly, but not too awkwardly. I thanked God for mountains and rocks, for tourists and pilgrims, for beer and golf, for thick and thin.

On the way down, I saw that the fundamentalists had gone to great lengths to antagonize the penitent, spelling out with rocks: ONLY JESUS FORGIVES SIN. An original cynic had painted a nearby stone: ALL RELIGION IS A CRUTCH. For a moment I could not locate the light, once again. For it will never be found with feet firmly planted, sure and certain as an unmoving stone, whether our certitude is religious or rational. The true pilgrim moves on.

Coming down the mountain was much more difficult than going up. I bit the dust several times, scraped up my knees, and cut my hands. Michael's rented walking stick, which I had almost teased him about, now seemed like a really good idea. Maybe a crutch is just the prop we need to reach an extraordinary height, like a mountaintop, or to descend to a lower depth, a place far deeper than we could ever experience without some type of support.

When we reached the parking lot, Michael wondered if the gift shop sold beer. The walking stick vendor had closed shop for the day, so Michael's deposit for the stick rental had now become the purchase price. It was not a bad souvenir from St. Patrick's Mountain. Not a bad holy relic, either, for that matter.

Lest things become too serious and solemn, Michael began to sing the song he had proudly composed the night before in

Dingle. It was inspired by an encounter with a young woman on the streets, a woman who had not asked him if he was a hairdresser. Michael had approached her and asked her to recommend a good place for us to go.

She asked him for clarification: "You want to sit and listen to the traditional music?"

His response surprised her. "Hell no!" he retorted. "I wanna dance!" He twirled her around, and she sent us on down the road toward a newly discovered Mecca of movement.

On the way, Michael began to sing "There's a Dingle in my Wingle." He had even created a special dance step that would *not* rival anything you may have seen in *Riverdance*. Or maybe it would. The beauty of the song he composed was that one could reverse the lyric and sing "There's a Wingle in my Dingle"—known by some as verse two. Though not a particularly moving composition, I noticed that it appeared to compel some people to move.

And perhaps that is the point of true pilgrimage.

Not that we are always moved.

But that we are always moving.

7

PEARLS OF GREAT PRICE

The kingdom of heaven is like unto a merchant seeking goodly
pearls; who, when he had found one of great price, went and sold all
that he had, and bought it.

—MATTHEW 13:45–46

Teach me, my God and King, in all things thee to see.

—GEORGE HERBERT, PRIEST, POET, BEER DRINKER

As a parish priest, I have participated in more than my
share of special moments in people's lives: weddings, funerals,
baptisms, you name it. We call these the "holy sacraments."
What makes them holy is that, if we ask—and sometimes even
if we don't—God gets involved. The Originator of all this ordinary stuff we take for granted somehow and some way gets
into it in order to bless us in a special way on these occasions.
The common materials of creation become indicators of God's
grace—external signs of an internal reality. The most unvalued
element can be ripe with holiness at any time and can become
the pearl of great price.

In a perfect world, these sacramental moments would consistently come across as quintessentially lovely Hallmark moments, but because we live in an imperfect world and we are imperfect people, they sometimes end up more like *Far Side* moments. Sometimes God's presence is unexpected and unpredictable.

In my early years in ministry, I preferred funerals to weddings. Not to sound cynical, but the former just seemed so much more hopeful than the latter. Perhaps Kinky Friedman captured my earlier sentiments when he courageously defended gay marriage during his Texas gubernatorial campaign, saying, "Why shouldn't they be allowed to be miserable like the rest of us?"

While I still think that the burial rite is a singular sacramental force, I am coming to appreciate matrimonial moments as powerful manifestations of true love, or at least, truly entertaining love. For when amateurs gather round to produce nuptials on parade, unintended comedy often ensues. In the end, such ordinary hilarity is not only extraordinarily endearing, it can be downright holy. Infused with loving purpose, common human folly can reflect the very glory and presence of God.

One of my favorite wedding moments occurred at a large society wedding at a lovely Episcopal church. The bride believed that her initial presence and graceful procession down the center aisle should be preceded by pause, pomp, reverence, and circumstance. She insisted that, just before her first step, two tuxedoed groomsmen should swoop down from the nether regions of the narthex and elegantly unfurl an eighty-foot white satin aisle runner. Upon this she would float all the way to the front of the church, thus keeping her feet from touching the common carpet trod upon by pedestrian wedding guests and supporting-cast bridesmaids.

At the rehearsal, those seasoned veterans of matrimonial mishaps known as church wedding coordinators informed the bride, clearly and unequivocally, "We do not recommend aisle runners. And if you insist on having one, we strongly encourage you to have it laid out, in place, and tacked down, *before* the service begins. Otherwise, it is a disaster waiting to happen." The bride would not be deterred, insisting on a pregnant pause, a dramatic unfurling, and a floating white pathway toward matrimonial bliss.

The wedding hour arrived. The grandparents and parents were seated. The groomsmen, groom, and I entered from the side and stood reverently at the chancel steps. The bridesmaids effortlessly glided down the plain carpet path. The runner unfurlers assumed their proud posts. The next seventeen minutes, which seemed like an hour and seventeen minutes, could best be summarized thusly: How many curls could a curl unfurler unfurl, if a curl unfurler could unfurl curls?

Not many and not fast.

How do you spell D-I-S-A-S-T-E-R? Let me count the ways. The nylon cord, meant to release the runner like a gentle wave upon the shore, was as forthcoming as a recalcitrant cat in a cage on vaccination day. The tuxedoed gents began to grunt, wrestle, yank, pull, cajole, and curse the stubborn shimmering fabric. This preliminary smackdown was followed by a series of high-powered buttock thrusts down the aisle and into the air, as if the carpet bouncers were auditioning for a *Buns of Steel* workout video. After butt-boxing pews, photographers, candle holders, and friends of both bride and groom, they huffed and puffed their way toward the now-frozen bride.

Noting the flustered bride's frustration at the obstacle course they had inadvertently created, the unfurlers would not be foiled. In a final stroke of brute strength and ungraceful incoordination, they grabbed the ends of the runner and yanked so hard that a battery of carpet tacks flew out of their positions tucked under the chancel steps and nailed the front-row families with the force of machine-gun fire on the front lines of battle. The wavy aisle runner was instantly transformed into a straight and narrow ski ramp of Olympic proportions.

By this time the organist had completely exhausted his entire matrimonial repertoire, including the theme from *The Thorn Birds* and the theme from *Shaft*. The silence was punctuated with uproarious laughter from everyone gathered, with the exception of the groom, who was already trained in the art of "when not to laugh," an important premarital training technique.

Rather than floating like a butterfly, the bride stomped down the aisle with the grace of a tank ramming a bunker. When she got to the trampoline portion of the runner, she planted her left foot and bounced right into the arms of her awaiting groom. My hastily reconstructed wedding homily focused on the sacramental beauty of sure and certain carpet tacks, and strong, supportive arms, not to mention a sense of humor when everything else fails.

My other favorite wedding moment occurred in the most unusual location in which I have ever been privileged to preside: the backyard of the Beer Can House. The Beer Can House was created starting in 1968 in a pregentrification blue-collar, working-class neighborhood in inner-city Houston, a land flowing with ladies' knickknacks and men's tank tops.

This folk art monument to one of the world's greatest pastimes—beer drinking—reveals a relationship that is as sacramental as any nuptial blessing. The story of the Beer Can House is really a love story. John and Mary Milkovisch were the retired couple who created and lived in the Beer Can House. Actually John built it, but Mary appreciated it. It is an endearing testimony to the power of love, even when conceived as sheer folly.

When John retired as an upholsterer for the Southern Pacific Railroad, he began to engage in the two activities that retired American males do best—puttering and beer drinking. Combine the two, and one has a potent force not unlike that exhibited by the Creator at the inception of the universe. Motivated by the complementary qualities of utility, beauty, ingenuity, imagination, and a hint of intoxication, one can fashion a masterpiece from the common stuff of life. Over the course of his eighteen-year retirement, it is estimated that John Milkovisch drank about a six-pack per day. This figure is according to Mary. John eloquently defended his capacity for far greater consumption by retorting, "I can drink more than six damn beers in one damn day." I do not doubt him. His dedication yielded thirty-nine thousand beer cans, which John stored in his garage.

One day, as the story goes, a small portion of wood siding had rotted away from an inconspicuous back corner of the modest bungalow. This was during the golden age of modern substances that seemed far superior to what nature had provided: things like Teflon, Formica, plastic, and that architectural wunderkind, aluminum siding. John decided he could fashion a section of durable metal siding by utilizing his greatest resource—beer cans. Taking several dozen beer cans, John crafted the world's first beer can siding. Standing back to admire his creative ingenuity, he saw that his beer can siding was not only functionally efficient but also a rather bold design statement. He proceeded to cover the entire house with a layer of lager labels, destined to shock the world, and, eventually, hopefully please his wife.

John soon began to imagine other art forms fashioned out of the various components of a six-pack, such as pull-tab curtains, for example. He attributed this stroke of artistic genius to "just one of those dreams in the back of my noodle." Beer can tops became wind chimes. Whole cans became the building blocks of quaint canopies, colorful walls, and patterned trellises. Inspired by beer, John's capacity for creative expression began to exceed that of his daily consumption. He utilized other common elements of human existence to create a world of wonder upon, around, and behind his house. Marbles, rocks, brass figures, metal pieces, concrete—no common utilitarian object was off-limits as John formed mobiles, curtains, sculptures, windmills, and other unknown hangy-downy thingamabeers from empty beer cans and their common Dollar Store cousins.

Till the day he died, John could not quite conceive of his creation as art, telling others, "Some people say this is sculpture, but I didn't go to no expensive school to get these notions." What began as a practical solution for inexpensive home repair became an acclaimed folk art monument to not only the beauty of beer, but also the powerful force of a loving partner. Mary not only tolerated his eccentric endeavor, she encouraged it. Several years after John passed away, I had the rare privilege of sitting with her in her living room as we planned a wedding ceremony for her backyard. Mary shared stories of true love for a husband who "thought beer cured everything" and who "didn't think anybody would ever be interested in this house—he just loved drinking his beer and just loved being outside and cutting up beer cans." Ah, true love.

As we sat in Mary's very traditional living room, filled with ordinary knickknacks ordered from common catalogs, my creative and entertaining friends David, a movie reviewer and aspiring author, and his fiancée Susanne, an appreciator of all things artistic, began to share their own dream: they wanted to get married here.

There were two reasons they so desperately wanted to be married at the Beer Can House. The first was their inherent appreciation for folk art, art created by common folk who did not go to expensive schools to get their original ideas. Susanne was the director of an equally unusual folk art installation called the Orange Show. The Orange Show is a small wonderland of exhibits, displays, and funky, artistic, unknown creations that pay homage to the orange, created to express one man's deep devotion to and appreciation for a most common citrus fruit. It is known as the Acropolis of folk art sites and is even more famous than the Beer Can House. It is also one of my favorite places on earth—a whimsical creation of a postman named Jeff McKissack, who was to oranges what John Milkovisch was to beer. McKissack, like Milkovisch, took ordinary components of human life and turned them into something extraordinary. When he received a building permit to build a beauty parlor, he parlayed that idea into a place of a rare and different beauty. Just as Milkovisch believed that beer cured everything, McKissack believed that the orange was the perfect food, a gift from God and the solution to most of life's ills. He wrote all about it in his book, *How You Can Live to Be One Hundred and Still Be Spry Even If Your Parents Are Dead.*

McKissack crafted normal building materials and found objects into something he believed would become a tourist attraction to rival the Astrodome. He was disappointed when the anticipated crowds never materialized. But after his death, a group of artists, architects, and all-around interesting people, including members of ZZ Top, got together to preserve the site for posterity.

At the Orange Show, there are mazes and mosaics, stages and steamboats, and a small museum with mannequins extolling fruity folk wisdom. The basic building is anything but basic—concrete, brick, and steel, decorated with gears, tiles, wagon wheels, tractor seats, and statuettes. One Fourth of July I attended a concert at the Orange Show, featuring Doctor Rockit and the Sisters of Mercy. From my skybox tractor seat under a canopy of discarded colorful tin, I drank a cold beer while beholding one man's version of paradise—a version not unlike my own. McKissack's creation served as the catalyst for the art car revolution, inspiring the famous Fruitmobile, one of the very first art cars in America. Now there is an Art Car Parade each May, sponsored by the Orange Show, attracting the most innovative art objects on wheels from around the world and drawing half a million curious onlookers. Although it took them several decades to arrive, the hordes of tourists now appreciate his efforts even if they do not know his name.

Beyond artistic appreciation, the second reason David and Susanne wanted to celebrate the sacrament of Holy Matrimony in the backyard of the Beer Can House had to do less with the art of folk and more with the folk of art. They believed that a relationship of unconditional love, celebrating the union of consumption and creativity, was precisely the kind of relationship they wanted to cultivate as a couple. They could think of no greater role models as husband and wife than John and Mary, and they wanted to exchange their vows where these two had experienced married life. Mary thought it was an unusual but lovely idea, much like what she had thought of John's initial undertaking.

When David and Susanne, devout Catholics, explained to their parish priest that they wanted him to officiate their wedding at the Beer Can House, he explained to them that they must have consumed large quantities of cheap beer before they had come to see him. He further explained that he was unable to perceive the sacredness of such a silly site, and that the church building was the only proper place for a proper wedding and the proper celebration of a proper sacrament.

Disappointed but undeterred, the bride asked a few creative types if there was any priest in town who might possibly be willing to officiate a wedding at the Beer Can House. For some reason having nothing to do with my drinking habits, my name kept coming up. I was honored to be associated with such things, considering this as great a compliment as when a former girlfriend repeatedly asked me, "Are you sure you're a priest?"

At the wedding, we processed out of Mary's traditional living room, through the front porch beer tab curtain, and around the yellow ladder embedded in the front yard that reaches toward the sky and is emblazoned with the Golden Rule: Do unto others as you would have them do unto you. We passed the beer can fence and marched across the marble-laden concrete patio and under the beer can mobile, and up the driveway toward the backyard. A band of gypsies played some of the most passionate and unexpected wedding processional music I had ever heard. We gathered under a beer can canopy as beer can chimes accompanied the traditional liturgy. We were surrounded by the power of ordinary sacraments.

Sacraments are really pretty simple, and you don't need to go to no expensive school to understand them. Sacraments happen when ordinary objects or elements, such as bread, wine, water, beer cans, or even two human beings, are infused with the power of love and made holy. Taken, blessed, appreciated, and given, the common becomes uncommon. The ordinary is transformed into the extraordinary. Artists are born. Masterpieces are created. The Source of Creative Love is manifest, for God hallows the unlikeliest of objects and the unlikeliest of subjects. That is what often makes the things we take for granted the pearls of the greatest price.

—

Early in life I recognized that there might be some sacramental possibility in this common grain-based beverage known as beer. It happened when I floated down a cool Texas river on a hot summer day with my second father, Hank Bartos. Hank always floated with a six-pack of Pearl tied around his inner tube, and he'd savor each sip as we slowly made our way around the bend. Hank explained to me that we floated in sacred waters, saying, "Billy, this is the area where they brew Pearl beer; this is the land of eleven hundred springs." Wow! The very idea that cool clear water could come up from the ground and be transformed into an adult beverage absolutely blew my mind.

I would later learn that the Pearl Brewing Company had been founded not far from that river, in San Antonio in 1881. Originally it had been called the J. B. Behloradsky Brewery, a great name not unlike other great names—Bartos, Milkovisch, and McKissack. Supposedly the name of the beer came from the German brewmaster from whom the new Texas brewery purchased the formula. This brewmaster, who had an eye for the sacramental, believed that the bubbles in a freshly poured glass of beer resembled fine pearls. By 1916, Pearl was the largest brewery in Texas.

Much has changed in the brewing world. Today, Miller, a much less interesting name, brews a mere pittance of Pearl Beer out of its Fort Worth brewery. Pearl beer connoisseurs— apparently not an oxymoron—insist that the formula must have changed, because it doesn't taste like it used to.

I suppose the ingredients could have changed, or maybe they no longer use the water from the land of eleven hundred springs. More likely it's that the brewing process is not experienced sacramentally. When the common elements of our lives are taken, blessed, and given, infused with love, in the process, they are transformed into something of supreme value. And we are changed as we experience them.

Only then can you end up with a pearl of great price.

8

THE ANGELS' SHARE

Do not neglect to show hospitality to strangers, for by doing so some
have entertained angels without even knowing it!

—HEBREWS 13:2

Always be generous in the bedroom. Share your sandwich.

—HOMER SIMPSON

*I*f beer is our bible, then Scotch is our creed. Both beer and
Scotch begin with similar proportions of the same ingredients,
but they end up with different quantities and levels of fortifi-
cation. While the Holy Scriptures contain an entire case of
"Tall Boy" tales about the multitudes' adventures in grace, the
creeds condense the story of faith to a few simple drams of the
divine drama. While fermentation is subtle and reasonable,
distillation is more dramatic and intense. Perhaps it's like the
difference between generosity and sacrifice—beer is incredibly
good while Scotch is downright transformative.

I have roots in Scotland. Supposedly, there is still a castle
in the Lowlands that bears the name of a clan who is kin.

However, since it is not located near any of my favorite distilleries, it did not appear on my seven-day itinerary when I went
to Scotland a few years back.

But there were two significant moments during my one-
week spiritual pilgrimage in Scotland in which I felt my ancestors, in some vaporous form, reach up under my kilt,
metaphorically speaking, and give me a good yank on the loins
to remind me of my ancient connections. As they say around
there, it was a poke to the naughty bits, and it was, if not
spine-tingling, enough to make a grown man cry. At the very
least, it got my attention and made me aware that I was, in
some sense, connected to a place that had been home.

The first epiphany occurred during the Edinburgh Military Tattoo. This military band, and drum and pipe, festival
takes place in an exquisite setting, on the Esplanade, starting at
dusk, in front of an illuminated Edinburgh Castle. Tickets are
hard to come by, and for good reason. It is a spectacle that resonates deep within the soul: primal, archetypal, even spiritual.

Tattoo, by the way, has nothing to do with lousy ink art
implanted on one's hidden parts. Rather, it was a decree from
the local military outpost to the town's taverns, informing
them that it was time for the soldiers to stop partying and
head back to the barracks for a reasonable night's sleep. It was
a kind of "Last call!" at the local inn, with the drums and pipes
of the regiment communicating a clear "Turn off the taps!" or
"Doe den tap toe." The expression was eventually shortened to
"Tattoo" and now has nothing to do with the shutting off of
ale taps and everything to do with opening up our ears to
some hovering-on-heavenly musical expression—courtesy of
the largest gathering of drums and pipes this side of Briga-
doon.

There have been but a few moments in my life in which music has swept me up into the celestial sphere. To watch, hear, and feel the massed pipers and drummers (historically fighters first and musicians second) kindled a deep longing to charge into battle alongside William Wallace or Robert the Bruce. I recalled, with tears in my eyes, that my name is not William Bruce for nothing. To say that it was a connecting moment is to say that downing twelve shots of Scotch might slightly alter one's state of consciousness. I don't know that my heart will ever beat with quite the same rhythm again.

The second movement of the Scottish symphony occurred when I entered the storehouse at the Glenlivet distillery, hereafter known as the Mother Ship. While I have never met a Scotch I did not like, over at the glen by the River Livet they seem to have perfected the art of distilling. It is quite the magical setting for alcoholic alchemy, understated and pastorally serene. I was ready to start my own private monastery in the village nearby, or at least price vacation property. Sure, sometimes I am in the mood for a fierce peaty-tasting, fire-breathing Scotch that will blacken the tongue, earthen the sense of humor, and make one hiss. Occasionally, I even prefer to sip some Scotch infused with sea salt from the outer islands, a drink that sneaks up on one's manliness like an unforeseen tsunami. But I always return to Mr. Glen Livet, for he never fails to smooth out the hard edges of life and remind me of my ancestral, if not celestial, home.

Upon entering the Glenlivet storehouse, I had what can only be described as an immanently transcendent experience. I breathed in deeply of a fragrance that was closer to heaven than any other over which my nostrils had previously flared.

What I inhaled was so sweetly uplifting it seemed to be the bouquet of beings not of this world.

It was not of this world.

For I was taking in that scent reserved for the heavenly host. I was sniffing the Angels' Share. So potently did it permeate the atmosphere that, with a few more breaths, I might have sprouted wings.

Scotch, like many spirits, is aged in an oak cask for many years. The aging barrels filled the entire storehouse. The wood is breathable and lets some of the liquid evaporate out. This part that is lost is called the Angels' Share.

For bourbon casks in the American South, it is said that up to 30 percent of the corn nectar evaporates through the wood and travels toward the angelic realm. I have always suspected that Kentucky had more than its fair share of angels, and like good southerners, they like to party. Since much Scotch whisky is aged in ex-bourbon casks, the Scottish angels are content to reclaim only 2 percent, far less than their heavenly hillbilly cousins. However, that 2 percent is pure alcohol, not to mention pure single-malt Scotch. Advantage MacAngels.

Our tour guide at the distillery explained that the natural breathability of the wood is a crucial part of the maturation process. If the Scotch were kept in a hermetically sealed canister, our kilted connoisseur said, the angels wouldn't be able to enjoy any of it, and the human drinker's enjoyment would also diminish. In other words, the resulting product would be pitifully inferior. Giving away a portion to the angels is a necessary part of the process. If the angels did not get their share, the humans would suffer equally, if not more.

Some might call this karma. Other, more scientifically minded types might call it evaporation. I prefer to call it a profound lesson on sharing, particularly when it comes to sharing with those we sometimes fail to see or whose existence we refuse to acknowledge.

Apparently such an idea is not original. The James B. Beam Distilling Company actually calls its charitable endeavors the Angels' Share. A percentage of their profits goes to worthy causes beyond their corporate well-being: basic social services, a ranch for developmentally challenged children, nature preserves, historic preservation, educational opportunities for those in need, and many others. Just think how much better the world would be, not to mention how much better the world would smell, if each us adopted an attitude of the angels' share. A shot. A share. And a difference. I'll drink to that.

—

I have noticed over years of ministry that, when the topic of giving is mentioned, some people get so defensive, obnoxious, and even angry, they almost drive me to drink. While some religious traditions have maintained that a share of 10 percent beyond one's own economic well-being is an appropriate giving goal, for the charitably challenged, any proportion can be a source of genuine irritation. It is always sad to find that some have hearts as shallow as their breathing habits, casks sealed so tightly the angels know not to hover around for long. But without the smell, we can hardly taste that which we have protected. Holding one's nose, like holding one's resources, is to greatly diminish the potential blessing—for all involved.

Usually when one speaks about sharing, sacrificial giving, or generosity, the folks who get nervous, stressed out, and defensive are the very ones who should be nervous, stressed out, and defensive. Conversely, I do not think I ever met a truly generous, giving person who was not at the very least deeply joyful and often incredibly happy. You can usually identify such cheerful givers whenever the topic comes up. They tend to look you right in the eye, smile a lot, and spend time pondering how they could do even more. They often sprout wings and seem to soar above the mundane worries that get most of us worked into pretzels. They tend to breathe deeply and seem to get a buzz off life itself. Or maybe they just inhale a lot of angel shares, or drink more Scotch than the rest of us. Whatever their MO, their casks seem never to run dry. Besides, these are the folks we'd all like to drink with, even if they didn't pick up the tab.

I learned about giving from my father. Our drinking habits were nothing alike, even though I still cherish that early photo of him downing a Pearl beer and smoking a cigarette in some forgotten Texas dive bar. He'd later become a teetotaler. Our theological, ethical, political, economic, and beverage choices diverged widely on many fronts, but when it came to generosity, he was the master teacher. I still aspire to reach a place where our giving habits converge.

For him it wasn't just about money. He gave himself. He spent many a Saturday morning mowing the lawn, weeding the beds, and cleaning the gutters for the widow who lived just behind us. Though she consistently tried to pay him, he refused to take a dime from her. As I got older, Mrs. Syptak would try to pay me, thinking an adolescent surely wouldn't refuse cold, hard cash. It was tempting, but in the end, I always refused, too. And I began to experience that core truth that it really is more blessed to give than to receive. Besides, she baked the best *kolache*s this side of Prague, and we never refused those.

Even though it wasn't just about money, my dad would never let anyone off the hook by saying, "It's not just about money." I think he noticed, as I have over the years, that often the people who say such things about money would prefer to hold on to their own. Those who protest too much might need to let go of a little more.

Every week I would see the check that my dad would write out to the Garden Oaks Church of Christ. While I could not calculate a precise percentage of his income, I was good enough in math, even at a young age, to understand a generous portion. There was one memorable moment in which he clearly defined his theology of generosity. My dad stood in the church pulpit and expounded the virtues of the tithe, giving away a literal 10 percent of one's income, and encouraging others to do the same. One man, heretofore known as "the Wingless Wonder," a man who preferred to seal his casks airtight, angrily cornered my father.

"Don't you know your Bible, Bill Miller?!" he yelled. "The tithe is in the Old Testament. We're New Testament Christians now, Bill. We don't follow the rules of the Old Testament. We're not bound by that teaching anymore!"

My father's response will forever remain lodged in my heart, not to mention my wallet. My dad smiled at the man and affirmed his theological position: "You're so right. The ten percent tithe was *before* God showed us just how much he loved us, by giving his own son Jesus Christ to die for us. The tithe was *before* God's ultimate gift. You're right, brother, the tithe is now completely *insufficient* as a response to God's incredible generosity. The tithe is not enough anymore. Thank you for reminding me of that."

And the man went away sad, for there were many casks in

his storehouse and they were sealed so tight it smelled like nothing in there. Like nothing at all.

Later on I did the math. I figured out that my dad consistently gave at least 20 percent of his income away to charity, mostly to the church. When he retired and had fewer resources, it was understandable that he would adjust his giving percentage. He increased it to 50 percent! When my dad died, they retired his wings. They are now displayed in the Human Flight Museum. I once tried them on and quickly discovered they were too big for me. One of my life's goals remains to grow into those wings.

Doris Summers had a nice pair of wings as well. Doris was eighty years old when she changed my life, particularly my understanding of "enough." At Trinity Church, we were entrusted with one of the most beautiful religious buildings in town, a neo-Gothic jewel designed by eminent architect Ralph Adams Cram. Being a good steward sometimes means simply taking care of what's been given to you and letting it age gracefully, like a well-tended storehouse. However, spaces that are grimy, leaky, stinky, ugly, cramped, and in a state of disrepair do not quite reveal the glory of God. We had not been such good stewards, and the time had come to own up to our role. The engineers, contractors, and architects told us it would take about $3 million to restore the building to its rightful reflection of glory. We were stuck at a million. That is, until Doris Summers got involved.

This eighty-year-old widow lived entirely on Social Security and a small clergy pension inherited from her late husband. One day Doris walked into her bank, right next to Trinity Church, removed her entire life's savings, walked across the street to Trinity, and gave it all away to restore her beloved church. Doris explained that her daughter had married well, her son with Down syndrome was well cared for, and she herself didn't really "need all that money." When the story of Doris's generosity began to get around the parish, virtually every one of us recalculated "the best we could do." Suddenly, it was a lot more than it had been. One hundred percent makes 10 percent look a lot more doable. We ended up with $3 million. The luster was restored to the jewel, and one gem of a lady had made it possible.

I know entire faith communities that live with such lofty intentions and integrity, giving up their very existence in the name of doing what is right and beneficial. The old Central Church of Christ was my spiritual home for several years just out of college. The parish had dwindled by the time I arrived but was still a lively and relatively diverse lot, especially by fundamentalist standards. Years before, the parish had lost its collective ass on a nursing home ministry that went bankrupt. The Christian Home for the Aged, not a very sexy project and unable to attract widespread support or deep pockets, went belly-up and left the mother church holding the bills.

There were really only two options: declare bankruptcy and pay pennies on the dollar to the creditors, or sell all of their church assets, including their church building and property, pay off every bill in full, and cease to exist as a congregation. The leadership decided that option two was the one of real integrity, even if it meant giving up everything, including their identity and existence, clipping their wings in the name of love. A conscientious developer—not an oxymoron—heard of their plight and partnered with them, offering a premium price for the property just above the appraised value, so they could pay off their entire debt. The remaining members merged with an existing congregation a few miles away, and the Central Church of Christ was no more.

Or was it? I, for one, still tell their story.

The story gets even better. The sanctuary space became a beautiful branch of the neighborhood public library. The offices and classroom space were turned into a funky coffee shop, delicious bakery, and a photography gallery, where years later I purchased my first real photograph—ironically, a George Krause photo of an old Philadelphia brownstone inhabited by a couple of winged creatures. In it, an imposing archangel watches over the city from a lower floor, while above a tiny cherub points onward and upward. And the old church parish hall? It became my favorite British pub in the city—the Black Labrador Pub. Not only do they serve Smithwick's on tap, but they offer the most impressive geographical distillation of Scotch this side of the River Livet.

When I meet friends at the Black Lab for a pint, or a single malt, I am pleased to tell them that in that room I stood at a lectern as an enthusiastic twenty-three-year-old, armed with my B.S. in Bible (appropriately titled), and lectured knowingly on the fundamentals of faith. I knew much more back then than I know now, of course. My friends are always pleased to point out to me that the pub is a much more profound use of the space. And actually, I have to concur. Between the bakery, the shepherd's pie, the ever-flowing taps, and the oft-uncorked bottles, I'd have to say the place still reeks of, well, angels. Not surprising, given its history. When one does the right thing at great cost, goodness and good times will often prevail.

One of my most memorable encounters with hospitality and generosity occurred on a train from Chester to Crewe in

England. I was traveling from Wales to Scotland. In Wales, I had read prolifically about Celtic spirituality in the library at St. Deiniol's College. In Scotland, I would drink prolifically and take in its essence, from the Highlands to the islands.

The train was crowded and cramped, and I found myself seated across from a large, tank-top-clad Irishman who was in a boisterous and extroverted mood (even for a Celt!). As soon as I sat down, he initiated a conversation that drew me into a fiery red ring of wavy locks, abundant freckles, and forceful brogue. When he found out I was from Texas, I thought he was going to stand and bow. Instead he stood and shook my hand as if I were a real celebrity, or even a hero. He immediately offered me a fistful of wine-flavored gummy candies and produced a plastic cup he had hidden in a beat-up backpack. He handed me the cup and the forty-ounce can of Bulmers cider he'd been gulping and said, "I'll share. Drink up."

I poured a polite quantity, barely wetting the bottom of the cup and handed the Bulmers back to him. He scowled and made what sounded like pirate gruntings, grabbed my cup back, filled it to the rim with cider, and handed it back to me. He grinned and nodded, as if to say, "That's how we share around here—all in."

When I told him I would be traveling on to Ireland after my time in Scotland, he stood up and shook my hand again. His eyes then sparkled as he spoke passionately about, of all things, the Alamo! "Remember the Alamo!" he cried out, raising a Bulmers in the general direction of Texas. "Many great heroes died there," he said.

My new friend continued, after a gulp of Bulmers of heroic proportion: "Aye, many a hero killed there: Davy Crockett, that one with the knife, and John Wayne. They were waiting for that general," he continued. "George Washington. To defeat Santa Ana and the Mexican Army."

He popped the tab on another cannon-sized Bulmers and, after downing a third of the can, filled my plastic cup to the rim. He looked at me with a mischievous Irish eye, and I wondered if he really did confuse his Texas, American, and Hollywood history, or if he was just pulling a Texan's leg. Either way, he sure knew his stuff when it came to sharing.

Sometimes it takes a moment, when the bubbles are sucked right out of our champagne, to remind us of the futility of saving it all for ourselves. Many years ago someone gifted me with a rare and expensive bottle of champagne. On occasion I have splurged on a fine Bordeaux or a well-aged Scotch, but this gift was in a class by itself. I made a conscientious vow to stash it away for safekeeping and enjoy it only when a worthy occasion would merit its ceremonial uncorking. For countless years it occupied that sacred tabernacle space in the refrigerator that some would call a vegetable crisper (that is to say, waste of space). It even made a move with me, securing its own private ice chest from Austin to Houston. I began to wonder if there would ever be an occasion worthy of popping the cork. I waited, and I waited. For a long time. Too long.

Finally, many years later, on a special night in October, two extraordinary things happened within an hour of each other. First, the Houston Astros, a team that I have followed since childhood, beat the St. Louis Cardinals to advance to the World Series for the first time in history. Second, I got a call from the senior warden of St. Michael's Church on Kauai offering me a job that would allow me to live in the most beautiful place on earth. This double whammy of good fortune finally propelled me straight toward the vegetable crisper. I hoisted the glowing liquid gold into the air and with all the ceremony of a priest raising a chalice at the altar on Easter Day, I popped the cork on the treasured gift.

Well, actually, I removed the cork, but there wasn't much pop going on. It was more like an impotent thud, like the sound of a single-serving can of Pringles being opened. I poured the celebratory bubbly and noted a complete absence of bubbles. The fizz had fizzled. The champagne had become "chump-pain." That's what happens when you save something for too long and fail to celebrate and share the gifts given so often along the way. In a flash, I recognized all of those extraordinary moments, special people, and memorable occasions that had slipped by over the years, every one of them worthy of a celebratory pour.

There is an old story told about a tide on a distant shore that had stranded thousands upon thousands of starfish on the beach. A small girl noted their plight, set aside her sand pail, and began to purposely pick them up, one at a time, and toss them back toward their home in the sea. A practical-minded adult came upon her and decided to impart to the naïve youngster some of the cold, hard facts of life.

"Do you really think it makes any difference?" scoffed the skeptic to the young girl, motioning toward the multitude of starfish still stranded on the sand.

Holding aloft a single starfish, she replied to the tightly sealed soul, "It does for this one," and tossed the creature back into the sea.

In medieval times, the monks who doubled as brewers called the yeasty froth that comprised the head of a beer "God is good." For within this undrinkable substance was the secret of fermentation. They finally figured out that if they skimmed it off the top and shared it with another brewing batch, the liquid would be transformed into something other than what it had been before. They recognized in this miracle of sharing that fermentation must be a divine gift, and a God-directed process. They also discerned that if they didn't remove this special portion, the miracle would not happen. Taking some off the top and sharing it with another made all the difference.

It still does.

God is good.

PART TWO

Women

Like a gold ring in a pig's snout is a
beautiful woman without good sense.

—PROVERBS 11:22

9

HAIL MARY

Hail Mary, full of grace, the Lord is with thee. Blessed art thou amongst women.

—CATHOLIC ROSARY

According to the autobiography of my second father and childhood across-the-street neighbor Henry Daniel "Hank" Bartos, *Give Me Thirty Minutes and I Can Be Ready!*, a grown man should be able to pack an entire tackle box with fishing gear and fully stock a large cooler of beverages in just under half an hour. If it takes him longer than thirty minutes, whether or not he has been forewarned, he is unworthy of wide-mouth bass, as well as wide-mouth beer.

In the larger-than-life photograph on the front cover of this favorite book, Hank sits comfortably in a lawn chair on a lazy summer afternoon. He is wearing Hawaiian-themed swim trunks and a mostly unbuttoned shirt, exposing a fine yeasty roll of beer belly. Atop his head is the requisite cowboy hat, but perched on his knee there is also a ball cap, known as a "gimme" cap. In Texas a real man worth his scalp should never be caught without some form of head covering. We are like Muslim women in that way. Hank's face is partially covered by a salt-and-pepper goatee, a scraggle of gray beard, and large, dark sunglasses. He's got a koozie in one hand hiding a cold Lone Star Beer, and, while the other hand is hidden by the kneecap, I would wager money there is a half-smoked cigar held there dangling toward the ground. Like a New Braunfels Buddha, Hank rests knowingly under sprawling shade trees with a meandering, deep blue Texas river in the background. The enlightened and contented expression on his face is just how I remember Hank: laid-back, loyal, and kind, with just a hint of "Y'all can all go straight to hell" and "I don't really give a shit what is stressing you out" mixed in for good measure.

In 1955, Hank and his wife, Rosemary, moved into a house at 1015 West Thirtieth Street in a mostly working-class, Eastern European neighborhood in Houston. Not long thereafter, my mom, dad, and older brother moved into a house at 1014 West Thirtieth, just across the street. I was born a few years later. As soon as I could walk across that street, I did. In fact, before I could walk I got Rosemary to carry me.

Every Friday afternoon for twelve years, until I reached that unfortunate state of awkwardness called adolescence, I would cross over and spend the night with my second parents, good Catholics and lovers of life, Rosemary and Hank Bartos. I'd return home to my far less colorful fundamentalist Protestant parents every Saturday afternoon, just after NASCAR and *Wide World of Sports* had been usurped on the Bartos's television by Porter Wagoner and Dolly Parton.

Hank's autobiography includes a few poignant paragraphs about their adorable little neighbor:

About now is where I feel I should insert our experience and sharing of our lives with a little fellow who lived across the street. Shortly after the Miller family moved in across the street, Billy was born. Rosemary was not working at this time, so she had a lot of free time on her hands and a lot of energy to use up. Our girls would babysit little Billy and we all found ourselves becoming very attached to this personable little guy. As he began to walk, he spent a lot of time with us and Rosemary would pick him up, walk four blocks to the bus stop and take him downtown to see various sights such as the zoo, museum, and library. Billy really looked forward to Friday morning, which was his day to come across the street and spend the weekend with us. Neither his mother nor Rosemary and I could figure out how the little fellow knew when Friday morning arrived since no one mentioned it. He would get up on Friday morning and begin to remind his mother to pack his small suitcase and tell her that he was going to see "Mary." He was just over a year old and was talking by that time. He was always cautioned not to go into the street or go beyond the edge of the driveway. He would stand on the edge of the driveway with his suitcase in hand and begin yelling "Mary! Mary!" for Rosemary to pick him up. He was too small to pronounce Rosemary so he did the best he could, just as long as he could come over.

I don't recall missing a single Friday for more than a decade. If there was one word that encapsulates my experiences with Rosemary and Hank, it was this: *abundance.* With Rosemary and Hank, there was always plenty—for an extra person, or an unexpected guest. On weekend nights, there was always an extra slice of pizza at the Shakey's Pizza Parlor, an extra bingo card at the Knights of Columbus Hall, an extra cheeseburger down at the bowling alley, and, on occasion, even an extra ticket to an important football game, like the Bluebonnet Bowl Hank took me to in the 1960s—Texas versus Ole Miss. "We're for Texas," Hank informed me; I still am.

With Rosemary and Hank, magic ice chests with a never-ending supply of soda pop appeared on cabin porches every summer vacation. With Rosemary and Hank, I first felt the refreshing sensation of floating down a cool Texas river on a hot summer day. Hank, with his six-pack tied to his tube, would always float just behind us. We'd know how close we were to the final bend of the river based on which beer Hank was on—by six we'd pull right into camp! With Rosemary and Hank, I first rose before dawn, drank my first cup of coffee, and caught my first fish, a perch suitable for mounting, by my estimation. They were kind enough not to throw it back until I wasn't looking. With Rosemary and Hank, I first downed a frozen daiquiri, recognizing its vast superiority to 7-Eleven Slurpees. They cut me off when I started singing Spanish love songs to the teenage girls in the next cabin.

Whenever I entered my home away from home, I would head straight for the lower kitchen cupboard where Rosemary kept three cookie jars well stocked with all my favorites. To this day I believe in the sacramentally sustaining power of the common cookie as a wonder food for the world. Saturday mornings, Rosemary coached me in my bowling league. At age three, when I couldn't pick up a ball with one hand, she taught me that there was no shame in using two hands—the pins fell, just the same. After working up an appetite with strikes and spares, we would hum mariachi tunes all the way to my favorite restaurant, a Tex-Mex wonderland. The cheese enchiladas, the world's most perfect food, were always on her. On Fridays, when seafood supplanted barbecue for all good Catholics, Rosemary did not miss a beat, bringing out the best shrimp creole west of Baton Rouge. Abundance abounded whenever I was with Rosemary and Hank.

My surrogate parents also revealed that when we engage life at every level and every turn, we are bound for extraordinary adventure. Life is meant to take us beyond what we already know as it spills over into the exploration and discovery of what we have yet to learn. Life is meant to lead us to the very edge even if we've been warned not to go there. When we stay on our side of the street, we miss out on much that God has made. Many days, Rosemary would take me by the hand and lead me down West Thirtieth Street to the busy thoroughfare of North Shepherd Drive. On our way, I would cross the little wooden bridges that many families had erected over their front yard drainage ditches, more for decoration than transport, but I would always pretend I was scaling a gator-filled moat and entering unexplored and uncharted territory. There was such joy in the simple crossing of a bridge. Rosemary taught me that.

She and I would eventually catch the bus and go to a place called "downtown," which was quite an urban adventure for a tiny tot. Filled with towering buildings, different kinds of people, and a pace that propelled me forward at warp speed, it made my head spin and made me feel like a man of the world—or at least a little more grown-up than I really was. We had a favorite Italian place where I would order the "bowl of worms," more commonly called "buscetti" and later correctly labeled spaghetti. This ritual helped stimulate my sense of adventure, in eating as well as every other facet of life.

Our adventures were not limited to the city or even to land. I remember the day Hank bought his first boat, a classic little wooden beauty that he kept in their garage. Hank and I used Elmer's glue and a scrub brush to get that baby seaworthy. Nautical technology in those days consisted of sticking a pole in the water, in an attempt to determine the depth, as one ventured forth. On our first outing on Galveston Bay, we dodged unforgiving oyster reefs, lengthy barges, and giant tankers that produced wakes that roiled up and down like the most harrowing roller coaster. When I caught a three-pound redfish, Rosemary and Hank made me feel that I had just landed the largest specimen ever seen on the Gulf Coast.

Venturing into the unknown with Rosemary and Hank, I won a giant kielbasa playing bingo, inhaled the mystery of the Mass in all its mystical glory ("Billy, you can stop kneeling now," Rosemary informed this penitent Protestant), and caroused at the bowling alley with a cast of characters named Lonnie Duff, Betty Battaglia, Bubba Marbury, and the inimitable Father Snyder, the parish priest at St. Rose of Lima. I had never seen anyone or anything quite like Father Snyder. He bowled in his clerical collar, drank beer like a sinner guzzling sacramental wine, and let forth with a barrage of profanity after every missed strike or spare. He utilized language that I did not even know existed but have now adopted as my very own. I am deeply indebted to Father Snyder, my role model for all that the priesthood should be—whether behind the altar or behind the bowling ball. Whatever it was, wherever we went, whomever we met—it was always an adventure, a new discovery, a broadened perspective, an expanding moment. To paraphrase the Twenty-Third Psalm: She leads me beside all kinds of waters, taking me to the most interesting places.

That same psalm speaks of being led along right pathways. Rosemary and Hank offered some guidance along the way as well. Life was not just about feeding my own belly, winning my own prize, or filling my personal dance card. It was also about doing the right thing—unto others, and unto the world. There are some things in life too important to ignore and worth standing up for: treating all people with dignity and respect, and sharing with those who are in need.

Two incidents from the mid-1960s significantly changed my perception of the world and our call as individuals to strive for justice. During this time there were still remnants of segregation in this sprawling, semi-southern city. Once, while I held Rosemary's hand at the bus stop, I spotted an older, beat-up, mostly unwashed bus that was filled with faces darker than my own. That bus did not stop to pick us up, zooming right on past, as if we were standing at the wrong stop. I cannot remember Rosemary's exact words, but I do remember their impact on me from that day forward. Whenever I would see one of those buses, no feelings of superiority welled up within me. Just the opposite. Sensing the inferiority of a people and place that would allow such an unjust duality to exist made me sick, sad, and uncomfortable. As a small boy, I knew that something was wrong with that picture, though I could not yet articulate the core value of Christian theology, that every human being is created in the image of God.

Several years later, the time came for the bowling alley, my other home away from home, to be integrated. African-American children would finally be allowed to sign up and bowl in our Saturday-morning youth league. I was bowling for the Cobras that year, when a venom-filled mother struck out at Rosemary in an attempt to shield her children from the inclusive realities of integration. Again, I do not remember the exact words my mentor and coach, Rosemary, had to say to this woman. But I do remember that Rosemary, all five feet of her, stood her ground. As I watched the uncomfortable drama unfold, Rosemary seemed to tower over the much taller and larger lady. Right there in the bowling alley, in that moment of truth, I got the message that doing the right thing and standing your ground in the name of justice and righteousness may cause others to take their balls and go home. And usually those who leave when faced with passionate reason won't be missed at all.

There was a neighbor lady who lived right next door to Rosemary. Her name was Maureen. Maureen was in very poor health, and her husband was a truck driver who was frequently out of town on weeks-long road trips. Every afternoon around five, Rosemary would pick up the telephone, dial her neighbor's number, and say, "Maureen, this is Rosemary—meet me at the fence." Then Rosemary would walk to the side fence and pass over to the other side a portion of whatever home-cooked meal Hank and I were going to enjoy that night. I figured out from watching Rosemary reach up and over the fence every evening that whatever, or whoever, is on the other side of the fence matters. Sharing is simply what one does whenever one has enough and someone else does not.

Years later, one Saturday afternoon, I drove from Austin back to Houston to attend an event for which I'll bet it took Hank more than thirty minutes to get ready—Rosemary and Hank Bartos's fiftieth wedding anniversary celebration. As I entered the parish hall of St. Rose of Lima Catholic Church, where Father Snyder had once celebrated the sacraments and consumed consecrated wine, I heard the sweet strains of a Czech polka band from Weimar, Texas. I beheld the ubiquitous keg of Lone Star Beer and the piles of Mikeska's Bar-B-Q from El Campo. I recognized some kindly faces that I had not seen in many decades, and I felt the blessing of coming home again, even if that home was a second home.

Rosemary was lovely in a stylish beaded black evening gown, and Hank had traded in his bubba-wear for a striking black tuxedo. They made the most beautiful couple, and a radiance seemed to surround the space in which they gathered, not unlike a Renaissance painting of the Holy Family. They beckoned me toward them for a photo. Joining us were their three daughters, Pat, Yvonne, and Margie. Just before the photographer snapped the picture, Rosemary said, "A picture with all my children."

Seven years later, Hank hovered near death in a hospital room, with Rosemary, his wife of fifty-seven years, by his side. Hank, who always felt that words were highly overrated, looked across the room and saw the love of his life. Then he spoke: "Rosemary, what do you think of me?"

Rosemary told him, "Why Hank, I think you are God's greatest gift in all the world." She then asked him, "And what do you think of me?"

"Oh, Rosemary," he said, "I think you are the Madonna, and I've felt that way from the very beginning."

For most of my childhood, I felt the same way. From her I learned that sometimes one has to cross over to the other side of the street to discover true virtue, to appreciate overflowing abundance, to openly pursue all of life's adventures, to courageously stand up for justice and righteousness, and to understand that there will always be enough to share with somebody in need. I was invited to preach the sermon at Hank's Rosary, a sermon that I titled "Crossing Over to the Other Side." On one level it was a sermon about heaven, about crossing over into eternity and finding an ultimate home with God. It also spoke about standing on the edge of the boundary that separates us from God's great adventure called life, knowing that God will provide someone to take our hand and lead us across to the most interesting places. With God's help, we can cross over every street this life has to offer—transitions, dead ends, new beginnings, the known, and the unknown—and not be afraid. In fact, on the other side, we might find a second home.

So, for one night, the Catholics allowed this Episcopal priest to cross over. As I said the Rosary that night, the words seemed strangely familiar, transporting me to a place I had once known. They are words I still say to this day, especially when I fear the unknown or what may lay on the other side.

Hail Mary.

Full of grace.

10

CHEERLEADER CHAPLAIN

Cheers to Father Bill!

—DALLAS COWBOYS CHEERLEADERS

*B*ack in the good old days, when Ann Richards was governor of Texas, I was invited to her office. It was just after the Rodney King incident in Los Angeles, and there was a heightened awareness of racial tensions throughout the nation. Texas was no exception, so Richards summoned about a dozen ministers from around the state to engage in dialogue about positive initiatives that would promote racial harmony and understanding.

While everything really is bigger in Texas, I noticed that Ann Richards's office was small and mostly unadorned. It had an interior design scheme that could best be described as "tough," not unlike the five-foot, two-inch (six-foot-four with hair) former schoolteacher with the disarming southern drawl who dared to run for public office in the union's most macho state, kicked some oilman's ass, and won handily. I noticed that there was only one art object on her office wall—a larger-than-life painting of Ann Richards wearing camouflage fatigues, holding a huge shotgun, and towering over a massive buck that lay meekly (as dead animals do) at her boots. The message was pretty clear to all who entered her office—don't mess with this tough Texan!

I was honored to be invited to the governor's office. I felt both important and insignificant at the same time. I was the only Caucasian clergy person who had been invited, and I considered that a rare privilege. However, as I looked around the room I saw a group of men who were much wiser, more experienced, better educated, and intimately more familiar with the issues at hand. I felt that my feedback might be vastly inferior to what they had to offer. Yet their comments pretty much affirmed what I would have said had I opened my mouth. So I left the governor's office that day retaining those mixed feelings of worthwhile significance and absolute ineptitude at the same time.

Maybe that's not such a bad duality. Perhaps a healthy tension between shortcomings and inadequacies on the one hand, and aptitudes and insights on the other, is just what the governor, and the Great Physician, ordered. My favorite Ann Richards quote is one that displays her keen insight into the minds of men and the ways of the world, not to mention her rare ability to tell the truth and have fun at the same time. The American Civil Liberties Union had filed suit against the state of Texas to remove a Christmas crèche publicly displayed in the rotunda of the Capitol. When her legal advisor informed her that the ACLU actually had the law on their side and that the state of Texas could not, in fact, display the baby Jesus, the Magi, the oxen, ass, angels, or any other overt symbol of Christianity in a public place, Richards became distraught. She said, "Oh, how I hate to see them take that Christmas crèche out of the Texas Capitol. That may be our last chance to find three wise men in that building!"

Ultimate wisdom originates in such awareness—knowledge of what is not as well as what could be.

Once upon a time I made a pastoral visit to a family who had a very young daughter. The family was quite faithful in their church attendance and the little girl would always come to the altar for communion and kneel at the rail to receive her blessing. The sanctuary of this particular church was quite impressive: neo-Gothic, cavernous, carved limestone sculptures, polished brass, stunning stained glass, marble altar covered with finely woven hangings, heavenly sounding choir, and clerics garbed in rich tapestries of gloriously colored vestments. As one ascended the steps to encounter a more immanent and tangible experience of the holy, found in a pinch of bread and a sip of wine served by ordinary human beings, those sacred surroundings still spoke of a transcendent and distant God. So the sacramental journey, at least in that space, became a sort of both/and experience. Was it immanent or was it transcendent? Is God wholly other or contextually incarnate? Survey says: all of the above *and* all of the below. When it comes to faith, we tend to want it one way or the other, while the truth is often found when we include both/and.

So, what the little girl found there beyond the chancel steps was both lofty and in your face, solemn and smiley, all at the same time. She was in awe, but joyfully so. She knew who I was and that I occupied a position of great authority, whether I was behind the altar elevating and offering the gifts of God, behind the pulpit expounding and explaining the word of God, or at the back door greeting and encouraging all the people of God. Her context for me was limited to those Sunday-morning sacred encounters.

On that day when I went to visit the family at their home, I rang the doorbell and the little girl opened the door. Her eyes grew quite large as she beheld who was standing before her. She smiled and ran toward the inner sanctum of her home. I could hear her shouting out to her parents: "God is here!"

While God is certainly here, and everywhere for that matter, present company should be excluded. While I have a loud, booming voice and can chant on key, I am not God, and not even worthy of a part in the Christmas pageant. I am not wise enough, nor do I know anything about sheep.

And yet, God gets by with a little help from God's friends. God employs, engages, and empowers the most unlikely candidates to speak, act, and serve in God's name. It is humbling and inspiring to know that God is much closer than we think.

—

In the gospel of Matthew, Jesus walked into the temple and began turning over the tables of those who sought to make a place of worship into a religious flea market. He was unhappy with those who turned a place of reverence, awe, and wonder into a place of inflated transactions, market monopolies, and "today only" deals. After he brought some good old-fashioned chaos and drama back into the religious equation, he began to work a few wonders of his own, healing those who were sick, awakening those who were slumbering, and even raising those who were dead.

While the Pharisees were not amused by his disorderly

conduct in the midst of their religious practices, the children were thrilled. Who needs coloring books to alleviate the boredom of religious observance when religious observance can make things more interesting, not less so? The children's eyes grew wide, not with rage but with wonder, and they began to shout "God is here!" and "Who-sanna Ho-sanna Hey-sanna!"—or something like that. The religious authorities, who were larger than Ann Richards in stature but much smaller in wit and wisdom, decided that the children were saying downright blasphemous things and complained to Jesus that he was allowing young minds to be corrupted with religiously incorrect thoughts. Jesus's response was to quote the Bible. Jesus knew that it always angers the religiously correct when you quote scripture that contradicts their own. So Jesus quoted Psalms 8:2, which says, "Out of the mouths of infants and babies you have prepared praise for yourself."

In other words, it is often the children among us who recognize the presence of God, while mature types fail to see the humor or the holy. While I may not be God, perhaps God chose to create me in God's image, to dwell within me like a spirit, and to use me as a vessel to accomplish some extraordinary purpose. God may be right here, after all.

Once upon a time, one fine Easter day, I wore a liturgical garment resembling a fancy Mexican poncho. It is called a cope, and it is a heavy, festive outer garment that makes one look like he is wearing his grandmother's couch in all its patterned glory, particularly if one's grandmother had a Baroque bent. This particular costume piece makes me feel just one miter short of being a bishop—it's that good. It is so heavy that I relied on our verger to help me put it on and take it off, as it is traditionally worn only during processionals.

Verger is a liturgical title given to the head cowboy in charge of the cattle drive. The verger tells us all where to go, often literally. The verger carries an instrument that closely resembles a cattle prod and is willing to utilize it to poke or brand anyone who dares stray from the proper processional order. I was particularly blessed at Trinity Church because our verger was a big behemoth of a man, named Joe, who was strong enough to lift the cope on and off my shoulders and look graceful in the process. He was also tough enough to carry what could be called a fairy's wand in procession, while wearing a velvet dress and a soft, squishy hat-type thing on his head. Our verger, by the way, was also the director of safety for the Anheuser-Busch brewery in Houston, which pretty much tells you everything you need to know about him. Not only did he keep us in line, in order, focused, safe, and out of trouble, but he also remembered his priest when he received his four free cases of beer each month. His eternal reward was greatly enhanced every time he dropped off a case of Bud, Bud Light, Ziegenbock, and even Michelob (whose theme song, "Life is kind of special," should be in the official Episcopal hymnal). There are many pop-tops in Joe's crown of glory.

So, rhinestone cowboys had nothing on me as I stood at the back door on Easter Sunday. I was wearing my cope—adorned with white silk brocade, ribbons of lush blue velvet, and heavily embossed gold symbols weaving their way around my upper torso. The most important thing I can tell you about wearing a cope is that it is fun, and fun is something we are sorely lacking in our far-too-solemn assemblies. It is not unlike those childhood moments where we would dress up and have a parade. In this case, the parade honors the presence of God among us, as symbolized by what we wear.

At the back door, after the service, a young mother approached me with her beautiful little daughter. I did not recognize them and thought perhaps they were not regular churchgoers. The mom was holding the little girl's hand. She seemed a tad hesitant to get close to me. In her innocent eyes was a look of wholeness, as if holding the fullness of immanence and transcendence in her gaze.

"She has a question for you," her mother said.

The little girl came closer. She looked at me with a combination of adoration and appreciation, with just enough reverence and awe to be uncertain but hopeful, perhaps even in love. She hesitated, but looking up at me, finally asked, "Um, are you a prince?"

It is my favorite question I have been asked in a religious setting—or anywhere else, for that matter.

I have been mistaken for a number of mythological characters over the years: the Donkey in *Shrek*, the Wolf in *Red Riding Hood*, even Brian the Dog on *Family Guy*, but never, until that day, a prince. And I have been asked many interesting questions while standing at the back door of the church after services: Does the bishop receive complaints on Sundays? What were you smoking? Do you speak English? Have you considered a career change? What the hell are you doing here? But that little girl's question was the best ever.

"No," I told her, "I am not a prince. I am a priest. And sometimes, when I wear a cope, we look alike."

Obviously the little girl had been reading too many fairy tales. She must have had quite the vivid imagination to mistake the likes of me for a prince, that stock character who always comes across as stunningly handsome, revoltingly romantic, noble in character, singular in purpose, *and* quite good-looking in tights. Such an idealized man who consistently comes to the rescue of any damsel in distress is hardly my persona. Neither am I like the prince in the Broadway musical *Into the Woods,* the one who cheated on Cinderella with the Baker's wife and defended his actions by admitting, "I was raised to be charming, not sincere." I am more sincere than charming, but occasionally less of either than I should be.

And yet, there was something about the little girl's sense of wonderment and starry-eyed hopefulness that has stayed with me for many years. She didn't fully accept my denial, which in turn made me question my own identity. She made me want to be more princelike, even if I usually more closely resemble the ogre's mule. She inspired me to exhibit more princely tendencies and pursue a more noble purpose—at least when I wear a cope. I still have to admit that I am not God, I am not a prince, and I am more of a wise guy than a wise man.

Once upon a time, the ministerial members of my Trinity Church staff gathered on Galveston Island for a retreat and planning session. We spent time evaluating our ministries, working through communication issues, and envisioning the future of our congregation. Since we had worked so hard, I treated everyone to dinner at a favorite seafood and steak place called Rudy & Paco. Paco was from Nicaragua and greeted every guest with a hearty embrace and the lyrical greeting "Welcome home, baby!" The food was always off the charts, in a home-style, Latin America meets Texas Gulf Coast kind of way.

After dinner, some of the younger members of our staff felt the need to "prolong this rare occasion of fellowship," that is, "get the priest to buy us more drinks since our spouses, partners, and children are sound asleep fifty miles up the causeway and we don't get out much these days." We ventured into a nightspot called The 21 Club. As I sipped a martini and engaged in devout religious rhetoric with my staff, a large bus pulled up to the door, and in marched/pranced/danced the entire squad of Houston Texans cheerleaders.

One of them was having her bachelorette party right there in the presence of God and the Trinity Church ministerial staff. I immediately felt the need to "prolong this rare occasion of fellowship."

I gazed upon a squadron of dazzling beauties as they walked, forty strong, through the front door. A man of true faith, my first thought upon seeing them was—well, never mind that first thought—but my *second* thought was "What a wonderful ministry opportunity!" I had never felt quite such a calling to share my faith at so intimate a level with a group of complete and total strangers. I knew how important evangelism was to my Lord and also my bishop, and I certainly wanted to set a good example for my staff, my parish, and you, the impressionably naïve reader. So I said a little prayer of preparation: "Lord, be in my heart, upon my lips, and in my pickup lines—I mean my testimonial witness."

The cheerleaders formed a tight-knit circle. As I approached, like Moses encountering the Red Sea, they parted and made a way for me on their circular couch. I was in! I proclaimed the gospel and preached the good news to them for fifteen minutes and felt in my heart of hearts that several were "not far from the Kingdom." Particularly the brunette Latin twins who were Pilates instructors.

A conversion experience was imminent when a large, unpleasant male approached and tapped me on the shoulder and said, "Sorry, man, but this is a private party!"

Inspired by the Holy Spirit, I replied, "Sorry man, but I am their chaplain!"

The formerly mean dude smiled and patted me on the shoulder and said, "Oh, sorry man, I didn't know. It's good to meet you."

"And it's good to meet you, my son," I said. I stayed there until I nearly talked the bride into allowing me to officiate the wedding.

Perhaps you are skeptical of my intentions. Perhaps you think that I had ulterior motives. Perhaps you are suspicious of my purity of purpose and impetus for indoctrination. If so, you are right, but if God were solely dependent on our motives and intent to accomplish God's purposes, the Kingdom of God would be confined to a small closet. Months later, one of the cheerleaders showed up at my church for a Sunday-morning service—with her boyfriend. A seed got sown, despite myself.

But I admit it. I am not God. I am not a prince. And I am not the chaplain of the Houston Texans cheerleaders. Dammit.

And yet, God chooses to use me, along with everyone else who is not always what they claim, or hope to become. None of us quite lives up to the claims we make for ourselves.

I am a spiritual person.

Really?

I am a follower of Jesus.

Is that so?

I am here to make the world a better place.

Uh-huh?

We are all flawed, and it will take us more than a full-time, lifetime job to live into God's loving purposes for our lives. Even the best among us fall far short.

Perhaps you have not heard about the virtuous Baptist preacher, the upstanding Methodist minister, and the highly principled Episcopal priest. All of them were invited to Oslo, Norway, to receive the first ever Nobel Piety Prize, an award given to the most overtly pious individuals on earth. They were all on the same flight, along with their wives, somewhere over the Atlantic Ocean, when an unthinkable and unfortunate event occurred. The plane developed engine trouble, crashed into the ocean, and everyone on board perished.

Each of the couples arrived at the Pearly Gates and came before the throne of Almighty God to be judged. The incredibly moral Baptist preacher and his wife approached first. The Lord said to the Baptist preacher, "Oh, brother, how unfortunate that you married a woman named Penny, symbolic of your love for money. You worshipped on Wall Street more often that at my altar. The almighty dollar was your ultimate motivator on earth. You are as materialistic as they come. Depart from me into the land of eternal debt, everlasting foreclosure, and terminal bankruptcy."

The Methodist minister swallowed hard as he and his wife were next in line to approach the judgment seat of God. God's voice boomed, "Oh, pastor, too bad for you. You married a woman named Candy, symbolizing the unfortunate fact that your belly was your God. You were addicted to food, consumed by your intense desire to ingest massive quantities of syrupy-sweet substances devoid of any nutritional value. You worshipped the God of high-fructose corn syrup and natural cane sugar and converted your children as well. Depart from me into the land of sea salt and raw vegetables and vegan chefs, where there are no pastries, pies, or pralines!"

About that time, the Episcopal priest let out a prolonged and heavy sigh. He finally moved toward the throne of God, recognizing that the time for his judgment had come. He turned to his wife and said, "I don't know, Fanny, but it's not lookin' good!"

A healthy awareness of our weaknesses and an ability to confess our shortcomings, coupled with an appreciation of our unique strengths and abilities, will give us just enough perspective, pause, confidence, and commitment to be used by our Creator. Our motivations are often impure. Our handicaps are obvious. Our failings are in our faces every day.

And yet, we aspire. We hope. We dream. We catch a glimpse of what others perceive in terms of our potentialities and what God can create with the raw materials of what we already have. To paraphrase Joseph Campbell, we live in a world heavy on celebrities but short on heroes. A celebrity is often the most unaware among us, as are those who idolize and idealize them. A hero is someone who is keenly aware that God can use us despite ourselves, and he gives himself to a cause greater than any one of us, to a purpose bigger than one's own limited and limiting life. The hero reaches beyond the self, and, in the process, admits what he is not, still hoping for what he might become.

Years ago, the Super Bowl came to my hometown of Houston. The biggest event of the weekend was not the game itself but an exclusive pre-party at the M Bar the night before the big game. I had no chance of getting in. The doorman did not recognize me as God, Prince, or Cheerleader Chaplain. Fortunately, I was with a good friend who is a muscular, better-looking version of Denzel Washington. He has degrees from Rice University and Stanford Law School. Only in his thirties, he is a partner in a major law firm. He is also a rugby star and a deeply committed Christian who has a heart of gold. I really can't stand the guy. My friend walked right up to the VIP admitting area, which was the only admitting area. Within a matter of minutes, he had sincerely charmed the keeper of the list. Father VIP was in! In life, as in religion, it's not really *what* you know, it is *who* you know.

Inside, the place was teeming with A-list celebrities: Diddy, Paris, that guy with the rainbow wig who appears holding a John 3:16 sign at virtually all sporting events, pretty much everybody who's anybody. I was unimpressed, until I spotted the Dallas Cowboys cheerleaders.

Perhaps I had been drinking. I remember engaging in a long conversation with the captain in an attempt to explain why the Dallas Cowboys cheerleaders should participate in the liturgical procession at Trinity Church the next morning. I envisioned a sort of Palm Sunday procession, with cheerleaders replacing the confirmation class, and pom-poms filling in for palm branches. I thought it was a brilliant idea. The cheerleaders, apparently, did not.

However, they were entertained by my gesture of theological inclusion. They autographed a photo of themselves and at the top wrote, "CHEERS TO FATHER BILL!" That photo now occupies a place of prominence in my treasure chest, right next to the ashes of my dog Sam, and my ticket to the BCS National Championship Game at the Rose Bowl (when Texas beat the University of Southern California in the final seconds of the game of the century). I am proud of that photo and that sentiment. Mostly. But it also causes me to shake my head sometimes and marvel at my own incompetent audacity, asking myself, "Who do you think you are?"

I can tell you this much. I am not God. I am not a prince. And I am not the chaplain of the Houston Texans *or* the Dallas Cowboys cheerleaders. Dammit.

I can also tell you this: Whoever I am, and whatever I might become, there is someone, somewhere, cheering for me—by name—believing that I am far more than I think I am. They must see something in me I don't see.

At least, not yet.

11

MISS HAWAII AND OTHER MISS TAKES

Charm is deceitful, and beauty is vain, but a woman who fears the
Lord is to be praised.

—PROVERBS 31:30

How fair and pleasant you are, O Loved one,
delectable maiden!
You are as statuesque as a palm tree, and your breasts
are like its clusters.
I say I will climb the palm tree, and lay hold of its branches.

SONG OF SOLOMON 7:6–8A

Although country singer Johnny Lee has played the legendary Grand Ole Opry in Nashville, Tennessee, only a handful of times, I should have known he would be starring the one and only time I attended. It should come as no surprise that the Urban Cowboy craze of the 1970s, fueled by Lee and his fellow country crooner Mickey "Mechanical Bull" Gilley, along with John "Bud" Travolta, had its origin one town over from my hometown of Houston in Pasadena, Texas: home of oil refineries, alligators, and tight jeans. This cowpoke period peaked just as I was going through my Alan Alda/Woody Allen/pale literary aesthete/smooth jazz aficionado with intellectual tendencies phase. I was drinking gin and tonic and wearing clogs when I should have been drinking Jack Daniel's and wearing boots. I missed the whole damn thing. It was not the first time I found myself looking at the back end of a galloping horse, wishing I had cowboyed up long before.

It should come as no surprise that that night at the Grand Ole Opry, Lee performed his hit tune and my personal theme song, "Lookin' for Love." In this catchy ode to aloneness, Lee bemoans a lifetime of "playin' a fools game and hopin' to win, tellin' those sweet lies and losin' again." Singin' about such melancholy all while never once ending any word with -ing. Apparently the consonant *n* is much more masculine than a *g*, and that lone apostrophe at the end adds singular force. Both Alan Alda and Woody Allen would have concluded with -ing.

Like Johnny Lee lookin' for love in all the wrong places, I have searched far and wide for ultimate love. Although I still share my bed with a single dog, along the way I have had my share of close calls and interesting encounters—some intentional, some accidental, some unforgettable, some lamentable. Such as the time I frantically rushed around Bangkok, Thailand, in search of Miss Universe. In the words of Maxwell Smart—missed her by *thaaaat* much!

I was well intentioned and properly motivated. My friend Jimmy Grace and I had visited the Taj Mahal in Agra, India, just a few weeks before. I was bewitched by the beauty of its design and even more so by the beauty of the love that built it. While its architecture alone has inspired reams of rapture over the centuries, what makes this marble monument so motivating is its moving tale of true love that lives on even after loss.

The beautiful Arjumand Banu captured the heart of the young Shah Jahan the moment he laid eyes on her. In 1612, at the tender age of twenty-one, she married him and became his favorite wife, the Mumtaz Mahal ("Jewel of the Palace"). Although numerous stories speak of this woman's inner beauty, her generosity, kindness, and wisdom, those stories don't hold a candle to the ever-radiant torch she held for her beloved husband. Shah and Mah, or Shahmah, like Brangelina after them, were inseparable. She bore him fourteen children, and it was in childbirth that she died in 1630, while accompanying her beloved on a military campaign. On her deathbed she asked the love of her life to build a monument so beautiful that the world would never forget the love they shared. It took twenty-two years, a thousand elephants, and twenty thousand laborers to construct the stunning spatial testimony to their deep spiritual connection. The great emperor spent his last years gazing from his locked quarters in exile across the river at his wife's final resting place. The beautiful wish of this beautiful woman had come to pass. Even now, the world has not forgotten and will always remember the profound love they shared for one another. I left the Taj Mahal inspired by beauty, determined to seek and find such beauty for myself.

I thought I had found my own personal Mumtaz later that night at the disco at the Sheraton in New Delhi, but she bolted prematurely for the Hyatt in pursuit of some Bollywood actor type. Our trip continued with a tortuous trek through Tibet, during which the yaks were starting to look good. After a few days on the island of Ko Sumui in Thailand, where we discovered female companionship was considered a business transaction, I was still looking for love in all the wrong places.

I recalled, not so fondly, the time I stood in front of my condo on Sixth Street in Austin, with my dog Sam, the world's greatest chick magnet. Walking toward me was the most stunningly beautiful young woman I had ever laid eyes on. As is my custom when I see something I want, I prayed. I remember the precise words of that prayer: "Lord, do you see that? *That* is what I'm looking for. Help a brother out."

God answered that prayer and, I am sure, still gets a chuckle out of it. Haley and I dated for almost a year. That is, for twelve torturous months, she terrorized my heart. She played me for the fool repeatedly, and I was too stupid not to play along. That was the last time I have been so overt in my pursuit of passion, or my prayer requests to God regarding my love life.

On the other hand, sometimes beauty tracks us down and slaps us into awareness before we know what hit us. Without any effort of our own, we are blindsided by beauty. Such as the time I met four Miss Hawaiis within a few days of each other. I was not even looking for love. I was looking for jazz musicians.

A jazz musician, with whom I collaborated for years to produce jazz festivals, had come to Hawaii to scout out local talent. Together we flew from Kauai to Honolulu, the only real population center in Hawaii. Our plan was to set out each night to explore the local music scene and see what sort of talent we might uncover. In a mere forty-eight hours we discovered a level of talent that neither of us had foreseen. We also met some musicians.

I had just checked into my hotel room in Waikiki when I found myself in conversation at the Ala Moana Starbucks with incredibly bubbly and quite lovely former Miss Hawaii #1. I happened to run into her the weekend her new CD, *Feel the Breeze*, was released, and I was able to catch a few songs of her set at the Sheraton later that night. I felt the breeze, in addition to the movement of the Holy Spirit.

My jazz musician friend and I also ventured over to the Jazz Minds Art & Café, and while there, I noticed a stunning blond woman checking me out. I often assume this is the case, when in fact it is not, but my friend was in a hurry to go to the next club and catch the last set of jazz pianist Tennyson Stephens, so he took the initiative and introduced us. The next day I googled the stunning blonde I had exchanged seemingly sultry glances with on the previous evening. I google all potential love interests to make sure they are not convicted felons, former adult film stars, or ordained clergy. I discovered that bachelorette #2 was not only a former Miss Hawaii, but had also won the swimsuit competition at the Miss America pageant! I also read that she came from a fundamentalist and quite conservative Christian household. Fundamentalists are notorious for winning swimsuit competitions. Sadly, our relationship remained at the aloof, strictly professional level. At least I think that's what she meant by "Stay away from me and seek professional help."

The week after my composer friend returned to Texas, I went back to Honolulu to attend the NFL Pro Bowl. At the big bash and official kickoff party (the event that costs twice as much as the actual game but is four times as much fun), I enjoyed delectable food, free-flowing beverages, and pom-pom-waving cheerleaders from every NFL team. Despite the presence of professional cheerleaders, my eyes focused on the most beautiful hula dancer I had ever seen, performing just behind the margarita station. Our conversation went like this:

> HER: So, what do you do?
> ME: I am a priest. So what do you do?
> HER: I am Miss Hawaii.
> ME: What shall we name our firstborn?
> HER: Go in peace to love and serve the Lord.

We also agreed to collaborate on a brilliant new idea that she had just inspired: a Hula Mass.

While the Hula Mass never got off the beach, after meeting all those Miss Hawaiis I decided that it must be a sign from God, and so I had an idea. As my friends will tell you, when I have an idea, it can be a most dangerous thing.

I may not be a fundamentalist, but I am a traditionalist and tend to think in Trinitarian terms. My trinity of thoughts at that time:

1. My church desperately needs money.

2. The men of my church desperately need a bonding opportunity.

3. I desperately need to marry a Miss Hawaii.

So, I decided I would organize a men's fund-raising event to support the many worthwhile ministries of our parish. I immediately contacted my new Miss Hawaii friends. The singer was in. The Pro Bowl party Tahitian dancer was in. The swimsuit competition winner reported me to Homeland Security, the FBI, the Honolulu Police Department, the Episcopal Diocese of Hawaii, and her Lord and Savior Jesus Christ. Although she declined to participate for religious reasons ("you are not very religious" is what I think she said to me), she did pass on my offer to another Miss Hawaii, a former Miss Congeniality and popular weather girl on a local newscast.

My holy nexus was coming together. A local Italian restaurant would cater the dinner. An active layperson in our parish offered his auto dealership showroom as the venue location. My youth minister agreed to bartend. A local keyboard player agreed not only to accompany the performers, but also to operate sound and lights. The three Miss Hawaiis would sing and dance. We sent out invitations offering the men of the community the rare opportunity to be "King for a Day." The trinity worked its way into our theme. We called this extraordinary event "An Evening with Miss Hawaii, and Miss Hawaii, and Miss Hawaii." Once again, God had smiled on me. So I thought.

While the majority of women in my church thought that the event was creative and worthwhile, others thought it reprehensible, offensive, and even "pornographic." The vocal minority accused me of having "half-naked girls writhing on cars while the men ogle them" and "vacuous bimbos of questionable moral character dancing on our husbands' laps." That scenario was not remotely what I had envisioned.

I was stunned. I had gone to a lot of trouble, and now I was *in* a lot of trouble. I had no idea why I was being labeled a liturgical Larry Flynt. I consulted many of my female friends whose opinions I highly value. After they laughed their asses off and pointed at me and laughed their asses off some more and pointed at me yet again, they offered me words of consolation, insight, and wisdom.

"You are such a jackass. You are getting just what you deserve. Just kidding."

Their responses were actually pretty unanimous and uniform. "This is not really about you, Bill," they told me. "And it's not really about Miss Hawaii, either. It is about our culture and its emphasis on youth, physical attributes, and airbrushed appearances—which amounts to a ticking time bomb just waiting to explode on any male foolish enough to carry a detonator. Not to mention, we now see a crucifixion in your future."

I even questioned the pageant winners about the criticisms, and their responses were pretty unanimous and uniform as well. "People who are not part of this process have a lot of their own prejudices and misconceptions that just aren't accurate," they said. They all pointed out to me that most pageants are about developing potential, furthering education, nurturing talent, and the empowerment of women. The Miss America Pageant, in fact, they proudly noted, is the largest source of funding for academic scholarships for women in the entire world. "Beauty is not just skin deep," said one former Miss Hawaii, "but it doesn't mean I don't have skin, and I am very comfortable in mine." Words of wisdom, spoken by Miss Hawaii.

These three women were all bright, talented, gracious, smart, and kind. They were happy to participate in a charitable cause. When you talked to them, they radiated beauty, and most of that beauty emanated from their eyes, which I hear may have some direct link to the soul. And yes, they also had good genes—and looked good in jeans, which is not such a bad or morally reprehensible thing.

Although a marriage proposal was not in the cards, in many ways, the evening with Miss Hawaii (times three) was a smashing success. We raised about ten thousand dollars for a worthy cause. Many of the women and men in our community rallied around the event and offered a helping hand. Friendships were forged. Bonds were made. Beauty was manifest in a myriad of ways.

One event had carried me through the firestorm of resentment, criticism, and fury. It affirmed my belief that God not only loves us but also has a highly developed sense of humor and will occasionally engage in an intervention just to keep all of us guessing. And praying. There were a few weeks before the event when I felt I must be a very bad person, and that I had engaged in behavior unbecoming of a priest. The proverbial pupu seemed to be hitting the fan almost daily during that time. I was working overtime to offer what I thought was a positive, creative event and was instead the target of much female wrath. I was completely stressed out. My anxiety level was at an all-time high. Every muscle in my body had tightened into knots the size of coconuts. I desperately needed a massage, but I could not afford one because I had spent all my money buying tickets for the fund-raising event and giving them away.

The auto dealer happened to invite me to the local Humane Society Annual Gala that particularly stressful week. I love the Humane Society in Kauai. My dog, Nawiliwili Nelson, came from the Humane Society. So I attended, thanks to my parishioner's generosity. When I walked in, a friend of mine was standing near the grand prize raffle area and talked me into buying one ten-dollar raffle ticket. I wanted to do what I could, my small part, to support the Humane Society. After I deposited my ticket in the bin, joining about a thousand other tickets, I saw that the grand prize was a three-thousand-dollar super-deluxe massage chair.

You would think that living here in paradise, no one would ever get stressed out. That would be an incorrect assumption. The cost of living is high. Many have to hold down second or third jobs just to survive. We're located in the middle of nowhere; living on a rock can create certain anxieties for people who like to run off when the going gets tough. Here, there's nowhere to go. Plus, people are just as dysfunctional and difficult to deal with in paradise as they are anywhere else.

So the massage chair was the most popular bidding item that night. I watched as scores of people purchased blocks of tickets and tossed them into the giant jar. People squandered entire paychecks to increase their odds of winning. I witnessed individuals fill out dozens of ten-dollar entries. Yet, as I mixed in my lone bet with the multitudes, I had an eerie feeling that God was about to reveal something interesting. I did not *dare* utter any sort of prayer. I knew that could only get me into trouble.

When they called out my name, I was not really all that surprised. I looked up, smiled, and said, "Thank you, Lord—yes, I get it." The Humane Society delivered the massage chair to my home the very next day. I attended the Miss Hawaii fund-raising event entirely stress-free, in a state of total relaxation.

Like the Bible says: "In all things, even if we are mistaken, God provides a loving massage for those that love the Lord, and are called according to His purpose, even if their motives are not entirely pure." Yep, that's what the Bible says.

—

I find it fascinating, if not scintillating, that in the New Testament, the community of the faithful is often described in terms of the human body, the kind with flesh on it. In the book of Ephesians we read that "from Christ the whole body, joined together by every supporting ligament, grows and builds itself up in love, as each part does its work" (Ephesians 4:16).

Just think, every human body part has an important function and plays an important part: the brain, the hands, the feet, the tongue, even boobs and butts. When I forget what part I am or I try to portray a role that is not in my DNA, spiritual or physical, or, when from a place of resentment and jealousy I deny someone else their God-given role, identity, calling, and gift, I stress the body. I make the whole in need of a massage. When I do such inauthentic things, I find that I am most unhappy, unhealthy, and unproductive, not to mention inhumane.

The truth is that there are some body parts I will never be. There are certain body types I will not be able to assume. There are certain gifts and callings that simply are not mine. I will never be a sumo wrestler, a Victoria's Secret model, David Beckham, a Chicago Bears quarterback, a Miami Dolphins cheerleader, or a Miss Hawaii. *I* am not properly equipped for any of those identities, but that does not deny their validity and importance. Knowing who I am and what I am frees me to recognize that others should be given the same courtesy and appreciation.

In the Celtic Christian tradition, the bodily senses, particularly the sense of sight, serve as thresholds of the soul. We can use our eyes to look at ourselves and at others in ways that appreciate and affirm, or in ways that diminish and denigrate.

Our eyes can view the whole of creation as revelation of the totality of God's glory (glory = *doxa* = beauty). Such is the lens of love. The lens of fear, greed, judgment, resentment, indifference, or inferiority does no one any good. God calls us to see others and ourselves through the lens of love. For the authentically spiritual person, the eyes always have it, and thus the ayes always have it. Truth is found in the affirmative. The negative often leads to ultimate heresy—denying God's presence in another. For the truly spiritual person, beauty is revealed in a myriad of ways. And we can see it only when we come to appreciate the God-given uniquenesses of each of us, however differently we are shaped.

—

Many years ago on a trip to Minnesota, I met the three-year-old daughter of my friends. Her name is Felicity. One morning we all went together to appreciate modern art, hunt for four-leaf clovers, and eat waffles topped with strawberries and whipped cream. When we got back in the car, her parents placed Felicity in her car seat in the back. All of these sensory experiences had left her fully engaged and overtly filled with great joy. She was smiling, beaming, loving life and all creation, aware and appreciative in her own tiny little way. Perhaps I am projecting, but she sure did look happy.

As I looked back at her and began to feel some of her radiance find its way into my heart, I told her, "Felicity, you sure are a beautiful girl."

She responded, "I know."

My prayer is that all these years later she still knows, that whoever she is becoming, however God is calling her, and whatever part of the body she assumes, she is beautiful. True beauty may reveal itself on the surface, but it always originates deep within the soul. To seek it is to look for love in just the right place.

To see it is to see God.

12

CHICKEN SOUP FOR THE HOOTERS GIRL'S SOUL

Those who wait upon the Lord . . . shall mount up with wings. . . .

—ISAIAH 40:31

And one was a doctor, and one was a queen, and one was a
shepherdess on the green

—"I SING A SONG OF THE SAINTS OF GOD"

$\mathcal{S}$ome unenlightened souls insist that the worst thing a daughter could ever say to her father is "Welcome to Hooters!"

I say there are many phrases she could utter that would be much worse, such as "Table dances are half off tonight" or "I'm going to law school" or "I'm going to seminary," or "I'm going to law school and my fiancé is going to seminary."

There are far worse plights in life and perceived blights on one's vocational history than serving buffalo wings while wearing orange shorts. After all, one of the great saints of modern history, a man who knew something about selfless sacrifice and ultimate service, the Reverend Dr. Martin

Luther King Jr., pointed out the true measuring stick of spiritual stature. "Everybody can be great," King said, "because anybody can *serve*."

Greatness, in the Kingdom of God, is in direct proportion to our willingness to be of service. Serving our fellow human beings, even if they are mostly a bunch of fowl balls, and even while wearing tank tops featuring a pair of owl eyes, is a most worthy endeavor. In fact, "sainthood" in the Christian tradition may just be our way of identifying folks who work in the spiritual "service industry"—that is, those who put the needs of others ahead of their own.

Jesus himself separated the sheep from the goats primarily based on one's willingness to be the waitstaff for those in need. If you ever brought somebody a meal, fetched them an item of clothing, or poured them a refreshing beverage, Jesus says, you have earned yourself a pair of wings. If you never gave a hoot about those who went wanting and were not at all mindful of the needs of others, you might go directly to that place where your beer is not kept cold by those floating Baggies of ice so lovingly placed in your pitcher by your favorite Hooters server. You might even go where there is no beer at all! Of his own calling and vocation, Jesus admitted, "I'm not here to be served; I'm here to serve." In other words, the customer always comes first.

—

I have found it to be both theologically and liturgically appropriate that what we call Halloween is really All Hallows' Eve, or the evening before All Saints' Day. When we dress up as a variety of characters on October 31 we are actually anticipating the many and varied saints we honor on November 1. The "saints" form a cast of characters as different, interesting, and unexpected as the best Halloween party you have ever attended. For All Saints' Day celebrates the consecration of all the saints—and that includes everybody from upper management on down. Or, given the reverse ranking system in God's mind, whereby the first are last and the last are first, that should probably be from lowliest servant on down. Both Eve and Day validate a variety of identities and callings—that is, who we really are, and even who we aspire to be. Plus, anyone who would consistently offer treats to costumed characters more deserving of tricks deserves a day of honor!

I will never forget my first Halloween costume, which was not my idea. When I was three years old, the teenage girls across the street dressed me up like a clown. They put so much lipstick on my face that I looked like a juvenile drag queen.

I moved on to store-bought costumes after that, but the cheap, unlined material that I wore made me feel less like Batman and more like a Giant Rash that was about to break out and destroy Gotham City. One year I was a hippie. That happened to be the year most of the folks in my blue-collar, Eastern European, South Texas neighborhood decided that hippies should be punished, if not shot. Such freethinkers who dared to challenge the establishment (that is, "good Christian") values were obviously tricksters undeserving of treats. I didn't even bother shouting "Trick or treat" by the third house, instead yelling "Make love, not war" to which one older woman bearing a broom responded, "Make love to this, you damn little commie." That year my friend Kevin, who went as a thug, ended up with lots of Butterfingers in his pumpkin. I ended up getting the finger a lot and a few pieces of cheap hard candy.

In my adult years, after my ordination to the priesthood, my costume dilemma was solved. For years, every Halloween, I dressed up like a priest. Partygoers could not believe how authentic my costume looked: black cassock, black cincture, real clerical collar, intricately carved pectoral cross, black Book of Common Prayer with gold gilding, and a look on my face like I knew what I was doing. You should have seen me make the sign of the cross—very professional indeed. My friends would often yell at me for my costume choice, but I would counter that, since I really do desire to live into what I wear, I am allowed to wear it, even for secular celebrations that most do not suspect are quite sacred.

I have had all sorts of interesting experiences on Halloween night while dressed as a priest. I have been asked to perform exorcisms and weddings on the spot. Once a bar manager in Austin asked me to judge a wet T-shirt contest, explaining, "You should know something about baptism, Father." For that brief evening, I was almost ready to argue the merits of full immersion over sprinkling—more, uh, revelatory.

I do not dress up on Halloween anymore. But I do always stand at my front door and pass out treats to all those creatively adorned souls who show up each All Hallows' Eve and reveal their chosen identities. I have been visited by a comprehensive sampling of all God's creatures: fire-breathing dragons, sparkling princesses, Spiderella, baby cows, Davy Crockett, the Ace of Spades, Star Wars stars, skeletons, ninjas, heavy metal musicians in search of beer (always my youth minister), that guy from the *Scream* painting, and even one little fellow, obviously seasonally challenged, who was dressed up like an Easter egg. He needed no defense as far as I was concerned, but his mother pleaded his case from the front yard: "It's what he wanted to be."

"Happy Easter!" I shouted as he rolled on down the street.

A few costumed characters have stood out over the years as personal favorites. One year a little girl stopped by who stole my heart. That year everyone else's costume seemed way overdone, as if having been conceived and executed by some Hollywood wardrobe department. This little girl had on no face paint or makeup and carried no accessories. She was beautiful with flowing dark curls and a playfully shy demeanor.

I greeted her at the door and asked the million Tootsie Roll question, "And what are you?"

She replied, "Oh, I'm just a little Spanish dancer."

With that apologetic pronouncement, she sashayed a step backward, and, placing a tiny hand on her red satin skirt with the flowery black lace, she twirled it up and around and down like a matador's cape. Her movement was far too subtle for an "Ole," not flashy or overdone, not overpowering with the force of flamenco, but with just a hint of a sultry night in old Seville. She ended her routine, not with a powerful tap of a heel to the front porch, but with a soft shoe point, a slight tilt of her head, and the most disarming smile I have ever seen. There was something about her humble choice of expression, her utter lack of pretense, and her willingness to dance into her identity and become just who she said she was that endeared that hallowed moment to me beyond measure. On All Hallows' Eve, she exemplified the simple, unadorned beauty of offering the gifts and identities and interests that make us who we are, and even who we aspire to be.

On the day of *all* the saints, God does not look for the brightest halo, the gaudiest or even the godliest mask, the most intimidating over-the-top costume, the most revealing raiment or stunningly sanctified cover-ups. No, God does not desire even the flashiest glow-in-the-dark deeds of power. God looks for our most honest and humble efforts. We are to offer all that we are, just as we are, not for our own sake or entertainment, but for others, for their viewing, and even living pleasure. As a southern theologian may once have said, "We has met the saints, and they is us!"

My second-favorite Halloween memory (other than the night I dressed up like a feather duster at the French Maid theme party) happened the night I opened the door and saw an entire family of chickens standing on my front porch.

"Who are you?" I asked this multigenerational assembly.

"Just us chickens," said the dad, who did not look quite like a rooster, but more like a big hen who'd taken a couple of testosterone injections.

"We are the Henlays," added the mom. I assumed that was their Christian name.

They were such a nice chicken family. There was a mother and father chicken, a boy and girl chicken, each seemingly pleased with such a family of origin, and there was even a baby chicken in a stroller peering out from behind a headdress and a tiny beak. The chickens and I bonded immediately. I was so grateful to them for being chickens. They just stood there in all their clucked-up lack of glory, a group of warm-blooded, fine-feathered, egg-laying vertebrates with outstretched forelimbs clutching paper shopping sacks decorated simply with bird seed. They were not trying to be the coolest, the trendiest, or the most powerful. They were not dressed up to scare, outshine, or out-battle anybody. They were just those chickens, not strutting any stuff, or if they were it looked so natural I did not notice. These were neither show-offs nor castoffs, just us chickens. They revealed a truth that should come home to roost in all of our hearts: that we miss much in this life by cutting ourselves off from others with our predetermined judgments of character, choices, and vocational callings—whether the waitress across town, the dancer next door, or the chicken down the street. Sometimes, it is the face in our own bathroom mirror that we leap to critique. Judge not, lest you not be picked to judge a really interesting costume competition.

This point was brought home to me one night while waiting for a cab in Las Vegas. Standing next to me in line, also waiting for a cab, and dressed to impress, was perhaps the most perfect-looking woman I had ever seen. Her hair was golden. Her skin was flawless. Her smile was intoxicating. Her radiance was resplendent. Her persona was personable. Her sweater was tight. Very tight.

I spoke to her with words that can be described only as probing the very depths of another's being. "Gonna party?" I inquired.

"Yes," she said.

Her affirmative reply obviously indicated that she was delighted by my attempt at social interaction. So I followed up with an even bolder question that attempted to explore more completely the entire breadth of her life journey.

"Where you from?" I wanted to know.

"Tennessee," she said, recognizing that one-word replies to my ponderous inquisitions would certainly have the captivating effect of making me want her even more.

I took a deep breath and uttered a prayer for guidance, wisdom, and courage. I finally asked her the question that would penetrate to the inner core of her being, all the way to the depths of her precious soul, "And what do you do?"

With the most disarming and charming southern accent she doubled the lexiconic and syllabic content of her previous replies. With two simple words she revealed all that I would ever need to know about her, and everyone who looked like her: "Nail technician."

Although there is but one letter's difference between "Man, I care" and "Man-i-cure," her response was enough to send me scrambling for a higher class of woman. "Hooters Casino Hotel," I told the taxi driver.

I am still ashamed of myself to this day for not recognizing the significance of her gift and calling. In certain ancient religious traditions the nails are, in fact, considered the windows to the soul, and don't even get me started on what I have come to discover as the sacred merits of the cuticle. Alas, what could have been. If our Lord's ultimate symbol of self-sacrifice and humble service was to stoop down and wash his disciples' feet, I can only imagine how close a full pedicure might transport me to the very heart of God.

In my lifetime, I have known two Hooters girls well. My friends Tammy and Shayna, though they shared a knowledge of dipping sauces, could not have been more different. One was as wise as an owl. The other was sillier than a flying bovine.

Tammy served my friends and me with a self-effacing humor that indicated she was in on the joke. She brought us buffalo wings not only to serve her fellow man, but to further her education. She was mindful of the little things that made her customers appreciate her. Her tips were sufficient to put a serious dent in her college tuition debt. Her interactions with the hungry hormone-laden hordes fine-tuned her communication and promotion skills and prepared her for a career as an in-demand marketing consultant. Tammy ended up marrying a popular radio personality. They had children and moved to the suburbs, and it would not surprise me at all if they dressed up like a family of chickens every Halloween. She had a "just us chickens" mentality that served her well, not only at Hooters, but also in life.

Shayna was endowed with the same natural beauty as Tammy. But she could not see the barnyard beyond the chickens, or her own potential underneath all the makeup. One summer she excitedly told me about her decision to quit summer school, which was a "waste of time," so she could concentrate on "bikini boot camp," which she believed had more lasting value. Shayna could have been "just a little Spanish dancer" type, but she did not want to attend rehearsals, work hard, or engage in service to others as its own reward, or even as the means to a greater end. She smoked a lot of cigarettes and partied into the wee hours of every night—until she got so drunk she fell down a flight of stairs and broke her arm, and could no longer carry wings, with one of her own in a sling. She hoped to go straight to the head of the class by dating her manager. Eventually she became pregnant, which got them both fired and led him to fly the coop. "I'm still hot," she told me the last time I saw her, which, like dipping sauce, is subject to individual taste.

Back in 2003, while the Yankees, Cubs, and Red Sox were getting all the attention, a most unlikely team was getting the job done on the field and ended up winning the World Series. No one expected them even to be in the Series, much less win it. The manager who started the season got fired. His replacement was way over the hill at age seventy-two. They had abysmal fan support. There are megachurches that draw more people than the Florida Marlins did. Their payroll ranked near the bottom in Major League Baseball. But something their former manager, Jeff Torborg, did back in training camp may have made the ultimate difference in the way the team played at the end. Torborg had printed up T-shirts for all the Marlins players. On the front it had a picture of the 1997 World Championship ring that the Marlins had unexpectedly won that year, too. Beneath the ring was this slogan, "Little things win rings." What is true in baseball is true in life, especially the spiritual life.

We tend to dwell on making it to the "big difference" of our dreams, while ignoring the many small things that can make our dreams, as well as those of others, come true: the practice, the hustle, putting the team ahead of your own needs, the cup of cold water given to one who is thirsty, the hot meal to one who is hungry, the kind word, the unexpected visit, a pair of shoes, a gentle manicure, an extra container of blue cheese dressing for your extra hot wings that doesn't even show up on the tab! When we serve our neighbor in these simple understated ways, we are actually serving Christ and becoming more saintly all the time. It may be an odd way for some of us to perceive success, but God is odd. After all, look at the ones God chooses to serve in God's name: an unlikely lot.

—

There's a big difference between self-satisfaction and self-sacrifice. The more we try to lord our own inflated self-image over others, the more ridiculous we appear and unhappy we will be. The more we attempt to buy, battle, or brag our way to a "get out of serving free" card, the less likely we'll discover the inherent joy that is found in bringing joy to others.

Chicken magnate Frank Perdue is said (whether apocryphally or actually I am not certain) to have discovered how such a self-centered pursuit can get lost in translation, not to mention reveal what really resides under our best-tailored costume. When Perdue tried to expand his burgeoning empire into Latin America, he figured his catchy slogan would leave no doubt as to who was in charge and at the top of the pecking order: "It takes a tough man to make a tender chicken." Billboards shot up all over Mexico featuring Perdue's self-gratifying sentiment. Unfortunately, or maybe fortunately, in Spanish the boast was rendered thus: "It takes a hard man to arouse a chicken."

In fairness to Perdue, the slogan, in Spanish, could also be interpreted as "It takes a sexually stimulated man to make a chicken affectionate." So in the Kingdom of God, our attempts to rule the roost or strut our spiritual stuff will come across as nothing more than cockle doodle doo (doo).

I now live on Kauai, also known as "the land of the free-roaming chickens." Hurricane Iniki, in 1992, blew away all the chicken coops and the local fowl were set loose. There are no natural chicken predators on this island (now that Colonel Sanders has moved to Maui), and, consequently, the chicken is the official mascot of Kauai. Chickens are everywhere, sometimes even in my church. On this island one hears "Cock-a-doodle-doo" much more often than "Aloha," "Surf's up," or "Cowabunga, dude" all put together.

The week before I moved to Kauai, my Texas friends, who knew what I was in for, threw me a going-away party. Standing at the front door and greeting all the guests at my friend's palatial home was my very own live rooster, purchased from a local feed store. Since it was virtually the same price to purchase the bird as it was to rent it, they bought it. My friends, thoughtful as they are, also purchased a matching T-shirt that was displayed alongside my new pet. The T-shirt read: HOOTERS GIRLS DIG ME!

I did not think much of or about my new wardrobe option until I met with the bishop of Hawaii in Honolulu shortly thereafter. He is a kind and wise man of God, a true servant, less cocky rooster and more nurturing hen. You would never see his photo plastered on a billboard in Latin America—or Hawaii—or hear him crow a clichéd spiritual slogan. He is steady, calm, and somewhat reserved.

Part of his duties as our spiritual leader is to interview incoming clergy to make sure that they are not psychologically immature, developmentally arrested, spiritually unsound—or authoring books about dogs or beer. Fortunately for me, he is a man who recognizes that each one of us has our own unique insights, gifts, and callings. Each of us serves in our own way. And just because we don't think alike, speak alike, see alike, or act alike, it doesn't mean that we are disqualified to be saints. Exhibit number one: he let me work here.

At the end of our very pleasant and affirming conversation, I still had a few hours to kill before I headed to the airport and boarded a flight to Kauai. I was hungry, so I asked the right reverend if he could recommend a good place to eat lunch nearby.

"Oh yes," he said, directing me to the Aloha Tower Marketplace, a short walk from St. Andrew's Cathedral. "There are all sorts of good places down there."

He paused, as if for dramatic effect, before he concluded, "like *Hooters*."

That man is a saint.

13

THE PATRON SAINT OF HARES

My religion and the spiritual side of my life come from a sense of
connection to humanity and nature on this planet.

—HUGH HEFNER

Although he knows a thing or two about bunnies, Hugh
Hefner is not the patron saint of hares. That honor goes to St.
Melangell of Wales. Melangell was the lovely daughter of the
mighty Irish king Jowchel, who attempted to marry her off to
a rich, old playboy. Melangell did not think that sounded like
a good time, so she boarded the first boat to Wales and hid in
the forest for fifteen years. Melangell devoted herself completely to her true love, the God of Creation, dedicating her
days to fervent prayer, sleeping on rocks, and sharing the wild
whimberries with the rabbits who frolicked in the nearby bogs
and heather.

One day, the story goes, the illustrious manly man,
Prince Brychwel Ysgithrog of Pengwern Powys, showed up at
prayer time hunting hares. His hunting dogs, Brych and
Throg, picked up the scent of a fine, fat hare and gave chase

as his servants began playing, on their hunting horns, an up-tempo version of "Who Let the Dogs Out?" The terrified hare leapt into a bramble bush that happened to be the favorite place of prayer for the fair maiden Melangell. The hare sought refuge under Melangell's skirt and calmly stared back at Brych and Throg, who began to retreat and whimper like castrated Chihuahuas. The hunting horns quickly offered a slow-tempo waltz version of "Here Comes Peter Cottontail" while the prince dismounted his studly steed and knelt reverently before the serene saint and her brave bunny. Recognizing the rare beauty he beheld, he offered a pickup line of which any prince would be proud, asking her, "Come hare often?"

Eliciting no laughter and realizing he had no chance, he asked her to tell him her pious tale of godly purpose. The prince was deeply moved and granted her all the nearby land that it might become a refuge of peace and protection for all creatures. The prince channeled his inner poet and told her:

> O most worthy Melangell, I perceive that thou art the handmaiden of the true God. Because it hath pleased Him for thy merits to give protection to this little wild hare from the attack and pursuit of the ravening hounds, I give and present to thee with willing mind these lands for the service of God, to be a perpetual asylum and refuge. If any man, woman, or bunny flee hither to seek thy protection, provided they do not pollute thy sanctuary, let no prince, chieftain or old rich playboy from Ireland or Chicago be so rash towards God as to attempt to drag them forth. And here's my number in case you change your mind.

It is easy for the rational fact-checkers of our time to dismiss such stories as mere legend without modern relevance, but that would be to underestimate the power of the patron saint of hares. To this day the local hunters in that part of the world always spare hares. The little church at Pennant Melangell has been lovingly restored, including a twelfth-century shrine said to contain her bones, a fifteenth-century oak screen with carvings that tell the story of her encounter with the prince, and a seventeenth-century inscription of a pun that reveals her ongoing power: *Mil engyl a Melangell. Trechant lu fyddin y fall.* Melangell with a thousand angels. Triumphs over all the powers of evil.

Perhaps the greatest testimony to the truth of her tale is the St. Melangell Center just up the road. Staffed by a female priest who is also a psychotherapist, it offers a real refuge from the world for those who are in need. Offering free counseling to anyone, the center provides opportunities for healing, renewal, and sanctuary. It has become a powerful place of pilgrimage for those dealing with terminal illness. As I wandered the gardens and enjoyed a home-cooked meal, I could sense a palpable, loving spirit that enveloped the place, like the protective skirt of a prayerful saint. If such intangibles are not enough to convince you of the reality of saints, perhaps the hares that still frolic in the bog, heather, and churchyard bear a more powerful testimony. Centuries later, bunnies abound.

Although stories such as Melangell's did not become as widely known as those of her male counterparts, she was one of several saints in medieval times who believed passionately in an alternative form of pleasure—the ecstasy of self-denial. It is a mostly foreign and dated concept for us moderns who have no clue that it is possible to do good, and feel good, by doing without. I'm talking James Brown "I feel good" good. Many of us princes and princesses today wouldn't know a hair shirt from a hare, a Pennant Melangell from a playboy bunny, and wouldn't touch a wild whimberry unless it was floating in a trendy martini. But these stories of self-denial and selfless concern contain an uncommon beauty and unique power. While they are too subtle to show up on reality television, the University of Wales at Lampeter offers a course about these almost lost legends, provocatively titled "Dead Virgins: Feminine Sanctity in Medieval Wales." Who knew that untold tales of untouched tails could wield such power still?

Appropriately, I discovered St. Melangell while studying Celtic spirituality at St. Deiniol's Library in Hawarden, Wales, not far from the sacred site where Melangell and her rabbit so fervently prayed. St. Deiniol's was founded by four-time British prime minister and champion of wayward women William Ewart Gladstone. Gladstone made it his personal crusade to scour the local red-light districts in search of lasses who had lost their way, as well as their virginity. These young women sought refuge, or at least survival, in the arms of men who knew much more about lust than love. Gladstone became personally involved in their lives, attempting to redirect them toward a purer lifestyle. Gladstone wanted them to know the One who truly loved them. Like the Prince of Powys, Gladstone set aside a sanctuary space where these women could find refuge and healing. He founded and supported the Church Penitentiary Association for the Reclamation of Fallen Women, which was not only a powerful and protective place of refuge, but also a great name for an all-girl heavy metal band.

Of course, whenever a red-blooded male is involved in such ministries, there are rumors of impropriety and whispers of ulterior motives. No exceptions here. Accusations abounded that Gladstone was just as interested in chasing their skirts as saving their souls. A jury eventually cleared him of all charges, but one has to wonder about the purity of Gladstone's intent, given his fervent obsession with this particular cause. Then again, if we fail to act for good because some portion of our motives is less than holy, I wonder if we would ever act at all. Was it Chesterton who suggested that we should never examine our motives, because they are always bound to be vile? Perhaps not vile, but certainly tainted. The truth is that we are capable of doing good, even if we are hoping for a few perks along the way.

This observation reminds me of the invitation I received several years ago to attend the fiftieth anniversary celebration of *Playboy* magazine at the Palms Casino Hotel in Las Vegas. Maybe it was a coincidence, a fluke of nature, a mailing list mix-up. Or maybe God was patting me on the back for being a parish priest for all these years. Regardless, "William Miller and Guest" somehow made the VIP list for a weekend that made every one of my male friends, including the ordained, jump up and down like the donkey in *Shrek* screaming, "Pick me! Pick me! Pick me!"

The previous year, while playing blackjack at the Palms Casino Hotel, I had become completely disassociated from the monetary value of my chips. Body-snatched by a Taiwanese billionaire, or perhaps an NBA all-star, I began to bet money like I had it to burn. The pit boss must have been paying attention every time I increased my bet and must have been checking out the cocktail waitress every time I lowered it. The end result was that I got upgraded to the Palms A-list of gamblers. My days of getting worked up over a comped $9.99 breakfast buffet had been replaced with an all-expenses-paid episode right out of

Lifestyles of the Rich and Famous. In fact, when I ran into Robin Leach, the host of *Lifestyles of the Rich and Famous,* at the front desk at the Palms, and told him boldly that I was the only priest invited to the weekend's festivities, he was so impressed it rendered him nearly speechless. He uttered a single word: "Certainly." Although it could have been "Security."

When the invitation arrived at my home, the parish rectory, I paused and prayed that God would grant me the wisdom to make the right decision about whether to attend this weekend of questionable moral character.

Of course, since, like most people, I pray typically to confirm a decision I have already made rather than to have God actually change my mind, I immediately began to reason with the Lord. Trying to look as pious as I possibly could, I shared that my true motivation for going would be to engage in research on the patron saint of hares. I also argued that I sought to be more like Jesus, who frequently hung out with folks of questionable character, like prostitutes and tax collectors. I also pointed out in prayer that I would have the opportunity to share my faith in, I mean with, bunnies. It was conceivable that through my presence, I pleaded, I might be able to recruit wayward rabbits to my new ministry, the Playboy Penitentiary Association for the Reclamation of Fallen Women. I felt that I was especially qualified to become the chaplain of this innovative religious endeavor. And I told the Lord that in addition to all of these sound reasons for attending, it was also possible that I might finally find a wife.

I am pretty sure that I heard the voice of God say to me, "Go, my son, for this may be as close to heaven as you shall ever get."

The entire weekend, I felt a little like a vegan at a chili

cook-off. I worked up quite the appetite, but I knew that my dietary restrictions prevented me from partaking. Sometimes fasting at a feast is much more enlivening and enlightening than feasting at a fast. To abstain and refrain rather than guzzle and gorge can occasionally be the more sensual, and spiritual choice. "Just enough" can heighten pleasure in a way that "too much" can dull our sensitivities. Self-denial can lead to a far deeper self-awareness.

Like the Christian admonition to be "in" the world but not "of" the world, I was fully present and engaged that weekend, but stood just a hare on the outside looking in. It was a surreal series of events.

As I was reclining by the pool one afternoon, Carmen Electra brushed up against my kneecap while filming a segment for a television news program. My knee has been wobbly ever since. Dennis Rodman and I approached the bar at the same time. The bartender, unbelievably, took Rodman's order ahead of mine. I had my picture taken with a dude who was a dead ringer for the devil, complete with red hair that had been fashioned into lifelike horns. The devil was there with his wife and toddler and seemed like a really good dad, which confused things even more than they already were. I played blackjack with a former Playmate of the Year, and I told Christie Hefner at the opening reception to "take me with you"—where, I was not sure. I talked my way into a private reception with Hef and "The Girls Next Door" some sixty stories up at the Ghostbar. My homiletical training in the power of persuasion finally paid off. After staring at Miss September for thirty seconds while she shared her insights on feminine sanctity in the modern age, I moved toward the much more enlightening shrimp cocktail buffet.

I attended my first ever Bunny Hop dance, found myself surrounded by fluffy white tails whenever I boarded the hotel elevator, and got in touch with my inner redneck at the grand finale concert featuring Kid Rock. I am pretty sure that sharing my personal testimony with Mr. Rock (as I call him) later led to his spiritual awakening and the recording of his greatest album, *Rock n Roll Jesus*. This musical milestone was a true step up on the inspiration scale from *Devil Without a Cause* and *Cocky*. *Rock n Roll Jesus* features such pious gems as "Blue Jeans and a Rosary," followed by the equally profound "Half Your Age." Perhaps his motives are only partially pure. No wonder I like him.

Over the course of the weekend, I established a good rapport with Hef's publicist, a guy whose last name was Miller and who really liked the title of this book. As an added bonus, Mr. Miller's wife took a liking to my partner in crime for the weekend, the winner of the "*Shrek* Donkey Pick Me" award, my friend Mark. Mark looks a lot like Elvis Presley, only taller, and Mrs. Miller was a big fan of Elvis, and now Mark. Spiritually serendipitous, for St. Elvis was also a mostly unknown and underappreciated Welsh saint, not unlike Melangell. In fact, legend has it that when St. Elvis heard Melangell's story, he composed a hymn titled "You Ain't Nothin' but a Hunting Dog."

Just outside Hef's private cabana at the Palms pool, publicist Miller and priest Miller struck up an animated conversation. Our verbal discourse did not go unnoticed by a reporter from the *National Enquirer* who figured out that I must be "somebody." Recognizing an opportunity for a wild hare chase, I told the reporter that I was *Playboy*'s chaplain, the actual patron priest of hares. She interviewed me extensively as I waxed eloquent in defense of nonpuritanical religious values, the refreshing honesty of Hefner's personal philosophies, and the divine beauty of God's most wonderful creation—the human form. I also pointed out the unnecessary and unspiritual trauma we inflict upon ourselves and others by dishonest repression of natural human tendencies and that we dishonor creation and the Creator with our inability to be comfortable in our own skin.

I don't think I fooled her, nor do I think I fooled myself. While I believe some of that, some of the time, I also believe that there is much more to life than filling every crevice of desire. One can often *do* more good and *feel* more good by not trying to feel *all* the goods. Try as I might to defend my motives, at the core of my being I was probably more interested in tail-chasing than truth-telling. But that does not mean that I am beyond the reach of a loving Creator who uses mere mortals to accomplish loving purposes, despite our often impure motives.

—

Back when I was a raging hormonal teenager, I was also a budding political and social activist trying to connect my faith with my politics, my spiritual commitment with my fervent physical desires. I was struggling with whether my libido should be banished to the repository of the repressed, or sublimated toward the storehouse of the soul. It's a choice that remains confusing. A psychoanalyst friend recently concluded that most issues we perceive to be spiritual are actually sexual, and most we identify as sexual are actually spiritual. During these impressionable years, a devout Baptist Sunday school teacher and peanut farmer from Georgia ran for president. I liked Jimmy Carter because he seemed to be pretty smart, cared about people, and tried to connect his faith to his politics, taking this connection seriously. Plus, he agreed to be interviewed by *Playboy* magazine. The interview created quite a stir, because, after all, why would a good Christian agree to be interviewed by such a suspect, secular publication?

My devout Baptist friend, Bobby, was a raging and hormonal teenager like myself, so we talked about the *Playboy* issue containing the Jimmy Carter article, concluding that our discussion would be much better informed if Bobby were to purchase a copy for us to peruse. Like millions of good Christian males before us, we longed for a *Playboy* magazine because we wanted to read the articles.

In the article, Carter admitted something that shouldn't have shocked any honest human being on the planet—that he had "lusted in his heart" on more than one occasion. Of course, there aren't many honest human beings on the planet, and even fewer honest Christians, who would freely admit that they had lusted with a lot more than their hearts. While Carter was probably too contemplative to take decisive action, and thus was a fairly ineffective president, he gets bonus points for his refreshing truth-telling. I think it was at that moment that I began to realize how threatening it is for religious people when someone dares to tell the truth. I also vowed that I would tell the truth anyway, whether people were threatened by it or not.

The afternoon Bobby rang my doorbell with the *Playboy* discreetly tucked under his arm, I had a feeling that our prayer time was about to undergo a paradigm shift, from petition to confession. He was by far the most devout Christian I knew. He prayed, read his Bible, shared his faith with other students, and played and sang strictly Christian music at all the school talent shows. He chose a career in music after he had prayed to God in seventh grade that if he turned on the radio and heard talking, he would become a preacher, but if he turned on the radio and heard music, he'd know he was called to a life of music ministry. He turned on the radio and heard music and became an accomplished performer, composer, and producer in the Christian music industry. The world is a better place today because my friend did not hear an evangelist when he turned on that radio.

On that day Bobby was a lot like me, a horny Christian teenage male whose motivations were not entirely pure. After teasing me for a few torturous minutes, he finally handed me the *Playboy*. I quickly thumbed through the magazine to find the pictures—I mean, the article. Not a single bunny left for my viewing pleasure! For my own sake, he said, he had removed all of the offending photographs from the magazine. He cared so much about the purity of my soul that he had edited out anything that might cause me to lust in my heart, but not before he had looked at every single one of the photographs, he said—or rather, he confessed. I was furious and frustrated, and I questioned his motives. But I don't question the fact that God can still use us—despite our motives.

Perhaps I will never be in the same saintly league as the patron saint of hares. Perhaps it is true that my motives are not 100 percent pure. But perhaps I can join a long line of males who just might make a difference anyway—Ysgithrog, Glad-stone, maybe even Mr. Rock and Mr. Hefner—anyone who can understand the power of the skirt to protect as well as reveal.

Besides, I am not convinced that the hare who sought refuge was entirely innocent.

14

MORE CLEAVAGE

Therefore a man shall leave his father and mother
and cleave unto his wife.

—GENESIS 2:24 (KING JAMES VERSION)

One day
He did not leave
After kissing me.

—RABIA OF BASRA, MUSLIM FEMALE MYSTIC POET, EIGHTH CENTURY

*S*extus Propertius is not, sadly, a Latin manual on the contractual obligations of marriage. He was actually a Roman poet who penned the line "Always toward absent lovers love's tide stronger flows." Hallmark has translated this as "Absence makes the heart grow fonder." The true lover understands that sometimes it is only in drifting apart that we endeavor to swim toward each other with much more intention, that we can commit to holding on forever and not letting go.

A former bishop of Hawaii once shared with me that, at a critical point in his life and ministry, one where he was expected to be the chief shepherd of a dispersed and diverse diocese of people, he discovered that he could not pray. The words, the connection, the feeling, the passion, the intimacy, the presence, the purpose, the point—all of these eluded him. The bishop, the spiritual leader upon whom so many depended for spiritual direction and prayerful counsel, was unable to enter into that place of interrelationship and interdependency that we call prayer.

I remember thinking, as the bishop shared the most vulnerable position he had occupied, or failed to occupy: Now here is a man who might have something to teach me about prayer. Here is a man whose insights about connecting, disconnecting, and reconnecting might go far beyond religious clichés and pious platitudes. Here is a man who has descended to the depths and has emerged on the other side, with a more authentic and lasting bond than he had before, a connection that can transcend perceptions and feelings and even realities. Sometimes to stand apart is to be able, eventually, to come together, in a more permanent place.

Or, maybe bishops are just human, too. Like a bishop who has learned about prayer by not praying, I sometimes find myself in the rather awkward role of being a divorced priest facilitating an eager young couple's premarital counseling. Although I was married for eleven years—not a bad track record for two incredibly individualistic individuals who got hitched at age twenty—it still may give pause to those who prefer that their guidance counselors made straight A's in guidance counseling. I must admit that I failed in my first and only attempt at lifelong commitment. Some may wonder what a divorced person could possibly offer those about to take vows of a lifelong commitment. What could such a relational failure have to teach an earnest couple hoping to connect at the deepest possible level? What could an avowed twenty-plus-years bachelor say to those pledging to uphold their relationship as long as they both shall live?

Maybe more than you might think. Sometimes distance is just the perspective one needs to see more deeply into the truth we seek. Sometimes those who have learned to let go have much to teach about the requirements for holding on.

Or, maybe priests are just human, too.

—

Relationships have sometimes been to me like prayer was to the bishop—distant, unspeakable, pointless. I sometimes feel like the endangered Hawaiian monk seal I often stumble across on isolated beaches here on Kauai. They are so named because they actually prefer the solitary life. They might, in rare moments of social intercourse, play with a seal pal, tease a sea turtle, or swim alongside a human paddling a sea kayak, but, at the end of the day, they go right back to their personal stretch of private sand, alone, happy, and content. Being on the endangered species list is not necessarily a bad thing, although the unendangered species might think so. Call me a monk seal, although that would be Father Monk Seal to you; I have learned plenty about relationships in my place of solitude and seeking.

I have learned that searching for Miss Universe is ultimately futile; one can make such a claim only after one has *actually* searched for Miss Universe. About such things, I do not speak metaphorically. I speak literally. For when it comes to the pursuit of rare beauty, I am a flaming fundamentalist.

Several years ago, toward the end of an Asian itinerary that took me from the Taj Mahal to Thailand, I finally took a step back and a deep breath in order to ponder the way in which human beings relate, or do not relate, to each other. During a trek through Tibet, a good friend, fellow priest, and blackjack partner and I bonded with a young Japanese salesman who lived in Bangkok. We were booked on the same flight to Bangkok from Kathmandu, Nepal, at the end of our trek. Our new friend, Tomo, offered to treat us to an insider's nightlife tour of one of the world's most notoriously sinful cities.

Back at Tomo's trendy high-rise apartment building, he insisted on showing us the many amenities offered by his residential complex. The Olympic-sized swimming pool and regulation Thai kickboxing arena were impressive indeed. But, as they say in Bangkok, "You ain't seen nothin' yet!" Tomo took us up to the second floor to see his personal pride and joy, the residents' very own bar. We were astounded that a single apartment building could offer a fully stocked, fully functioning bar, but not nearly as astounded as we were a moment later when Tomo instructed us to shift our eyes from the massive cocktail inventory to the wall opposite. On that side of this watering hole for the weary, working masses who called this place home was a sight one simply does not see every day. Behind the floor-to-ceiling window, forty scantily clad, attractive young women sat seductively smiling, each holding a personal identification number.

Once we located our tongues on the floor below, we were able to speak again. Tomo's English was decent but not particularly nuanced. When we tried to describe the kind of bar we were really looking for—a bar where girls might give you a number, a normal bar where equals gathered for conversation and camaraderie, a place where all people, regardless of sex or vocation in life, were treated with dignity and respect—Tomo looked absolutely perplexed. Such a concept seemed as foreign to him as a World Series ring to a Chicago Cub.

Attempting to appease the foolish, uptight Americans, he described our options. Every bar he described was but a variation on the same theme. Their undeniable purpose was for connection, but not the kind I had anticipated. The local bar scene seemed to be a simple excuse for unequal consumption and unethical consummation. The romantic notion of living happily ever after had been replaced by a very different kind of happy ending, one that involved a monetary transaction and a most definite violation of the Apostle Paul's admonition to be not "unequally yoked."

Having failed to fully appreciate Bangkok's charms, we boarded a plane for the island of Ko Sumui, a much quieter, calmer resort destination where the most titillating sensual experience was sprawling outside on a comfy pillow while drinking ice-cold Thai beer and munching on barbecued tiger shrimp. We agreed that Bangkok must have been some sort of unrepentant urban aberration, a nightlife anomaly that would be offset by the more normal social encounters of the island. A local told us about a reggae bar just outside town that sounded like the ticket to return to bar-hopping normalcy. "Stay till eleven," he advised; "that's when all the girls show up." What we discovered was that that was when all the working girls showed up—and there didn't seem to be any other kind.

I spent the rest of my time in Thailand face-to-face with the intimacy of my snorkeling mask. My sole source of scintillation for the duration came from traditional Thai massage on the beach. Other than tiger shrimp, traditional Thai massage is the best thing about this exotic land. For twenty bucks, a licensed therapist will walk on your back for two hours and stretch your entire body into proper alignment.

Things were so weird in Thailand that I decided that I would consistently err on the side of the surreal. So, with a three-hour layover back in Bangkok (just enough time for someone like me to do something extraordinarily stupid), I did something extraordinarily stupid. On the flight in, someone loaned me a local newspaper where I read that, on the very day of our layover, at the very hour we would be puttering around the airport Starbucks waiting for our connecting flight, none other than Miss Universe herself would be making an appearance at a shopping mall called the Emporium.

While most rational human beings would read such an article and think to themselves, "Isn't that interesting, Miss Universe is at a shopping mall in Bangkok," a nonrational being like myself reads such an article and thinks to himself, "Isn't that interesting: my future wife is at a shopping mall in Bangkok."

I hired a cab.

Armed with nothing more than a newspaper photo of Miss Universe, I began to plan how this unlikely scenario would unfold. My timing would be impeccable. I would swoop down from the Orange Julius on Mall Level 3 (in Thailand these are called "the Orange Julia formerly known as Orange Julius"). She would be autographing head shots for the masses, but she would pause and lock eyes with the perfect American stranger, as if she had been waiting for me her entire life. We would have a brief chat that would reveal her deeper spiritual aspirations and her long-held desire to be a preacher's wife and live in Texas, where she would raise cows and I would barbecue them. Then I would propose to her. She would accept, and we would live happily ever after on the island of Ko Sumui with a weekend apartment in Bangkok, where I'd get a traditional massage every Sunday afternoon just after the karaoke service at the Anglican cathedral.

What actually transpired was a slightly different version of reality, known to some as "reality." My cabdriver, first of all, insisted that what I was really searching for was not Miss Universe, at all. No, what I really wanted, and what would give my life true meaning and happiness, was a suit crafted by his favorite tailor. I would get "very special price," which, of course, was "good today only." My cabdriver and his wife would also get a very special commission, which would allow them to live very happily ever after.

Finally convinced that I had no desire for a tailored suit, he proceeded to tell me that what I was really searching for was a massage. He knew just the place where I could get the very best massage in the world, a massage that would give my life meaning and happiness. And yes, I could find a wife there, too. And yes, there would be a happy ending to the story, after all, just not the kind of happy ending I had imagined. I insisted that what I really was searching for was Miss Universe and that I really could find her at the Emporium mall on that very day at that very hour.

We arrived at the Emporium just as Miss Universe was departing. I was able, however, to speak to a Miss Universe executive, which is a job that I believe I would like to have. After I explained to him that I was from the Kingdom of Texas and was personal friends with the "Shah of Midland-Odessa," he informed me that I could catch her at the Times Square mall in just a few hours. I explained that I would be on a plane to

Hong Kong at that time, and the Miss Universe executive proceeded to give me the name of the hotel where Miss Universe would be "resting" between appearances. My cabdriver, by this time, was impressed with my tenacity, or perhaps he was merely afraid of what such an unstable, obsessed human being might be capable.

At the hotel, I persuaded the manager to call Miss Universe's room. Her representative was *not* persuaded that Miss Universe should join me in the lobby for tea. I had to settle with an intimate chat with the official driver of Miss Universe. As I sat in the back of his Mercedes and told him my tale of woe, he seemed genuinely moved and somewhat entertained. He took my card and told me not to worry, that he would make absolutely certain that Miss Universe got the message and called me immediately upon my return to the United States. Several months later, I was crushed when someone handed me a newspaper that indicated Miss Universe was dating Derek Jeter. He must have known a shortcut to the Emporium.

There is a Buddhist saying that much of our suffering as human beings simply lies in our dissatisfaction with things as they are, things over which we really have no control. Thus, our frantic searches often lead to nowhere, and nothing, and no one. Such obsessive journeys create even more stress, anxiety, and unhappiness. The search for the perfect woman, perfect man, perfect woman who used to be a man. The search for the perfect lover, the perfect partner, the perfect friend. The search for the perfect job, the perfect family, the perfect faith community. All of these elude us.

A more meaningful search is one that is less obsessed with locating the perfect and more content to understand and make love to the imperfect. To deal with the hand that is dealt, to love in the relationships we have been given, to survive and thrive in the life that has been entrusted to us—a sacred, sacramental trust that even mere mortals can vow to honor and uphold all the days of their lives. The grass may be greener on the other side, but that is probably because it has not been lived on. If we were truly committed to the grass we walk upon each day, we would take care to water, fertilize, feed, protect, and give it the attention it deserves so that it could be as lovely and as lush as humanly possible. As Jesus once said: Love the one you're with.

—

The older I get, the more traditional I become, at least when it comes to the language of relationships. Call me a dinosaur, but I think nuptial vows, for example, should always include the "plighting of our troths." It is just as romantic as it is archaic to tell a beloved how much we desire to "plight thee my troth." Pledging one's fidelity does not have quite the same ring to it.

Traditionally romantic language in biblical literature should gain the same respect. It is annoying when a perfectly potent—though perhaps dated—word is replaced by a more modern, more impotent term. Take the passage about men and women from the book of Genesis, for example. In the lusty old King James Version we read: "Therefore a man shall leave his father and mother and *cleave* unto his wife." Now, the vastly inferior, supposedly improved text informs us that a man shall "cling" like Saran Wrap, or "is joined" in the same way one links up with the American Automobile Association. The word *cleave* is much stronger and has the powerful force of fierce bonding, fiery fusion—a deep and abiding connection. It is a word worthy of reclamation.

My favorite story about the biblical word *cleave* is told by the storyteller, former fundamentalist evangelist, Unitarian minister, and progressive radio talk-show host the Reverend Chuck "Soul Talk" Freeman. Like me, Chuck grew up in a fundamentalist denomination that is so fundamentalist, it thinks the other fundamentalist denominations are going to hell. Long ago, when Chuck was the youth minister at the Fort Stockton Church of Christ in Fort Stockton, Texas, the literal middle of nowhere, he attended a gathering of youth ministers. All of these young men, and I do mean men, had gathered in Lubbock, a city only slightly less holy than Abilene and Nashville for the good folks of this particular denomination.

The elder statesman of youth ministers, Brother Wilbur Williams, was tapped to give the keynote address to the budding clerics. Like the Apostle Paul to young Timothy, Brother Williams admonished them "in the Lord." Brother Williams chose as his topic the alarmingly high divorce rate among the young, seemingly unfaithful upholders of the faith. Brother Williams had plenty of ammunition. Jesus, for example, while making no statements on homosexuality, had plenty of derogatory comments about divorce. But Brother Williams decided to go back to the very beginning of Holy Scripture, to the book of Genesis, and chose as his text for his sermon my personal favorite, the King James Version of Genesis 2:24: "A man shall leave his father and mother and *cleave* unto his wife."

This wise veteran of marital affairs began to expound upon the chosen text, admonishing and encouraging the men to remain faithful in their relationships. With his voice rising to an oratorical crescendo, he explicitly pronounced the prevailing theme of his urgent message: "My young brothers in Jesus Christ, I declare to you this day that what we need in our relationships, what we need in our marriages, what we need in our churches, and what we need in this world is simply this: MORE CLEAVAGE!"

Even in a sea of far-too-serious fundamentalists, somebody has a semblance of a sense of humor. There was much rib-poking, tittering, and snickering at the solemn evangelist's exhortation. But Brother Williams would not waver from his righteous indignation directed at his younger bosom buddies. Undeterred, he traveled on down the less titillating path: "Young men, this is no laughing matter! I cannot overemphasize this point to each of you today. It is the core issue of our commitment to Christ and our loyalty to God, and our faithfulness to one another. Do not be deceived, young men! What we truly need in these desperate times is: MORE CLEAVAGE!"

By this time the dual-edged overstatement had elicited outright laughter and hearty guffaws among the naughty novices. But Brother Williams, unaware of the suggestive power of his oratorical insights, would not be deterred. Continuing with his pointed pleadings, his voice rose to a feverish pitch. He pounded the pulpit, rose up on his tiptoes, stretched forth his arms with palms outward and upward, and shouted: "Young men! I implore you! I beseech you! I pray to God that you understand this inerrant point! What I need! What you need! What God needs! What the world needs! MOOOOOOOOOORE! CLEEEEEEEEEAAVAAAAAAAAAAAAAAAAAAAAAAGE!"

Amen, Brother. I feel closer to God already.

15

GERTRUDE GETS THE LAST WORD

A Rose is a Rose is a Rose.
And Evelyn is Evelyn is Evelyn.
Amen.

*T*wisted and delicious is the irony that a fundamentalist preacher concluded his eulogy at my mother's graveside service by quoting a Jewish lesbian feminist. Although the pastor added one indefinite article and omitted a single rose from the original quotation, the literary and liturgical reality remains that on that sunny All Saints' Day in 1996, Gertrude Stein got the last word about my mother, Evelyn Madyne Miller. Poetic justice aside, the parallels between the two women are striking.

Gertrude Stein—lover of Alice B. Toklas, intellectual, playwright, poet, biographer, convener of keen literary and political minds, brilliant, but admittedly not much to look at—was born in Allegheny City, Pennsylvania, and lived most of her life in Paris, France.

Evelyn Miller—lover of Thomas C. "Bill" Miller, former assistant flag girl in the Hearne High School Marching Eagle Band, telephone operator, Sunday school teacher, funeral home receptionist and greeter, consoler of grief-stricken families and friends, occasionally intellectually challenged, yet a real looker—was born in Edge, Texas, and lived all her life in the Lone Star State.

Gertrude Stein—avant-garde experimentalist with rhythmic, stream-of-consciousness writing, a sort of cutting-edge cubism for the literary world, cultivating phrases such as "Out of kindness comes redness and out of rudeness comes rapid same question, out of an eye comes research, out of selection comes painful cattle" and "Sugar is not a vegetable"—used perplexing metaphorical images originating from a cultured context where Picassos inspire the pen.

Evelyn Miller—Avon-guarding experimentalist with lyrical, stream-of-consciousness yelling, a sort of "rudism" for the common woman, employing phrases such as "Aw, foot!" "Thunderation!" "Well I never in my life!" "Gimme a nerve pill!" and "That looks like somethin' the cats done drug up and urped on!"—used perplexing rhetorical images originating from a countrified context that could have inspired *American Gothic*.

Gertrude Stein was thought to have coined the term "Lost Generation" to describe the expatriate Americans wandering aimlessly in Europe after World War I.

Evelyn Miller was thought to have utilized the term "horse's ass" to describe certain church people who spend more time slinging shit than engaging in social or spiritual transformation.

Gertrude Stein, informed and opinionated on all issues, consistently conservative, bordering on fascist—perhaps only because fascists were in vogue in Europe at the time—considered Roosevelt's "New Deal" a bad idea, and she did not vote or campaign for him.

Evelyn Miller, uninformed and opinionated on most issues, consistently voted for the Democrat—perhaps only because there were no Republicans in Texas at the time. She once admitted that she would have campaigned vigorously only if Pat Boone had run for public office.

According to Stein, "The important thing is that one must have deep down as the deepest core within oneself a sense of equality."

According to Miller, and a message communicated effectively with a syrupy sweet southern accent, "Y'all be sweet."

Stein believed in herself as revealed in *The Autobiography of Alice B. Toklas,* which was really the autobiography of Gertrude Stein, whom she described as a "confident genius."

Miller believed in God as revealed in *Hurlbut's Story of the Bible for Young and Old,* and described him as "beyond me."

My favorite Stein quote described the city of Oakland, California, but could be said about most of the places we visit in our lifetime: "When you get there, there's no there there."

My favorite Miller quote came toward the end of her life after Yolanda, her chemotherapy nurse, called our home in tears to tell my mother that she had been her "favorite patient ever." My mother's response: "Well y'all tell *Lasagna* that she sure was nice to call!"

Gertrude Stein died of stomach cancer at age seventy-two.

Evelyn Miller died of liver cancer at age sixty-nine.

Stein's last words, directed to Alice, were "What is the answer?" Since Toklas did not respond, or at least did not respond fast enough, Stein followed up with "In that case, what is the question?" Brilliant.

Miller's last words, directed to her husband of forty-seven

years, my father, were "I need some," followed by "I love you, too." Brilliant. Even more so.

So, there at the end, as a final observation on the meaning of my mother's life, the preacher picked up a single red rose from atop her casket and held it toward the bright autumn noonday sun. Oblivious to his literary source as well as the liturgical meaning of November 1, when *all* of the saints are given their due, even Gertrude and Evelyn, the preacher did know of whom he spoke. His laughter confirmed such knowledge. And his object of affection uniquely represented the object of all of our affections that day. Although no one there knew much about Gertrude Stein, everyone there knew about Evelyn Miller and recognized that the preacher, in this case, was anointed and inspired, even prophetic.

To say simply "rose," as Stein observed, is to invoke a whole host of images and emotions and understandings implicit in the name itself. To say simply "Evelyn," as the preacher observed, is also to invoke a whole host of images and emotions and understandings essential to the name itself. As the preacher proclaimed, my mother, Evelyn Miller, was a unique, authentic human being. She was who she was. Like it or not, she dared to be the one she was created to be. Such singular truth will always be the last word about any of us.

Theologically speaking, each one of us is created in the image of God. This statement implies that God is large, conflicted, unique, broad, quirky, contains multiple personalities, and possesses one unusual sense of humor. I have also heard this theological reality stated as "Every person is a unique *eachness* within the all-encompassing *allness* of God." Some would go so far as to say that, come Judgment Day, God's ultimate question will pertain equally to our eachness and God's allness.

God's final question, and thus the beginning of eternity, will go something like this: "Evelyn, were you Evelyn?" If the answer is honestly and authentically "yes," then God's response will be equally affirming: "Well done, thou sometimes good, occasionally faithful, but frequently entertaining servant."

My relationship with my mother, like all human/dysfunctional relationships, alternated between poignant and pungent. There were times when she would lovingly rearrange every hair on my head, so that I "would not look so stupid." There were other times when she would utilize that same hairbrush to "beat the living tarnation" out of me. To this day, I continue to work with my therapist on my unhealthy obsession with my hair. And without my mother's hairbrush to beat it out of me, my friends all tell me that I have become a virtual aquifer of tarnation these days, supplying my entire community with enough tarnation for all.

Evelyn conveyed to me at an early age that God knew my name, loved me dearly, had a special claim upon and calling for my life, and paid particular attention to my predicament when I spoke to him using King James English and called him "Thee." Apparently that was some sort of nickname that only the privileged few knew. Concurrently, my mother frequently insisted that I was the veritable spawn of Satan himself and could lay claim to the title "meanest kid on earth." I would point out to her, after these moments of hyperbolic shaming, that I was ranked only number 3,187th of the meanest kids on earth. She hated it when I made light of her condemnations.

Despite her verbal reminders that I was a sinner in need of grace, I loved her dearly. I remember the first Christmas that I decided I would not rely solely on my father's conscientious trips to the department store during his lunch break to purchase a bottle of my mother's favorite perfume. Each year he would kindly label the gift "from Billy," although I had never smelled or even seen it before. It would be meticulously wrapped by someone whose wrapping skills far surpassed my own in technique but not in creativity.

On that Christmas, I decided that I had reached the age of gift-giving accountability. So my friend and I disobeyed our parents and walked all the way to Woolworth's on the corner of Forty-Third Street and Ella Boulevard, where I purchased for my mother one scented candle ("You can't go wrong with a scented candle," she always said, words spoken I am sure from a decade of receiving crappy knickknacks from those who meant well) and one pair of house shoes whose appearance could only be described, in early 1970s terminology, as "psychedelic." Right there, in a furry house shoe, the god of black light posters and the spirit of hallucinogenic drugs converged to create a wonder of psychedelic podiatric art—all for only $4.99. Timothy Leary would be proud.

The scented candle was certainly the safe choice, like perfume, and my way of hedging my gift-giving bets. But for the house shoes, I was gambling on that groovy ghost of Christmas present. I wrapped the colorful shoes in an old model airplane box to further prolong the sole suspense. When my mother unwrapped them on Christmas Day, she exclaimed, with a force unique to appreciative mothers, words that would come to be immortalized in print: "Psychedelic house shoes! Just what I've always wanted!" She wore them with the same anti-establishment élan that those of us on the tail end of the Age of Aquarius committed to our low-cut, bell-bottom jeans. After my mother died, my father and I spent an entire afternoon rummaging through her vast clothes closet to separate the items for the resale shop from those reserved for posterity. Hidden in a shoe box originally dedicated to some brand of fancy high heels, we uncovered one pair of well-worn, vintage 1970s, psychedelic house shoes. Some thirty years after the "Great Woolworth's Adventure," they retained their mind-blowing coloration, though faded into a "purple haze" of sorts. My mother's enthusiastic and appreciative embrace of such an unusual gift showed me the difference our gifts can make in the lives of others, especially when they are uniquely chosen and authentically given.

My mother, like many human beings, did not enjoy perfect health. Her pill regimen required its own suitcase whenever she would travel. She was high-strung, highly charged, anxious, and sometimes depressed. In other words, she was my mother. Her high blood pressure rating is still the stuff of legend at the Medical Clinic of Houston. Technically, she should have been dead, but her well-respected internist admitted that systolic and diastolic numbers were now "all relative" thanks to Evelyn Miller.

She also had an "enlarged heart," a condition I would use to my advantage whenever the assistant principal called me into his office at the Frank M. Black Middle School. When Mr. Sanders, the assistant principal whom we affectionately called "the Duck," attempted to expel me from school yet again because it had come to his attention that I was "the meanest kid on earth," he told me clearly that I could not return to school without the accompaniment of a parent or guardian. I would return the next day accompanied by my usual bologna sandwich and Twinkie, end up back in his office, and plead for mercy because, if my mother found that her prophetic utterances regarding my incorrigibility were, in fact, correct, it would certainly cause her "enlarged heart" to break, thus killing her before she had the opportunity to kill me. My persuasive speech, an adolescent testimony to my calling as a preacher, caused the Duck to repent of his initially unforgiving judgment and embrace grace and compassion. He allowed me to return to Mrs. Simpson's English class; it was a victory that seemed strangely defeating. Nonetheless, I still preach with a keen awareness of my incorrigibility—a trait that has served me well among sinners.

Not long after the psychedelic house shoes incident, my mother's condition empowered me to apply such bold initiative to prayer. Back during the 1970s, when adolescents were encouraged to explore alternative realities related to everything, including religion, my mother came down with a serious kidney infection that required hospitalization. My new friend (even though he was a Baptist and thus probably going straight to hell for his liberal tendencies) and I attempted to find some common ground between our raging hormones and spiritual convictions. Our conversations in seventh grade began as religious debates over the requirement of full-immersion adult baptism as a necessity for salvation. I argued the affirmative based on hard-core evidence as revealed in the New Testament, evidence I found to be irrefutable. My friend, Bobby, argued based on one's "personal relationship with Jesus Christ" (damn relativist!) and also the hypothetical possibility that a person could be saved while dwelling in a drought-stricken desert. He had me there.

So Bobby and I, having resolved many of our religious differences, decided to pray for my mother's healing. Bobby was a guy who took his religion so seriously that his mother never called him "the meanest kid on earth." He believed strongly in a powerful, active God who offers evidence of his presence in our daily lives, often dependent on our fervent and faithful prayers.

He began our prayer session by informing me, "I am not going to pray for your mother unless you really believe that she is going to be completely, miraculously healed."

"Sure, I believe," I said, hoping we could get through this and return to our conversation about eighth-grade girls.

"If you truly believe," Bobby continued, "then you will call your mother and tell her that she has been healed and is coming home today."

Well, that sounded about as in-your-face as a psychedelic house shoe. I tried to think of an out, but my adolescent brain was not nearly as evasive as it sometimes is now. So I told him I would.

We prayed. Fervently. Expectantly. We prayed with a powerful degree of adolescent faith, which is probably the best kind since it doesn't know any better than to believe wholeheartedly. After the "Amen," Bobby handed me the telephone. "Call your mother. Now."

I called my mother at the hospital. I told her that Bobby and I had been praying for her and that God had healed her completely of her kidney infection because that's what we had prayed for and we believed and claimed that victory in Jesus's name and, on top of that, she would be coming home from the hospital today.

There was a long pause on her end. Then she said, in a somewhat unsettled voice, that we boys "sure were sweet" and that she knew that God would "eventually make me better," but that the doctor had been in her room late last night to tell her to get comfortable because this looked like a tough infection, and she was really sick and should plan to be there awhile.

"No, Mom," I told her, with Bobby holding his New Testament against my ribs like a powerful weapon, "you have been healed and you are coming home today."

Later that afternoon, my mother called my father to report that the doctor had just left her hospital room after telling her, "Evelyn, I don't understand this at all, but the tests show no trace of the infection. You can go home today." We picked her up an hour later.

That day I learned that, despite our meannesses, inadequacies, and misunderstandings, in the words of the Apostle Paul, "The prayer of a clueless teenager availeth much." And that to engage in prayer is to play with fire. I still don't quite get it and don't understand how it works. All I know is, in the words of Bobby, "It takes big cojones to pray." I think I get that part.

While the adolescent prayer incident gave my mother and me a bit of pause, it did not change our basic personalities or interactions. From that day forward, she simply paired her berating of my hairstyle, attitude, vocational pursuits, and wardrobe choices with a spoken appreciation for "Billy's hotline to heaven," my ability to occasionally place myself in the oncoming path of a miracle or two, and my knowledge of what it's like to "touch the hem of Jesus's garment." Who needed such pressure? I think I'd rather have been known as "the meanest kid on earth." Those were much smaller shoes to fill.

While her kidneys improved, her personality disorders remained the same—quirky, irritating, laughable, and lovable. Although she had linguistic challenges throughout her life, she led the charge in thundering pronouncements. She could turn a curious phrase, for sure, but could not "pronunciate" (her word) worth a darn.

Just before her first trip to Mexico, she asked me to teach her a few basic phrases in Spanish. What follows is a literal transcript of lesson one, our *only* lesson:

ME: Mother, repeat after me: Buenos días.

MOTHER: Beenus Speedo.

ME: Buenas tardes.

MOTHER: Ganus Holiday.

ME: Cómo estás?

MOTHER: Communist stockholder.

ME: Hola.

MOTHER: Taco.

ME: Mucho gusto en conocerle.

MOTHER: Much gaucamala and an enchilada.

ME: Una más cerveza, por favor.

MOTHER: Supercalifragilisticexpialidocious.

She spoke a lot of English with a heavy Spanish accent on that trip.

She could not master certain phrases, but she could effectively communicate her opinion, particularly related to interior design, contextual morality, and proper ethical behaviors. For example, there was the time my very sweet and mild-mannered sister-in-law, Maelene, took up crocheting. She had painstakingly labored over a wall hanging that she then had the audacity to hang on her own wall! The wall hanging made its debut in her living room during a baby shower my sister-in-law was hosting for a group of women from her ladies' Bible class. My mother took one look at the artistic creation, pointed at it like it had committed the unpardonable sin, and asked the gathered group of prim and proper young women, "How do y'all like that rag up there on the wall?!" Subtle art criticism is a rare gift indeed.

Once, while visiting my parents in Houston, I had taken my new bride out for ouzo and Greek food the night before at a ship channel dive called the Athens Bar and Grill. The Athens Bar and Grill was way off the beaten path, but an underground favorite, one of the more unique establishments on the Gulf Coast. It was dark, musty, and looked like a Mediterranean cave. Whenever a Greek ship was in port, the sailors filled the space, and, after a few shots of ouzo, they would undertake a redesign of the restaurant's interior, creating a few wall hangings with the leftovers from their barroom brawls. The belly dancer had an actual belly, so you knew she was the real deal. The waitstaff spoke in Greek, and patrons only spoke when spoken to, and only after a shot of ouzo. The owner said his name was Zorba, and you got the impression that was his actual Christian name.

When my mother found out I had taken my unsuspecting and innocent young bride to some place called the Athens Bar and Grill, she was incensed, and not in the Orthodox way. We sat down to dinner the next night, and my mother turned on the television set, located about two feet from the back of my head, tuned in to an obnoxious game show, and turned the volume up so loud it made me want to buy a vowel, such as AAAAAAAA! Not being shy, just like my mother, I stated that I would prefer to enjoy my dinner in peace and quiet, or at least have the opportunity to engage in meaningful and coherent dialogue with my family without game-show groans overpowering every thought.

My mother's response was weighted, deliberate, and certain. It was as if her inner ancient Greek philosopher had emerged from the cave of enlightenment and was about to share the most profound observation the world had ever heard.

"Well," she began, "some people watch game shows . . . and some people go to bars!" She lowered her pitch on "bars" as if to indicate that all bargoers should immediately descend into the bowels of hell, without passing Go, or collecting dinner, or a fabulous prize.

To this day, I have never heard anyone articulate the basic difference among human beings any clearer. Evelyn was absolutely right. There are two kinds of people in this world, two kinds of spiritual paths, two ultimate callings that manifest their particulars in how we choose to spend our time. There are those who watch game shows, and there are those who go to bars. Choose this day (*pitch lowered for effect*) whom you will serve.

Toward the end of her life, the woman who always had plenty to say about everything suddenly had little to say about anything. When it came to life, she had much to offer. When it came to death, I suppose she was as stumped as the rest of us.

And yet, she communicated quite effectively, though with few words. Just a few weeks before my mother died, I drove from Austin to Houston to pay a visit. The hospice had not yet delivered the bed that would take center stage in our living room for her final days. When I arrived, my father walked back to their bedroom and I heard him tell my mother, "Somebody's here to see you." I had stopped at the Fiesta Mart on Interstate 10 to buy her some flowers. When it came to end-of-life issues, I was pretty clueless, but I knew, as sure as I was that she would appreciate a certain pair of house shoes, that I could not go wrong with flowers.

That night, she was unable to move under her own power, so my father picked her up from the bed, like a doll. He stood behind her, and, with arms cradled around her to support her, he practically carried her to the living room, where I was standing and waiting for her. They moved so slowly, as time tends to do toward the end. It seems to stand still, in slow motion and yet gone before we know it. My mother tried valiantly to place one foot in front of the other, ultimately depending on my father for all forward movement. She was heavily sedated and had the look of death upon her face—her eyes drawn in, dark and devoid of expression, her mouth partially open, her cheeks sunken, her wispy thin arms rigidly at her side until my father said to her, "Look who's here."

Slowly, painstakingly, with great effort, she looked up and saw me. In a moment of transformation, her entire face came to life, her eyes filled with illumination and recognition, her mouth broadened to the loveliest smile, and, with all the strength she could find in her frail, tired body, she tried desperately to reach out her arms to embrace me. Her arms would go only as high as a cross might allow, parallel to the floor, held out directly to her side.

In that rare moment of life in the midst of death, as I walked toward this rigid and radiant figure, I saw such beauty. Such love. I even saw Jesus. There before me was Crucified Love and Risen Hope in the one who had given me life. As we embraced, I felt a connection that said, without words, "You are the most wonderful child on earth." That was the last time she was able to stand. But from that moment, in that moment, on that moment—I still stand.

She was feisty to the end. Until the spirit leaves the body, the body is full of spirit. I recall the conversation my father and I had with her after the doctor had pronounced her death inevitable and imminent. My dad asked her about her desires for a funeral service, carefully phrasing it to include his own service, "whenever that time may come." She, who had read so many Bible stories to me when I was a small boy, could not think, in that moment, of an appropriate passage of scripture. She loved the hymn "Beyond the Sunset," she said. When my father mentioned the possibility of forgoing flowers and instead honoring the deceased with a charitable donation, for a fleeting moment Evelyn Miller got back into the ring. Coming back to life and reclaiming her old self, she bellowed, "Whoever heard of a funeral without flowers! Of course I want some damn flowers at my damn funeral! That's the dumbest thing I ever heard of! Well, I never in my life!"

There were flowers at her funeral. At the visitation at the Pat H. Foley Funeral Home, where she had lovingly offered consolation, "fixed" the hair of the deceased (some things never change), and arranged the flowers based on her personal preferences, her viewing room looked like a floral shop in a tropical paradise. The flowers spilled over into the hallway and reached all the way to the next viewing room. During the service, they filled the entire church. During the graveside service, there were so many sprays you could barely see the coffin or the gathered family.

I gave her yellow roses. She was blond, vibrant, different, and Texan through and through. My yellow rose of Texas, I suppose. My father chose red roses to place atop her casket. They were particularly beautiful—open and in full bloom. It was such a flower, such a rose, that Brother Harris held up to the light on that All Saints' Day in November 1996.

After we left the graveside, my childhood friend David stayed behind and kindly kept watch for a while. His stepfather had hired my mother at the funeral home years before, so he knew all about such things. After most had departed, David gathered up three of those red roses we had placed upon my mother's resting place, took them home, and carefully pressed them in a large family Bible. Months later, he showed up at the front door of my father's house with three perfectly pressed red roses—one for my father, one for my brother, and one for me. "I just thought you all would like to have these," he told us, "something special to remember her by."

I still have that rose. And every year on All Saints' Day, although sometimes on Boxing Day, because that, too, seems like an appropriate day, I take it from the safe place where I keep it, deep in the recesses of my closet, in an old shoe box that once housed something priceless in its own right. I often hold it up to the light and look at it and admire its singular beauty. And I remember that every flower is as unique as each person. So I give thanks for a timeless truth that I am just beginning to understand:

A Rose
Is a Rose.
Is a Rose.
And Evelyn.
Is Evelyn.
Is Evelyn.
And that is the last word about any of us.
Amen.

16

THE CLUELESS HEART

Love bears all things, believes all things,
hopes all things, endures all things.

—1 CORINTHIANS 13:7

Over the years I have found most Valentine's Day gifts to be unimaginative and uninspiring. Since my usual Valentine's Day activity consists of sharing cheeseburgers with my dog, followed by the inevitable farting competition, I can stand safely at a distance and be amused by what I see occurring around me in the name of true love.

One late Valentine's Day afternoon, driving home from work, I found myself on a street lined with the largest concentration of flower shops in Houston. I watched as an army of last-minute lovers darted through bumper-to-bumper traffic to purchase some sweet something for a sweetheart. These risk-taking Romeos sported various expressions on their frantic faces, ranging from desperation to confusion to relief. I saw one guy clutching what resembled a tiny bouquet of weeds, staring at them fearfully as if he already knew that he was going to pay the price for not paying the price. I saw another guy lugging the world's largest stuffed pink lion with a tacky velveteen heart pinned to its chest. I could only hope he liked sleeping with stuffed animals—on a couch.

Then I spotted the ultimate winner of the "What were you thinking?" gift-giving competition. He was a dude with a cheesy, self-satisfied grin, carrying a prepackaged themed gift basket. In this case the theme was "Redneck Role Playing." I swear I saw in his basket a bag of pork rinds, a bottle of Mad Dog 20/20, and a pair of handcuffs. I believe this basket is known informally as the Git R Done Picnic Combo. All I can say is that if she appreciates that gift, then I am dating the wrong woman.

My favorite Valentine's Day gift that year was one that I received unexpectedly from an unlikely suitor. Her name was Imogene Horton. To say that our relationship got off on the wrong foot is to minimize the impact of planting a foot on the south side of a northbound priest. My first impression of her was that she was a hypercritical, judgmental, nonhumorous, unforgiving bag of wind. If you have ever read *How to Deal with Difficult People,* Imogene's photo appears in the chapter titled "NO DEAL!"

Imogene was the church librarian, a no-nonsense retired high school English teacher who took meticulous notes and no prisoners, especially with regard to my own grammatical, homiletical, theological, liturgical, and relational activities and articulations. She believed the only appropriate words in the English language were those in circulation before 1645, and that unless one worshipped in formal, stilted Elizabethan phrases, one was wasting one's time, and risking God's displeasure.

On my first day at Trinity Church, she marched into my office in possession of a serious scowl and informed me: "I am Imogene Horton, and I am *quality control* around here." For the next few years, not a week went by that Imogene did not criticize, offend, judge, alienate, or upset somebody—often me! The negative energy surrounding her was almost palpable and not particularly pleasant.

When her husband, Patrick, died, Imogene shocked me by saying, "Ain't it sad?" I knew that some sort of internal transformation was taking place. For Imogene to utter an *un-Oxford* vernacular phrase, particularly in the context of her own grief, was not unlike a Texas politician actually admitting that he is an idiot.

Over time, Imogene began to lighten up. The tension accompanying our verbal exchanges and her physical presence began to dissipate. Our eyes met more frequently. A smile crept onto her unsuspecting lips on more than one occasion. She would still sling barbs of outrageous criticism my way, but they were less poisonous, more like Nerf-tipped arrows, clever and teasing more than punishing and derogatory.

Then came the Valentine's Day when she approached me in the church hallway with a mischievous gleam in her eyes and a flirty smirk on her face. "Father Miller," she intoned, "I have a special Valentine's Day gift for you. It is just for you. And it has your name written all over it. Now, hold out your hand." I held out my hand, and Imogene placed into my palm one of those tiny pink candy hearts that have been around for decades, the kind that read: BE MINE, HUGS AND KISSES, CUTIE PIE, VALENTINE, I LOVE YOU, or SWEETHEART. I could not believe that (1) Imogene Horton was giving me a Valentine's Day gift, and (2) the gift was a precious little candy heart with a tender sentiment inscribed there upon.

"Now read it," she instructed as she cast an almost co-quettish and certainly coy glance in my direction, and friskily pranced her way back toward the church library to continue cataloging antiquated commentaries. I opened my palm and beheld, printed in bold red letters on a tiny pink heart, a one-word sentiment: CLUELESS.

That tiny Valentine's Day offering still occupies a place of honor, not only in my treasure chest, but also in my heart. When I announced I was leaving Trinity Church to move to Kauai, if I hadn't known better I would have sworn that Imo-gene's eyes got a bit misty with emotion. Shortly before my de-parture, Imogene presented me with three additional gifts. One was a small stuffed lion. The very fact that Imogene Horton was giving away a stuffed animal was proof of the exis-tence of a loving, and life-transforming, God. Imogene was a fan of C. S. Lewis and the Narnia series, as was I, so she at-tached this note: "May Aslan go with you." And Aslan still goes with me, wherever I go. He sits on my desk in my office at St. Michael's. Whenever I see him, I feel more lionhearted, and more hopeful that people can change. People like Imo-gene, for example.

In addition to giving me Aslan, Imogene wrote a poem. In her previous life as a cross between a fire-breathing nun and a thorn-covered thesaurus, Imogene would, no doubt, have composed a poem to convey some obscure theological, liturgi-cal, or literary criticism. Not this time. The topic of Imogene Horton's poem was *pink flamingos*! Such an irreverent and un-conventional tribute to a plastic lawn ornament would have garnered a failing grade and a sea of red-lettered derision in her own English class a few decades prior. Not now! Imogene Horton was not only in on the joke, she was empowered by the Holy Prankster herself.

This gift basket surpassed the one I had seen held aloft by the country Casanova back at that crowded flower shop. Imogene had enclosed a personal note of gratitude and goodbye. This note began with a sentence that was so ludicrous and off target that I was not sure whether to laugh derisively, scoff haughtily, accuse her threateningly, or point a lethal weapon toward the church library. The very nerve of this woman! After all I had put up with in relation to her antics. Despite everything, I had forgiven, loved, and stayed the course with her through all those critical judgments and self-esteem-deflating glances of displeasure.

Her note began, "I am so glad I did not give up on understanding you."

What? Come again. Have you lost your mind, woman? You are so glad that *you* did not give up on understanding *me*? You lunatic of language and tormentor of truth, have you not reversed your subject and object? You have our relationship completely backward! Your words are inaccurate, inverted, illogical, and offensive. Your statement is as faulty and fallacious as that damn candy heart sentiment you gave me back on Valentine's Day! Do you not recognize that I am the one who never gave up on understanding *you*? That I am the one that kept on loving *you*? That I am the one who looked way past your faults and into that tiny remnant of an actual beating heart! Obviously, somebody here is entirely *clueless*! And it ain't me!

"I will miss you terribly," she concluded. "Love, Imogene."

I would miss her terribly, too. And I love her, still: for who she is, who she was, who she is becoming, and who she shall be. And, for speaking the truth in love. And for never giving up on understanding me.

I heard recently that Imogene was undergoing chemotherapy for lung cancer, and that she had lost all her hair. On her first Sunday back in church she wore a hat. On her second Sunday back in church, the entire congregation, men and women, wore hats, just to support her. I heard that a few of them were topped with pink flamingos. When it comes to true love, those are some people who obviously have a clue. Like Imogene. And on rare occasions—like me.

Love, more than anything else, stays the course. It does not give up. While it may not result in a complete derailment, it might involve a clueless collision or two along the way. Over the years, I have learned the most about love from people who have been most difficult to love. And likewise, I am sure. Imogene Horton was one. Lynette Logan was another.

As soon as I arrived at St. James in Austin to become vicar of a historically African-American parish, a number of parishioners warned me about the diminutive, outspoken, elderly white woman who had joined their church during the civil rights movement. "She's a tiny little thing," they forewarned, "but she carries a big cane!"

Lynette Logan had never been married. She had lived alone for many years. She was in poor health, in and out of the hospital. "It's that damn diverticulitis again!" she would announce as I stopped by for a visit. She came to church as often as she could, but most weeks I would deliver Communion to her at her home.

While I was not the object of her wrath as frequently as some previous priests had been, she nonetheless lit into me on

more than one occasion, unleashing a torrent of unpleasant-
ness. She once threatened to sabotage an entire capital funds
campaign because her one wish had not been granted. The
capital campaign was intended to repair a church building in
such a state of disrepair that whenever it rained, I needed an
umbrella to stand behind the altar. While we were making the
necessary repairs, Lynette reasoned, why not add a covered
parking area right by the front entrance for her entering and
exiting pleasure, just like the large downtown congregation offered. Never mind that the large downtown congregation was
ten times our size with twenty times our resources. Never
mind that the architect had said that not only would such a
scheme be a visual, design, and construction disaster, but it
would also cost as much as the entire renovation and expan-
sion project. Why confuse the issue with such facts, Lynette
demanded to know. She nearly poked my collar off with her
cane the Sunday that I informed her that her covered parking
plan was not going to happen. She eventually got over it, although I still have not quite gotten over her.

Over time Lynette and I became pretty tight. We even bordered on enjoying one another's company. Her crusty exterior
started crumbling, revealing a softer inner side, a kinder and
gentler way of expressing her religious fervor. When I looked
into her eyes, I began to recognize that there was a lot about
her that I did not know and much of her story that I had not
heard. I was reminded that too often we are far too quick to
cast judgment and assume we know the whole truth, long
before the whole truth has had time to reveal itself. First impressions are highly overrated, as are the first hundred, really.

One day, after Communion in Lynette's home, she told
me to remain seated on the couch as there was something she

wanted to read to me. "I'll be back shortly," she pronounced as she hobbled off to fetch some show-and-tell piece that had special meaning in her life. When she returned, winded from rummaging through a pile of papers and making the long round-trip trek to her bedroom, she reminded me that she had never had her own children. She shared that, long ago, she had befriended a young boy who had Down syndrome, and that they enjoyed a special relationship for many years. She recalled fondly their days playing in the local park. She had written a poem about it, dated January 2, 1972. She held the poem in her hand, so tenderly, I recall, so unlike the way she had held her cane that Sunday when she nearly knocked me out. In her most maternal voice, though it was much more childlike than parental, she read to me aloud:

> *There was a child once—*
> *greatly loved—*
> *who would come running*
> *with arms flung wide*
> *Star-eyed and laughing,*
> *To where I stood waiting*
> *And fling himself*
> *Into my open arms*
> *With such a collision of love!*
> *So would I go when calls my Lord,*
> *Laughing, with joy,*
> *To run into his arms!*

A great collision. A clueless heart.

I have often returned to such truthful images of true love. They give me hope and strength for the journey, the journey that often takes a while to get on track, much less cover any real territory. Like a friend said in his rehearsal dinner toast to his bride-to-be, "I just want you to know that you make my stomach churn!"

Most everyone in attendance agreed the groom *meant* that she gives him sweet little butterflies fluttering around with their precious tiny wings inside his tummy. He just got his metaphors a bit mixed up and his manner of speech confused. I beg to differ.

Who made butterflies the official mascot for love? I vote for butter as a much more likely expression of true love. Butter that was formed, over time, from a questionable substance that was coaxed out of a cow in a most intimate, if not awkward, procedure. It is then churned slowly until it becomes something tasty and beautiful and makes my ass look big, but that's okay because you love me so much that I make your stomach churn.

We are far too quick to think we get it. Then, when we find that we *don't,* we are far too quick to assume we never had it and never will get it. That's not how love works. Love works and waits. Love takes time to hear the rest of the story and even to rewrite and edit the tale as it unfolds. Love takes the initiative and stays the course. In love, if you want to be understood, you understand. If you want to be heard, you listen. If you want to be forgiven, you forgive. If you want to be loved, you love. First impressions, fleeting feelings, initial misunderstandings, casting premature judgment, giving up too soon—these are all roadblocks on the way to encountering the "greatest of these"—which is love. So go ahead and play the fool. In so doing, over time, you will look far less foolish.

We are all amateurs trying to find a clue. Finding our way in love is not unlike the little girl who once answered the phone when I called her father, a former professor of mine. I asked her if she could deliver the simple message to her dad that "Bill had called." There was a prolonged silence, and I repeated my question as to whether she could deliver the appropriate message. "I don't know," she admitted. "I'm just a kid."

When it comes to love, we are all novices attempting to understand and communicate something that is far beyond our capacity to comprehend. Of one thing we can be sure. There are no secrets, but there are clues. Clues like patience. Forgiveness. A sense of humor. Heavy compliments. Rare criticism. Taking the initiative. An occasional and creative gift basket. Handcuffs.

Such love calls for a long-term commitment. Space for evolution and change. The willingness to hear and write the rest of the story. Risk. Sacrifice. Compromise. Lots of butter. And perhaps an occasional butterfly. To love is to press on, despite the hurtful collisions, the churning stomachs, and the clueless hearts.

These days, I am less of a player, but I am still in the game. I have not given up on true love, loving truly, and telling the truth in love. I owe my perseverance to a few rare souls whom I initially misjudged and eventually learned to love. They are those who never gave up on me. Some of them still haven't.

I say to each of them:

I miss you terribly.

Love, Bill.

PART THREE

Song

The Lord is my strength and my song.

—EXODUS 15:2

17

GIN AND JUICE

If they act too hip, you know they can't play shit.

—MILES DAVIS

*W*ith the exception of that irritating electronica crap, there is no musical genre beyond the realm of my appreciation. You name it—I will listen to it, and I will like it. From classic country to classic rock to classical, from gangsta rap to Gregorian chant to gospel, from Philip Glass to Barry Manilow, from Snoop Dogg to the Gourds, from the haunting sounds of Faure's Requiem to a belted-out Broadway show tune, from four-part harmonies sung with evangelical fervor by people with really big hair at a Gaither Family gathering to the stripped-down subliminal groove of grunge, from a sultry smooth *Soul Train* standard to an in-your-face party at the Headbangers Ball, I will pay money to hear it. And I will enjoy every musical moment.

However, if you were to force me to choose my favorite music genre, I would land firmly in the city of New Orleans and choose that most American indigenous and improvisational musical experience, called jazz. I have my reasons, and they are personal, sensual, theological, and spiritual. For, ultimately, it is only when we set aside the score and start improvising that we allow the Spirit to move freely in our music—and in our lives.

Good theology, like good jazz, begins with a clearly articulated vision, a major theme, and a core truth. That powerful truth must resonate at a subconscious level so that the soul can hum along from memory, as if the truth had been heard long before. This truth gives life to a singular theme that does not stand in isolation. To have meaning, a variety of players must make the theme their own, bringing their stories into the dialogue through communication or confrontation with the laid-down truth. Given an individual's unique gifts, the particular instrument with which one is blessed, and the soulful singular response of personal appropriation, there are then a host of improvisations on the theme.

While one begins with a core truth, multiple melodic, harmonic, and dissonant influences take hold. Each artist responds, incorporates, moves on, begs to differ, and eventually returns. While repetition may reinforce a religion without relatedness, improvisation is the integration of inspiration into the whole.

In the end, the ensemble comes back together, each artist having made the theme his own. The theme is not discredited. Rather, it is fuller, richer, more varied, and livelier than it was before. What was old is new. What was new is old. What was known becomes unknown so that it might now be known in a new way. The "standard" may stand the test of time, but even standards allow for and insist upon improvisation. That is, if it is *true* jazz, and if it is *truly* truth, spiritually speaking.

Personally, I just like jazz, and I like those who play it. I find them to be cool and interesting cats, for the most part. They are the kind of musicians who are always in on the joke, especially jokes like:

1. How can a jazz musician end up with a million dollars? Start with two million dollars.

2. What is the difference between a large pepperoni pizza and a jazz musician? A large pepperoni pizza can feed a family of four.

3. What do you call a jazz musician without a girlfriend? Homeless.

For many years I have worked with a variety of jazz musicians to create imaginative, entertaining, and, hopefully, inspirational jazz masses. My more musically learned collaborators will sometimes tell me that my ideas are unworkable, if not compositionally suspect.

I once proposed the Tribute to Barry White on the Feast of St. Valentine to focus on the Trinitarian significance of "You're the First, the Last, My Everything" and a mass titled "Practice What You Preach." My partner convinced me to focus on the sacred works of Duke Ellington instead. At times he would merely tweak the concept but, in so doing, completely reorient it toward a more profound truth, such as the time I proposed "The Spiritual Side of the Reverend Al Green: Sensually Speaking." He insisted on doing "The Sensual Side of the Reverend Al Green: Spiritually Speaking." Fortunately, we ended up doing John Coltrane's *A Love Supreme,* a more profound celebration of the genre.

Sensually and spiritually speaking, I am not sure that there is an art form, other than mud wrestling, that speaks so completely to the whole person—one's mind, body, heart, and soul.

If you were to ask me to name the most sensually pleasurable experience of my existence that did not involve a cheese enchilada, I would immediately be transported to an evening that begins with a descent down the stairs and into the womb-like entrance of the Village Vanguard in New York City. There, I would listen to the best jazz, by an artist you have never heard of, while sipping a series of Tanqueray and tonics.

I once dreamed of engaging in such behavior with frequency. Years ago, I was one of three finalists to become the rector of an Episcopal church in Greenwich Village. The four-story historic brownstone rectory that would have become my home was a mere eight-minute walk to the Vanguard. I had already planned my service of installation, which would include John Coltrane's monumental, transcendent work, *Ascension*. The after-party, of course, would be held at the Village Vanguard. Truthfully, such a composition would have gone over in that parish about as well as the Barry White mass. As George Foreman said, long before he sold out to the grill industry, "Boxing is like jazz; the better it is, the less people appreciate it."

The previous and longtime rector's name was (believe it or not) Father Goodness, and he looked, according to the parishioners, like he was "straight out of central casting." It did not help matters that the longtime Presbyterian minister just down the street was named Pastor Shepherd. Given such illustrious clerical history, Padre Tequila did not have a worm's chance in mescal!

Just after college, I went to work at a residential treatment center for children with mental health challenges. The pay was horrible but I enjoyed my job immensely. I played kick ball— *and got paid for it*! (I mean it was good to feel that you were making a positive difference in a child's life.) While there, I learned much about mental health, child development, and family dynamics, principles that would later serve me well as a youth minister and as a priest. Some of my fellow employees were stellar, possessing graduate degrees, profound insights on the human condition, and a capacity for healthy social intercourse with human beings of all ages. Then there were others who were themselves in need of residential treatment. While I would never cast the first Valium (in fact, I would swallow it), I would point out that some folks got issues.

One such employee was a woman we shall call, in the jazz tradition, Ms. Armstrong.

It was no secret to my fellow employees that I was a jazz aficionado. Ms. Armstrong proudly boasted to me one day that her uncle was the well-known "Wild Man of the Tenor Sax," Arnett Cobb. Cobb was a jazz legend, not only in Texas but around the world. I immediately made a solemn bow before Ms. Armstrong. I knew Cobb's story and was a great fan. Arnett Cleophus Cobb had grown up in Houston's rough-and-tumble Fifth Ward neighborhood. His grandmother taught him to play the piano, but, for some curious reason, he switched to the violin during his teenage years. At Phillis Wheatley High School, he found himself the only string instrument in an eighty-piece brass band. He decided that if he was going to go to all the work of learning to play an instrument, he would like to actually be heard. He switched to the saxophone and eventually developed such an uninhibited, boisterous "I *will* be heard" style of playing that even his fellow jazz musicians found it over the top.

Arnett Cobb had replaced another Texas tenor legend, Illinois Jacquet, in Lionel Hampton's band in 1942 and eventually went on to form his own band. He was nominated for a Grammy Award in 1979 for Best Jazz Instrumental Performance and shared a Grammy with B. B. King in 1984 for Best Traditional Blues Performance. In 1986, Arnett founded the Jazz Heritage Society of Texas.

He was certainly an accomplished player, but what impressed me the most was the *way* that Arnett Cobb played the saxophone. He had been hit by a car when he was only ten and another auto accident in the 1950s had crushed his legs. At every performance, Arnett Cobb would hobble onto the stage, prop himself up on his crutches, pick up his saxophone, and wail on that instrument like it was attached to his soul. It was a searing sound, magnified and amplified by the visual image of a man who had been forced to improvise for most of his life. What he had lost in leg movement, he made up for with a frenzy of arm, finger, lip, and mouth movement. It was an inspiration to hear, *and* to see, Arnett Cobb play the saxophone.

In 1983, the time came for me to depart the residential treatment center in Houston to attend McCormick Theological Seminary, on the South Side of Chicago. I have never been shy about asking for favors, so I asked my coworker Ms. Armstrong if she would please consider asking her jazz legend uncle to play for my going-away party. I would certainly pay him whatever he asked and it would be worth every penny to me, I told her. I had already secured a friend's historic mansion near downtown as the party's venue, and having some old-school jazz blown by the legendary "Wild Man of the Tenor Sax" would be the perfect send-off to the Windy City.

Only a day later, Ms. Armstrong informed me that not only had her uncle Arnett agreed to play my party, but that he was bringing his good friend, the only slightly less legendary big band leader Milton Larkin, to play trombone and belt out a few soulful vocals. I hugged my coworker Ms. Armstrong with the force of heavyweight champion George Foreman. I felt like I had died and gone to jazz heaven.

Securing the talent of Milton "Tippy" Larkin was as big a coup as getting Arnett Cobb. I had followed Larkin's career for years. He was born in 1910 in Navasota, Texas, the same small town that had produced blues legend Mance Lipscomb. Like many musicians of the time, he was self-taught on a variety of instruments. The Milt Larkin Orchestra, founded in 1936, was sometimes billed as "the Greatest Band of All Time," primarily by those who played in it! Although they never achieved national acclaim, the band featured some world-class performers including Cobb, Jacquet, Eddie "Cleanhead" Vinson, and "Wild Bill" Davis. The band drew big crowds to Joe Louis's Rhumboogie Club in Chicago, and Larkin eventually led the house band at Harlem's famed Apollo Theater in New York.

While Larkin was a great musician, musical mentor, and bandleader, what made me respect him all the more was a decision he made in the 1930s and '40s that cost him much wider musical fame. Although he had a large fan base, he stopped recording during the period of his greatest success to protest the ridiculously low wages being offered to black musicians by recording companies. As a result of this decision, as well as his absence from the music world while playing trombone in the army band during World War II, most people have never heard of Milt Larkin. Unearthing a recording of Larkin or his band is a rare feat.

Larkin's commitment to ethics and social justice did not end when he retired in Texas in 1977. He founded the non-profit organization Get Involved Now, or GIN, as many a jazz musician was fond of calling it. GIN offered free jazz performances for those who rarely got to hear live music, such as children's hospitals and nursing homes. The jazz musicians of Houston finally organized in 1990 and named themselves "the Milt Larkin Jazz Society" in Milt's honor. While never achieving legendary status or universal acclaim, his good works and his courageous stand for social and professional equality had already made him a legend in *my* mind. I could not believe my good fortune. What an honor and a privilege to have these two jazz giants, Arnett Cobb and Milt Larkin, play at *my* going-away party. I immediately printed up the musical-themed invitations and distributed them to everyone I knew, and even a few people I did not know but wanted to.

A couple of days before the big bash, I had received more than a hundred positive RSVPs, with many of my friends wondering how "Ol' Midas Touch Miller" managed to get Cobb and Larkin booked for the gig. I was only a bit concerned that I had not spoken directly to either man, though I had repeatedly offered my contact information to Ms. Armstrong. She assured me, repeatedly, that she had passed along all the pertinent information and they were all set to do the gig.

The party was planned for Saturday night. On Saturday morning, I got a call from, guess who, Ms. Armstrong. She stated, mustering all the sadness she could, that her uncle

Arnett had had a heart attack and was now at St. Joseph's Hospital. She was so sorry that he would not be able to play my party.

I have always believed that the first step in making appropriate ethical decisions, such as whether to inflict bodily harm on a person, is to glean all the pertinent facts, to discern as much truth as possible, before deciding upon and implementing a course of action. I called St. Joseph's Hospital and inquired as to whether Mr. Arnett Cobb had been admitted. As I had painfully suspected, Cobb had *not,* in fact, been admitted to the hospital. I took a deep breath, said a short prayer, called myself the fool that I was, and remembered that the local NPR jazz affiliate had recently done a feature on Larkin's organization, GIN. Though I really wanted to down an entire bottle, instead I called the station and asked the deejay if he had any contact information at all for the organization. He gave me Milt Larkin's home telephone number.

Milt answered the phone. I first asked him if he knew anything about playing a going-away party for a guy named Miller, if he had ever heard of Ms. Armstrong, or if he and Arnett were warming up for an evening gig at a historic mansion on the edge of downtown. He knew nothing about any of that. I told him the whole, sad tale of woe. There was a long pause on the other end. Milt Larkin finally spoke.

"Well," he said, "this is kind of unusual. More unusual is that I don't have a gig planned for tonight, so I'm free. Tell you what, young man. I will put something together for you, maybe a nice guitar trio or something like that. But I'll be there. I'll play the party. Now, I don't mean to be skeptical or anything, but would you mind, just so I know you are real, would you mind bringing a cash deposit by my home?"

Are you kidding? I would have taken him my firstborn child at that point, I was so grateful.

I drove over to Beldart Street, located in an unfamiliar part of town. I turned into the driveway, and standing there, repairing the side of his car, was Milt Larkin. He waved me onto the driveway and looked at me with a kind, reassuring expression on his face. He shook my hand firmly and spoke with a soft, welcoming, soothing voice. By this time, his wife, Catherine, had come crashing through the front door and was shouting at me like I was her foolish prodigal son and had finally found the sense to come home. Apparently Milt had already told her my tale of woe.

"Is that you, Bill? You get in this house right now. You poor thing. Milt told me what that crazy woman did. Let me get you a beer!" It was love at first pour.

For the next hour and a half I sat in their living room, and we shared our stories with each other. There was a tenderness that permeated their spirits, their home, their conversation, and their concern. I did not want to leave. They took me into Milt's memorabilia room, which, for a jazz buff, was not unlike being escorted into the Holy of Holies by the high priest himself. Milt and Catherine showed me countless photos with a "Who's Who" of the jazz and blues royalty of the world, newspaper clippings, reviews, awards, and charts. A whole lifetime of making music was on display, and more important, a whole lifetime of making a difference.

Catherine was still fit to be tied over what had happened to me. "This woman *was* a *black* woman, wasn't she?!"

I laughed and said, "Yes, ma'am. I may be a fool, but I ain't *that* big a fool!"

In the Larkins' presence, not unlike what I experience at the altar each Sunday, I had an overwhelming sense that everything was going to be okay. As I stood up to leave, I thanked them again for their hospitality, and I thanked Milt profusely for playing the party that night, knowing that one half a bill is way better than a no bill, especially when the half is someone like Milt Larkin. But Milt had one other surprise for me.

"Oh, I almost forgot to tell you. I talked to Arnett. He'll be there with me tonight."

He was there all right. Propped up on crutches. Playing with wild abandon and windy force and absolute joy. The theme was clearly articulated that night. By Arnett. By Milt. By Catherine. By me. And by everyone present. And what do you know? That theme was this: improvisation. When you improvise on improvisation itself, you know that you have come close to the presence of God.

I moved to the South Side of Chicago. For the next three years, I'd feel a lot of wind, and it was damn cold. I would hear more blues than jazz, but it was all music to my ears. Arnett Cobb passed away. My parents sent me the newspaper clipping in Chicago. Milt and Catherine and I maintained a most unpredictable friendship. During my years in Chicago, I got a Christmas card from them every year. Every year Catherine would address it to "Bill, our Son," and she would never fail to mention how proud they were of me.

Years later I returned to Texas and was ordained a priest at the Church of St. John the Divine on River Oaks Boulevard in Houston's most exclusive neighborhood. Until I worked there, it was a neighborhood I was mostly unfamiliar with, but people made me feel at home. The night of my ordination service, Milt and Catherine Larkin showed up, the only African Americans in attendance, which didn't seem to matter to them in the least. During the reception, she told everyone who was within earshot that I was their "son" and that they were so proud of me. They had one more surprise that night before they left. "We're Episcopalians, too," they told me; "have been for years." I should have known that anyone who would name his charitable organization after booze would be a Whiskey-palian.

Not long thereafter, Milt celebrated his eightieth birthday. The *Houston Post* ran an article titled "Milt Larkin at 80: Where's the Fanfare?" bemoaning the fact that there was no city-wide celebration to honor such a talented and stellar citizen. I joined a few friends and family members at the old Musicians Union building on the edge of downtown, not far from where we'd had the going-away party, to celebrate Milt's birthday. Throughout the evening, Milt stayed out of the spotlight, quietly welcoming people in his unique, soft-spoken, reassuring way.

The climax of the evening was not a proclamation from any elected official or a sleek video presentation paying tribute to his musical legacy. Rather it consisted entirely of his daughter taking the makeshift podium and thanking her father for teaching her how to love. She spoke about her work with at-risk mothers at a community center in the same part of town that had been so unfamiliar to me. At the end of the evening, she called all "family members" to come forward for a "family photo." I remained in my seat until I heard Catherine's voice: "Now get on up here, Reverend. I told you that you are our son!"

One of these days, for the final time, I am going to move to a new city. And instead of having a big going-away party, I believe that there will be a welcome party given in my honor on the other side. I believe that there will be music, and I believe that it will be jazz. There will be a trio: Milt, Arnett, and Gabriel. And Catherine will be there, too, offering me a beer and saying, "Welcome home, son."

Before that time comes, I hope that my life and my faith will continue to reflect what a friend once said about jazz: "It's a surprise that tastes good." I hope that there are more Ms. Armstrongs to make up stories that lead to life-changing encounters with extraordinary people who hear the music in ways I can only imagine. I hope that I cultivate my own talents, learn to better play the instrument with which I have been blessed, and take a stand whenever one needs to be taken, even if it means that I make less music, so someone else might make more. I hope to listen more carefully to major themes. And what I really hope to do is that most spiritual of all endeavors: improvise.

I plan to have a drink occasionally.

I plan to get involved.

Now, that will be the true tonic for my soul.

18

WWJD

What Would Jesus Drink?

And as he reclined in Levi's house, many tax collectors were also
reclining with Jesus and his disciples—for there were many who
followed him. When the scribes and Pharisees saw that he was eating
with sinners and tax collectors, they said to his disciples, "Why does he
eat and drink with tax collectors and sinners?" When Jesus heard this he
said to them, "Those who are well have no need of a physician, but those
who are sick; I have come to call not the righteous but sinners."

—MARK 2:15–17

I'm a long gone Waylon song on vinyl.
I'm a back row sinner at a tent revival.

—ERIC CHURCH, "SHE LOVES ME LIKE JESUS DOES"

*J*esus came to call, not the righteous, but sinners. It is the
best news I've heard since Pabst Blue Ribbon became the hip-
ster's choice—now I can drink cheaply and look cool at the
same time. Finally, I am qualified to do something other than
drink beer. The really good news? So are you.

The party scene in the second chapter of Mark, with Jesus surrounded by the cast of characters assembled at your local dive bar, is my favorite image of Jesus in all of scripture. The Greek word that is translated "sit" in so many more staid versions of this full-on rager actually means "recline." Here we see the essence of "Come take a load off" religion, what Jesus meant when he said, "My burden is light, my yoke is easy, my beer is cold and free." The gospel of Jesus Christ, the good news for a broken and bored world, is summarized in this scene and with these words: "Y'all come on in and get comfortable!" The mission of those who have already accepted the invitation to come in can be summarized in this simple, celebratory sentiment: "The first round is on Jesus. After that, we all buy a round!"

At the party pad of Matthew the IRS agent (also known as Levi), Jesus is chillin' with his friends and followers. Our Lord and Savior kicks back, lays back, and throws back, along with everyone else. The members of this ragtag gathering would never be found on the guest list for high tea with the high priest down at the local temple. These are also not the kind of folks who would get worked into a competitive frenzy at the mere mention of a casserole competition for a typical parish potluck.

Nope, these were the folks who were outside the rope of the nicest nightclubs, whose lives were seemingly so messed up that they were considered "beyond the pale ale" by those whose religious preferences were much more refined and exclusive. These are the people who brought saltines and squeeze cheese, a can of bean dip, and a paper platter of Vienna sausage sandwiches, with white bread crusts intact, to the party. They found the lyrics to "99 Bottles of Beer on the Wall" to be challenging, and their version of sacred music was crooned by the likes of Lynyrd Skynyrd and Billy Ray Cyrus. These were the outcasts, the ones who drank their wine out of a box, defended the legitimate sporting merits of professional wrestling, and argued that *Hee Haw* was an artistic achievement worthy of PBS syndication. They put the "un" before the "couth" and the screw cap back on the bottle—that is, when they were not drinking straight from it.

Their singular spiritual insight consisted of the only one that really mattered—they knew that they needed him. They literally hungered and thirsted for some justice and righteousness in their lives, for something more than what they had previously known. They desperately longed to hear some good news for a change, news that could change some things for good. And because they were not all consumed with proper protocol and the subtle nuances of off-limits conversation, they were the most likely candidates to share such good news with others, and even invite them to the party. This whole religion thing is really pretty simple: We are so astounded to discover that our names are on the guest list, and that we can get in because we're with him, that we tell the world and invite all those who previously had no clue that religion could be so much fun.

Jesus partied, but he partied with a purpose. A profound gospel story about Jesus comes from the second chapter of the Gospel According to John. Jesus, his disciples, and his mom had all been invited to a wedding in Cana of Galilee. Back then, the wedding banquet was the social event of the season. At this particular party, whistles were just getting whetted when the wine ran out. This matrimonial faux pas was like McGooley's Irish Pub running out of both green beer *and* Guinness stout before Happy Hour on St. Patrick's Day.

Jesus's mom steps in to save the day, telling Jesus, "They have no wine." You gotta love that. The Virgin Mary comes across in the Bible as being one of the most reticent of players, typically slow to speak, mostly silent, and rarely getting worked up over anything, even when she has plenty of reason to. But God forbid they run out of booze at a party to which she has been invited! Such a predicament calls for the power of the Most High to be unleashed on both the caterer and the bartender.

Jesus rolls his eyes and says, "Thanks a lot, Mom. I guess that whole virgin birth thing was not nearly enough for you."

I wonder if Jesus, like most of us, never quite measured up in his parents' eyes. He summoned the waitstaff to fill six gigantic stone jars, typically used for religious purification rites, to the brim with water. Once again, Jesus confused the sacred and secular, having no use for such artificial, unnatural, and unhealthy boundaries. Jesus then performed his first public miracle.

(There is an ancient apocryphal text that actually records an earlier similar miracle. Jesus, in the disciples' presence, had turned twenty cases of light beer into actual beer. Although the disciples were very impressed, they all agreed that no one would ever believe *that*, so they kept it quiet, not to mention noncanonical.)

Here we read that Jesus turned the water into wine. Nothing says "I care" and "I represent God" quite like 180 gallons of the world's finest Bordeaux. After tasting the good stuff that Jesus had somehow crushed, separated, fermented, and aged in the same amount of time it took Mary to say, "Thank you, Jesus!"

the chief steward told the bridegroom, "Dude, at most parties they serve the good stuff first. Then when everyone is sloshed they start serving the Boone's Farm. But here's to you, my man, for you have saved the best for last!" The gospel of John concludes the story by telling the reader, quite clearly, that this was the first of his signs, and that it revealed his glory, and that his disciples, who had witnessed the whole thing, not to mention having partaken of quite a bit of it, believed in him.

So I believe. I believe that several important theological truths are revealed by both the party at Levi's house and the miracle at Cana, including the idea that it is far better to believe in something or somebody than to believe in nothing or nobody. The one who has little to celebrate, celebrates little, while the one who has much to celebrate, celebrates much. There is a bit of prodigal son in each of us.

When Jesus gets involved, the fruits of his labor are not only fermented but abundant and of the highest quality. When Jesus is invited, the party will go on for much longer than we had planned and will include people we had assumed would not be invited.

—

When I was a child growing up in a more restrictive, fundamentalist religious tradition, I became acquainted with a well-known preacher and teetotaler named James Burton Coffman. Brother Coffman believed fervently that booze was strictly off-limits to the believer. He rose to fame having written and published a set of commentaries on every single book in the Bible, all while having no knowledge whatsoever of Hebrew or Greek, the languages in which the Holy Scriptures were originally written. This extraordinary feat would be much like my writing an encyclopedic and personal account of my giving birth to a giraffe. Other than the fact that I am a male and not a giraffe, I am certainly well equipped to enlighten the entire hoofed animal kingdom.

Brother Coffman, who held sway in certain society circles in the South (having founded a fundamentalist church in the heart of Manhattan, a feat not unlike founding a Pizza Hut in the heart of Rome), was challenged by his host at a party. The Baron Enrico di Portanova (whose claim to fame was enclosing and air-conditioning his entire backyard in Houston, and who once said that the most important things in life were "sun, sex, and spaghetti") pointed out to Brother Coffman that his own Lord had certainly imbibed throughout his life. Thus, how could Brother Coffman, for religious reasons, abstain? The preacher responded with full pulpit-pounding fervor: "Well, Jesus is more liberal than I am!"

Brother Coffman, go straight to the head of the seminary class. You are hereby awarded the Glenn Beck Award for Completely Unintentional Religious Insight. Despite your linguistic limitations, you have somehow managed to condense the entire Bible into a single slogan. You have uttered the most profound revelation ever spoken about our Lord.

Jesus is more liberal than I am.

Jesus is more liberal than I will ever be. Jesus is more generous, giving, broad, tolerant, unorthodox, grateful, grace-filled, and accepting than I could possibly become. Jesus, the original bleeding heart, has so much love for the likes of you and me that he invites and includes, affirms and upholds each one of us as his child, even entrusting to us his message, hoping we will share it with the same lack of discrimination that originally got *us* a place at the table. Far too often, the assumed followers of Jesus not only refuse to party, but do all in their power to keep others off the guest list. The good news is that such bad news does not come from God, despite any human claims to the contrary.

—

Religious truth is rarely found in the context of negativity. Telling people what they cannot do or cannot become is to misrepresent God's call. As a bumper sticker once said, "God loves everyone, but prefers fruits of the spirit to religious nuts." And as the Austin Lounge Lizards sang, only a religious nut would assume a corner on Christ, a sentiment captured in their hit song "Jesus Loves Me but He Can't Stand You!" Such assumptions are so far from the truth of the gospel and are as ludicrous as they sound. A religion of "NO" is no religion at all. There are no bouncers at the banquet of Christ, and anyone who assumes such a position does not work for God and does not speak for Jesus.

There have been times in my life when I have needed to be reminded of such an inclusive God-ordained reality. Several years ago, I was invited to ride in the Gay Pride Parade in Houston. Houston, by the way, was the first major American city to elect an openly gay mayor. This is Texas for you. Just when you think you have it all figured out and stereotyped into a corner, these Texans go and do something no one would ever expect. I accepted the invitation to the parade because I felt that it was important for the people of God to show up and stand up for those who have been intentionally and historically left off the guest list for far too long.

I was so excited by the opportunity that I even wore my clerical collar. The last time I enjoyed such a festive view from atop a parade vehicle was when I donned my cowboy duds at age seven to ride in the Houston Livestock Show and Rodeo parade. There were as many chaps in this procession, but some of these pokes had forgotten their jeans! I waved to tens of thousands of people who lined the parade route, including many of my parishioners, gay and straight, who cheered wildly when I passed. I was feeling very good about the world, the church, myself, and my community, when the mood took a sudden turn for the worse.

I noticed that two police officers, riding bicycles, had moved in right next to me, attempting to create a barrier between me and the crowd. They did not look like they were in a very festive frame of mind, possessing the serious demeanor of no-nonsense Secret Service agents, out to protect and defend. Soon enough, I heard, and I saw, the source of their overprotective instincts.

On our left was a small, angry mob that had shown up for the sole purpose, but not the soul purpose, of shouting down everyone else with words of condemnation. They saw themselves as the official spokespersons for God. If that is true, this is a God I want nothing to do with. I have never encountered such an evil, un-Christlike spirit in any group of human beings in my life. Some of them were so scary that they were foaming at the mouth, filled with rage, hatred, and vitriol. They hurled epithets that seemed more in the spirit of the crowd that taunted Jesus than of those who followed the crucified Savior of the world. They carried banners that offered such endearing sentiments as "God Hates Fags," "AIDS: God's Justice for Queers," and "Homosexuals Will Burn In Hell."

You can imagine how excited and delighted they were to see me riding along in my clerical collar, representing a very different kind of God. I don't remember precisely what they said to me, but the spirit with which they shouted seemed to originate from the bowels of hell. Not one to back down from or ignore a confrontation with injustice, yet not wanting to fuel their hellacious, hate-driven fire, I found myself simply staring them down, pointing at them like a gospel preacher and shouting back, "May God have mercy on you all!"

I have no idea where those words came from, because my intent was to say something far less charitable and loving. My words did not shut them up, but I did see one of them look away, and several of them seemed to be taken by surprise.

We finally passed them by, the dark clouds of intolerance giving way once again to the sunnier dispositions of those rooting for the home team, even if they didn't play for them. The police officer closest to me said, "Sorry about that, Father. What *some* people do in the name of God."

Indeed, it could only be outdone by what God will do for *some* people. Such as sacrifice his very life for those who could not care less about his. Such as having a bleeding heart for those who would just as soon draw his blood by nailing him to a cross. Such as look at a mob of vitriolic vipers right in the eyes and love them anyway, hoping against hope that they might see some light, and cast off some darkness. Such as pray for them, saying, "Father, forgive them, for they know not what they do." That is the kind of God who speaks for me, for you, and for everyone, even those without voices, those who have been condemned or crucified for being true to the calling and identity entrusted to them.

There is nothing virtuous about castigating the opposition. There is nothing religious about railing *against* anything or anyone. Those who follow Jesus have never been defined by what or who they oppose. Followers of Jesus are always defined by what they are *for* or *who* they support.

—

One of my more memorable experiences as a youth minister was on a return trip from a Junior High Confirmation Camp. I was driving one van out of three, all filled with smart kids who not only had decided to make a mature commitment to Christ, but also understood that to be upright did not mean they had to be uptight. In case there was any confusion about that necessary distinction, Gates Elliott was prepared to shatter all of our spiritual misconceptions.

I noticed that one of the other vans had slowed down as it had pulled up alongside us. Gates decided to make a statement about his willing vulnerability in Christian community, dedicated to exposing and offering every part of himself to his Lord and Savior Jesus Christ. He expressed such commitment by revealing to all of us, not necessarily the deepest part of him, but certainly the widest. As the van kept pace with us, Gates engaged in that adolescent rite of passage known as mooning, whereby one directs one's naked posterior in the general direction of those you are hoping to impress or disgust, and hopefully, to the teenage mind, both.

Gates was a large young man. He was the biggest lineman on his football team. When it came to his mooning prowess, size mattered. And what we beheld on that sunny afternoon in a church van was the blinding light of unconditional affection, the revelatory power of the whitest, widest, most expansive full moon any of us had ever seen. Such a sight would have been sufficient to indelibly imprint itself, not only on the van window, but within our subconscious minds for the rest of eternity.

But it didn't end there. What followed shook the very foundations of our faith, not to mention my ability to steer, keep a straight face, and not get run over. Gates's expansive statement of unguarded endearment came face-to-face, or rather cheek-to-cheek, with the clear glass surface of the van window. The force of his celestial-sized posterior shattered the pane into a thousand shards of surrender. Gates's behind moved onward and upward, toward the heavenly realm, before realizing that the wind it felt was not the movement of the Holy Spirit but the reality of doing sixty miles per hour with your butt sticking out. We saw the moon quickly retreat back into its proper planetary alignment, safe within the confines of the van and its now wide-open exterior space. While blowing out a van window, Gates Elliott had blown our minds, not to mention our travel budget.

We pulled off the road and gathered in a parking lot to assess the damage, both to our vehicle and our collective psyche. We prayed for Gates, although we did not lay hands upon him. I preached an impromptu homily on the power of God to break through whatever separates us from our truest selves, even when we reveal that we are bigger asses than any one of us would like to admit. We all agreed that we had witnessed the moon of our lifetimes, thus none of us would ever moon again. All future moons would pale, although not literally, in comparison.

Over the years, I completely lost track of Gates, though I

had thought about him often, especially when we would sing hymn number 436, "Lift Up Your Heads, Ye Mighty Gates!" Apparently he had drifted away from the daring days of his adolescent "in your face" faith, gone to work for an investment company, and was seriously dating a serious Christian—as in way too serious—about him, about her faith, about everything. She was not able to make that distinction between the upright and the uptight. Apparently she was one of those narrow-minded and judgmental Christians who think that it is harder for those who disagree with them to get into heaven than it is for a giant posterior to pass through a van window.

Many years later, Gates tracked me down and came in to talk to me about his life. As we visited and caught up, Gates said something even more revealing and profound than what he had offered during the days of his youth. He told me that, after dating this woman and experiencing her rather restrictive religious tradition, he was pretty sure what he wasn't. But that was insufficient. It was not enough for him to know what he wasn't, he said. He needed to know what he was! He understood that knowing what he did not believe would only get him so far. He wanted to break on through to the other side of real truth, and real life, to know what he *did* believe. Gates Elliott wanted to define himself in terms of what he was *for,* not what he was against.

I knew at that moment that Gates Elliott was not far from the Kingdom of God, was very close to the very heart of Jesus Christ, and that God would use him to break through many barriers and shatter a lot of limitations in this life, not only for himself, but for many others.

As Gates began to seek, he began to find. He broke up with the girl who would have never approved of mooning as an expression of faith. He began to read and study and con-template. He started coming to church and getting involved. He surrounded himself with people who weren't afraid to think outside the van window. He figured out, as the book of Romans reveals, "If God is for us, who can be against us?" And if God is for us, then we are for everyone. Gates fully embraced that theology.

Gates eventually quit his job with the investment company, went to seminary, and was ordained a priest. He married a fellow priest, a lovely girl whose love is expansive and inclusive. They now minister in Mississippi, where I will bet Gates continues to shatter illusions and help people break on through to that place they were previously afraid to be. I marvel at how far Gates has come, through faith. And I am often reminded, when I think of him, of the words of George Clinton, of Parliament Funkadelic fame: "Free your mind, and your ass will follow!" Free your ass, and perhaps your soul will follow, too.

—

Years ago I attended a church conference at St. Bart's in New York City. This church was known for practicing a radical kind of welcome and hospitality for all people, as evidenced by the Krispy Kreme doughnuts they served every Sunday. Before I departed on my trip, my Altar Guild directress, who knew me like she knew the back of her fair linen altar cloth, came into my office, shut the door, and asked me in hushed tones, "Now, Bill, are you going to get into any trouble while you are in New York City?" I reassured her, saying, "Mildred, I am not going to have time to get into any trouble—my days will be completely filled with worship services, plenary sessions, and workshops."

Mildred smiled, knowingly and skeptically, saying, "Mmm. Hmm. And what about your nights?"

Not wanting to disappoint my Altar Guild directress, I hooked up with my old friend Jason Donovan while in New York City. I had known Jason since my youth ministry days. While Gates was shattering windows, Jason was in my office working on his "God and Country" Boy Scout badge. Too bad there was no badge for partying, because Jason would have earned it in record time. At that time, my office was a shared space in the church, which also functioned as the senior pastor's vesting sacristy. Every Sunday morning, Father Hall would put on his vestments for the worship service, right there in my office.

There is an old joke about how one can tell what kind of church you are in simply by observing what adorns the wall of the sacristy—that is, that place where the ministers gather before the service to prepare for worship. If it is a Roman Catholic church, you can be pretty certain that on the wall you will find a picture of the Blessed Virgin Mary. If you are in a Baptist or Methodist church, on the sacristy wall you will most likely find a picture of our Lord Jesus. If you are in an Episcopal church, on the sacristy wall you will most assuredly find a full-length mirror. Draw your own conclusions. Jason certainly did, as we spent more time comparing our biceps in the mirror than we did figuring out the relationship between patriotism and faith. He was proud to be an American, but even prouder of his physique. However, my biceps continue to dwarf his, even to this day.

Jason's self-confidence had only increased by the time he got to New York City, and he had arranged for us to meet up with three of his female friends at a quaint little Italian restaurant in the West Village. We followed this feast, where we had miraculously turned full bottles of Chianti into completely empty ones, with a trek toward the increasingly chic Meatpacking District and the infamous bar "Hogs & Heifers." If you saw the movie *Coyote Ugly*, a masterpiece in cinematic achievement based on this bar, you will be familiar with the concept. You park your "hog" outside so you can be entertained by the "heifers" inside. The female bartenders, who are much better looking than the cows I have known, dance on the bar in cutoff shorts and cowboy boots, insult most of the male patrons, occasionally pour shots down the throats of unsuspecting stiffs who need to be loosened up, and encourage other female customers to remove certain items of clothing and toss them onto the ceiling. Apparently, this is someone's idea of a good time.

In fact, it must be a lot of people's idea of a good time, because when we got to Hogs & Heifers around 11:30 P.M. the line stretched down and around the block, with no end in sight. I rarely play the priest card, but because there are few enough perks in my profession (other than free wine every Sunday), I boldly approached the doorman, who was bigger than a bull. In fact, I do not recall ever encountering a more intimidating human being in my life. He was a heavily tattooed, full-bearded, black-leather-clad giant of a man. He looked like he could bench-press a Harley and a heifer, if not an entire herd. He was the Bouncer among all Bouncers, and his demeanor resembled that of a grizzly bear who had been teased one too many times.

"I am Father William Miller, a priest from Texas," I told him. "I am here with several potential converts, and we would like to come in to your bar and eat and drink with sinners, as is the custom of our Lord."

His eyes grew large, and I prepared myself to be pounded into the pavement. Instead he laughed, and said, "Okay, Father, I'm gonna have to see some ID."

I showed him my business card and my driver's license. He looked at the card, the driver's license, and me, and said, "Well, I'll be an [expletive expletive expletive]. No [expletive expletive expletive] has ever tried that one before. [Expletive expletive expletive]. Come on in and have a good time. And put in a good word for me with the Big Guy, would ya? [Expletive expletive expletive]."

And so, Lord, on this day I humbly beseech Thee to bless Thy servant Bubba the Bouncer. Open the door of Thy Paradise unto him, that he may enter in and safely graze upon the goodness of Thy welcoming Love, and drink unceasingly from the tap of thy ever-flowing and most bountiful Blessing. And may there be Harleys and Heifers on Earth, as there are in Heaven. Amen.

Once we got inside, a Jewish girl who was in our group turned to me and said, "I'm not really sure what religion you are, but if your God has the power to get us into this place, I think I am converting."

He's that kind of God with that kind of power. Hangs out in those kinds of places. With all kinds of people. You'll know the place by the sign: SINNERS WELCOME.

So come on in and have a good time.

Don't forget to invite others to the party.

I can't drink 180 gallons all by myself.

19

A DIFFERENT KEY

I celebrate myself . . .
I am satisfied . . . I see, dance, laugh, sing . . .
Divine am I inside and out, and I make holy whatever
I touch or am touched from;
The scent of these arm-pits is aroma finer than prayer.
This head is more than churches or bibles or creeds.

—WALT WHITMAN, "SONG OF MYSELF"

I'm beautiful in my way
'Cause God makes no mistakes

—LADY GAGA, "BORN THIS WAY"

*W*hen I find myself in need of forays into strange new worlds, I frequently head north and east, all the way to Gardiner, Maine, to visit my good friend Father Jacob "Jack" Fles. Even though Jack likes to hold hands and pray out loud, unscripted and emotional behavior that makes me uncomfortable, I love him anyway.

Our lives could not be more different. Jack, for example, has a liver condition that prevents him from drinking. I have a heart condition that requires me to drink habitually. Jack is a devoted husband to his beautiful wife, Becky, and a caring father to his three wonderful children, Keegan, Broghann, and Jacob Jr. I have a dog named after an outlaw country singer who smokes pot and wears pigtails. I prefer solitude and privacy and appreciate doors that not only latch but lock. Jack prefers the company of everyone. His compound is inclusive and expansive, his whole life one big, open, unhinged gate. I like things to be organized, thought through, time tested, and well planned. Jack backtracks a dozen times a day, flies by the seat of his pants (if he has remembered to wear them), changes directions constantly without consulting MapQuest, and prefers chaos to stability. I am a neat freak almost to the point of obsession. In my guest room at Jack's house, there is sawdust on the floor from a previous century's renovation, and what lurks below in the kitty litter box could reveal archaeological insight into ancient Egyptian civilizations.

At 5:45 A.M. on one visit, Jack barged into my room, turned on all the lights, tossed a can of Coke and a bag of pretzels on my bed ("Breakfast," he said), then placed little eighteen-month-old Jacob on my chest. "You guys get acquainted," he said. "I'm gonna go to the office for a bit." He quickly proceeded to leave the scene of an impending crime.

For the next two anguishing hours, little Jacob implanted tiny pretzel spears into every exposed portion of my anatomy. Meanwhile, Broghann, his older sister, sat at my bedside and grilled me on Harry Potter and *SpongeBob SquarePants* trivia, absolutely astounded by my ignorance of popular tween culture. She then began singing, with the gusto of a recent religious convert who has seen the error of someone else's ways, "BILL IS A WEIRDO! BILL IS A

WEIRDO! BILL IS A WEIRDO!" I was so moved that I joined in the chorus.

While Broghann's insightful intonement may have captured a core truth about myself, I reminded her, as I frequently remind my adult detractors, "That's *Father* Weirdo to you!"

God does not necessarily call us to be normal. God distinctly calls us to be different. God made me just as unique as God made you. There is no one on earth created quite like either one of us, with precisely the same purpose, passion, or perspective. God's call will lead each of us on divergent paths, marching to different beats, taking us to different places. We will sing our respective songs respectfully, but in a different key.

Sometimes we will have to endure cases of mistaken identity by those who may not understand, recognize, or approve of the direction God is sending us in. Even my godson James has been guilty of such interpersonal errors. Years ago, James and his family moved from Austin, Texas, to Jackson Hole, Wyoming. I had not seen him since he was an infant, and he was about six years old when I stopped by for a visit. As I drove up I saw, standing in the doorway, a radiantly mischievous towheaded boy in possession of the world's most engaging smile. Obviously a godson after my own heart, he was holding a welcome gift, an ice-cold bottle of Grand Teton Pale Ale.

As we gave each other a big hug, I asked him, "Do you know who I am?"

"Yes, I do!" he exclaimed. "You're my grandfather!"

Only because of the beer did I not take offense. He further atoned for his sin by telling me after my blessing over our buffalo burgers, "That was a good one."

On this same visit, I began to recognize that our vocational paths and intellectual interests would diverge more than they would intersect. James has a scientific mind and is very fond of snakes. I have an artistic mind and am fond of ballerinas. Over lunch, James pleaded with his mother to create a pond in their backyard so that they could attract more snakes. On my next visit, he greeted me with the news that his python was missing but would most assuredly turn up in the guest room where I was sleeping. I slept in my car.

Years later, when James was eleven, after we had planned another visit, James enthusiastically informed his grandmother over the phone, "Grandma, I'm so excited. My *God* is coming!" Apparently my godson thinks that I am ancient and wise. Soon enough he will figure out that I am just old and immature, but, if he has learned anything at all as my godson, he will love me anyway. As we grow up together, we will celebrate our differences as individuals whose lives are distinct yet dependent. God made us that way. And as soon as there is a ballet about snakes, we are *so* there.

As God's sons and daughters, each one of us is called to sing the song that we can sing, the tune that resonates from deep within. Sometimes we sing such songs as solos. On other occasions, we will perform as part of a more harmonious whole. The song of myself listens to the inner voice that reveals ultimate identity, core truth, authentic self, personal relationship, and singular connection to my Creator, and affirms that such a song is unique and distinct. But the song of myself also understands that multipart harmonies and multilayered complexities all come together in relationships and experiences, in connections and communities. Such a sweeping chorus does not diminish but only enriches the song.

There will be those, over the course of your lifetime, who will ask or demand that you change your tune. The song you sing may be dissonant or unfamiliar, with lyrics in a language they do not understand, harmonies too unpredictable, a melodic style they cannot appreciate, or a beat they cannot follow. They may ask you to turn yourself way down or even to silence yourself. Some will want you to sing along only on their song, and only in unison. Remember that there is only one Conductor, one initial Source of inspiration. There is one judge of your tune and your talent—and it is not Simon Cowell.

On occasion, someone will either criticize or shake their head in bewilderment at the medley that has become the song of myself. They do not understand how I can appreciate a diverse blending of styles, realities, and truths. The idea that one can appreciate Bob Wills *and* Barry White, R&B *and* rap, Gregorian chant *and* southern gospel, just does not compute for those who assume that we are all artists constrained by a single style.

When people ask me what I do, for example, I tell them that I do many things and have many interests. When I tell them that I own a music venue, pastor a church, and write books that combine spirituality and beer, they sometimes put their fingers in their ears and tell me they've never heard and do not want to hear such a tune. They tell me that I can't be a priest *and* be a single person who goes on dates, that I can't serve Jesus *and* live on a beautiful island, that I can't preach about justice and righteousness *and* be a partner in a bar that caters to bikers and cowboys. They maintain that such diverse lyrics and multilayered compositions are simply not allowed in this life, and certainly not in the church. They insist that I have to be a one-hit wonder.

Sometimes people will interrupt me mid-verse and begin an interrogation that demands to know just who I think I am, and by whose authority, and with what credentials, do I attempt to do what I do. I have been asked what makes me qualified or gives me the right to collaborate with a musician on a jazz mass, for example. After all, they point out, I am not a musician, do not have a degree in music, and know little to nothing about music theory. And yet I dare to compose, collaborate, and even sing. I tell them the truth: nothing qualifies me, except that which qualifies anyone to sing any tune—some melody in the heart, some passion and interest, some willingness to listen and learn, the belief that with God, anything is possible and that a lack of qualifications never disqualified anyone from anything. God does not call the qualified. God qualifies the called.

When I hear such discordant criticisms, I sometimes sing the second verse of the song of myself, the one that follows "Bill is a weirdo" and goes like this: "YOU ARE NOT THE BOSS OF ME! YOU ARE NOT THE BOSS OF ME! YOU ARE NOT THE BOSS OF ME!" The revelation that "they're playing our song" does not cater to the hater. When my spirit and God's spirit combine in a duet that is unique, beautiful, and true, the critics' panning of our performance is increasingly irrelevant.

There is an old Gaelic blessing that reads like the lyrics of a Randy Newman song. It recognizes the age-old reality that not everyone is going to buy your records or applaud your attempts to evolve as an artist:

May those who love us, love us
And those that don't love us,

May God turn their hearts.
And if God doesn't turn their hearts
May he turn their ankles,
So we'll know them by their limping.

The ancient Celtic Christians gave thanks to God in their prayers for making a world that was not uniform and for giving us songs that are not always sung in unison. The music that is mine may not be hummed by the adoring masses, but it can still stand atop the only chart that matters.

Yet as both Barry Manilow and Walt Whitman have conveyed, there is mutuality in our music making. The whole world may get involved. Whitman acknowledged a more complex and complete truth about his vocal capacities:

I am of old and young, of the foolish as much as the wise,
Regardless of others, ever regardful of others,
Maternal as well as paternal, a child as well as a man,
Stuffed with the stuff that is coarse, and stuffed with the
    stuff that is fine.

We compose our lyrics regardless of others, and yet at the same time ever regardful of others, ever mindful and willing to incorporate. A band is bigger than its front man or lead guitarist. Even the solo career is supported by a cast of thousands—writers, arrangers, producers, investors, technicians, and roadies. While my song may originate from within, it is fine-tuned from without. There is an external dimension to my music, a connection beyond the inner sanctum. There is call and response, and there is always a chorus that all are invited to join.

—

I once had occasion to revel in a case of mistaken identity that eventually led me to a larger connecting truth. One of life's greatest mysteries is what we used to call simply "the phone company." Years before four-year-olds were texting their grandparents on their own cell phones about how often they went poopie, there was a telecommunications phase during which various long-distance providers would call people at home each and every evening, trying to get them to switch their service. This was before the invention of the "Do Not Call" list, one of the federal government's most brilliant creations.

At the time, I lived in the rectory of Trinity Episcopal Church and the home phone number was actually listed by that name. The church owned the home, paid the bill, and had set up the account before I even moved in. I should preface this story by revealing that I have always believed in the reality of evil forces in this world, and that they are frequently manifested in the telecommunications industry. I do not know why. Perhaps there are fewer background checks of new hires, or maybe stay-at-home demons can do such work from the confines of their dungeons.

All I know is that I once spent an entire day trying to purchase a simple phone charger from a company we shall call "People in Contempt of Service," or PCS. I spoke to various "service representatives," "virtual assistants," "replacement parts supervisors," and "customer care coordinators" before I was finally given a number that would connect me with the head honcho, the one who would solve all my problems. The number: 1-800-584-3**666**. I am certain it is mere coincidence that Satan, the sign of the Beast, and the company's CEO share anything in common at all, but I *was* tempted to ask for "the head beast in charge," or if "Mr. Lou Cifer" was there.

Combine my disdain for the "phone company" and contempt for telemarketers with a confusing directory listing and the result is a series of endlessly entertaining conversations. After answering "Hello," I was queried with the following:

> *May I speak to Mr. or Mrs. Episcopal?*
> *Is this Trinity?*
> *Would Miss Evi Scopal be available?*
> *I am trying to get in touch with Tiny Esposito.*

Most frequently, unbelievably, the human being on the other end of the line would simply ask the straightforward, nonsensical question: "May I speak to Trinity Episcopal Church?"

At first I was annoyed by such moronic inquiries, but then I decided to go along for the ride and see how many ridiculous turns it might take. Forgive me, Lord. I would take great delight in referring the telemarketer to the Altar Guild, the Wedding Coordinator, the Sexton, the Chancellor, and the Official Church Mouse. I would sometimes completely confound the party to which I was speaking by giving them a brief history of Anglicanism, the relative merits of each movement and following necessary corrective, and occasionally recite or even chant the Great Litany, and sometimes quote the entire Burial Office, Rite One, Elizabethan English, of course. I once told the telemarketer that I would have to put God on hold and that the Almighty would punish all those who were responsible for call waiting, banishing such fools to a place of eternally unlisted numbers. Every now and then, I would qualify my response by indicating that I could not speak for the entire community and that our official long-distance phone policy would require a vestry resolution, an endorsement from the Archbishop of Canterbury, and the coming of the Apocalypse. Once, I cut to the chase and asked the interrupter if we could pray together right now over the phone regarding this most important decision. If I was in a big hurry, I would simply ask, "Have you accepted Jesus Christ as your personal Lord and Savior?" How do you spell d-i-a-l-t-o-n-e?

Eventually, I began to feel guilty about my telemarketing response campaign. I came to recognize that those telemarketers *were* calling Trinity Episcopal Church whenever they dialed my number, just as they would be calling the church whenever they dialed the number of any one of its members. Whether one can figure it out through directory assistance or consulting all the entries in the community phone book, there is a collective reality that informs, shapes, expands, and commits us to something far greater than the sum of any individual part. We are all different extensions, connected through one line, the source of our group identity.

The ringtone I choose must reveal much more than my personal tastes and preferences. The identifying sound is the result of tradition, history, people, and place. The connection was made before I ever came along. I may be occupying a space for a given time, and even assigned a number all my own, but it doesn't belong only to me. It belongs to those who preceded me and to those who will come after, regardless of what technology is fashionable at the time.

To pursue a spiritual identity is to have my repertoire expanded for a greater good, to learn the old songs of an old community, to teach the new songs of a new community, and to realize there is good reason to gather round the campfire when we sing rather than stay in my cabin and compose on my own. Our songs are impoverished by every connection that we deny and enriched by every rooted reality that we admit and engage.

It took me many years to come to terms with my Texas roots, to understand that we cannot define ourselves solely by what we have rejected or edited. As an inclusive progressive person who grew up in a diverse cosmopolitan city, I was not at all sure that I wanted to be identified with the entire "F y'all" state. But I cannot help where I am from or change the context in which I was formed. The truth is, over time, the Texas myth gets into the Texas man, however much I might try to fight it. At some point I gave up, traded in my clogs for cowboy boots, took my inner Touchy-Feely Man out behind the shed, and although I did not beat the shit out of him, I did turn him loose, kick him in the ass, and send him on his way back to the land of the overly sensitive. Eventually, I embraced my heritage for the heartburn-inducing, sad country song that it might on occasion be. Deny as I might, I not only remember that tune, I wrote one of the verses.

I now get a lump in my throat when I sing along to "The Eyes of Texas." It's a simple sentiment with a borrowed tune, but that makes it no less powerful—perhaps even more so. "Do not think you can escape them" is just the down-home truth. I get teary-eyed when I hear Johnny Bush sing "Whiskey River," and overcome with emotion when Waylon and Willie join forces on "Luckenbach, Texas," especially if I'm

hearing them sing it *in* Luckenbach, Texas. Hell, I even find
myself longing for home when Sissy (Debra Winger) sidles up
to the bar at Gilley's and asks Bud (John Travolta), "Are you a
real cowboy?" And when they dance off into the sunset to
Johnny Lee's "Lookin' for Love," just go ahead and shoot me
(and I mean that in the positive Texas way!).

There are people who refer to themselves as Texans who
have never set foot in a dance hall or floated down a Hill
Country river while depleting Texas-sized inner tubes filled
with Lone Star Beer. There are some people who may be *in* the
place, but are certainly not *of* the place. They are the ones who
not only have no idea how to dance "The Cotton-Eyed Joe,"
but have no clue where in the refrain to shout out "Bullshit" in
unison. Not that it matters, since they wouldn't know it if they
stepped in it. I would wager such folks are a few verses short of
the complete tune. There is nothing virtuous about singing the
same monotone pop as everybody else, from everywhere else.
A steady stream of elevator music may offend no one, but it
will make your soul shrivel up and die.

For seven and a half years, I was the priest of a historically
African-American parish in East Austin. The stories, characters, histories, experiences, challenges, and triumphs of the
people of that place became completely interwoven with my
own. The greatest blessing of my life has been to have my vocal
and spiritual range expanded by a full octave, and that's what
happened when I was at St. James. After those years, I will
never see the world in the same way, and I will never sing
without some syncopation of rhythm. My life's song is better,
richer, fuller, and deeper. I still can't dance the Electric Slide
worth a damn, although I might be better than your average
white boy, which isn't saying much. But when I hear that old

hymn "Lift Every Voice and Sing," I do not hesitate. I know not only what I am supposed to do, but what I *must* do. I stand, and I sing with full voice and even fuller soul. I know the words. More important, I have a clue what they mean:

Lift every voice and sing,
Till earth and heaven ring,
Ring with the harmonies of liberty;
Let our rejoicing rise
High as the listening skies,
Let it resound loud as the rolling sea.
Sing a song full of the faith that the dark past has taught
*   us;*
Sing a song full of the hope that the present has brought
*   us;*
Facing our rising sun
Of our new day begun,
Let us march on till victory is won.

While I will never be able to claim this song as some can, I can still sing it and mean it.

For the last eight years I have lived on the island of Kauai in Hawaii. I now know some things about this people and place that I did not know eight years ago. The more I listen the more I learn, and the more my own song is enriched and transformed. I now know more about the struggles and the injustices of the native peoples. I have experienced the stunning beauty of the mountains, the mesmerizing depths of the ocean, and the spirit of aloha shared by those who have called Hawaii home since long before I arrived. I have learned about the songwriting skills of Queen Lili'uokalani, who wrote "The Queen's Prayer," a prayer about forgiveness and God's mercy, even as she was imprisoned in her own palace by occupying U.S. forces. We often sing her prayer in Hawaiian, just after we confess our own sins, acknowledge God's forgiving absolution, and prepare to share "Peace" with all who gather in community. I now understand more fully how confession and forgiveness lead us to practice peace among all people.

When we stand and sing Queen Lili'uokalani's beautiful anthem of love and farewell, "Aloha O'e," her sentiments seem to well up and overflow from my own soul. I have nothing against Elvis Presley and *Blue Hawaii,* but these tunes are timeless. When I join in the chorus of what for some has become a kind of national anthem, "Hawaii Aloha," singing " 'Oli e! 'Oli e!" (Rejoice! Rejoice!) my heart is completely filled with joy.

O Hawaii, O sands of my birth
My native home
I rejoice in the blessings of heaven
O Hawaii, aloha

May your divine throngs speak
Your loving people, O Hawaii
The holy light from above
O Hawaii, aloha

God protects you
Your beloved ridges
Your ever glistening streams
Your beautiful flower gardens

Happy youth of Hawaii
Rejoice! Rejoice!
Gentle breezes blow
Love always for Hawaii.

I wasn't born here, but, as they sometimes say in Texas, "I got here as fast as I could." I cannot claim this song solely as my own, but such sentiments are now part of my musical and spiritual DNA. It is part of who I am becoming.

When various oppressive religious regimes wanted to disconnect the Celtic peoples of faith from their traditions, their histories, and their land, they banished common community gatherings that were known as *ceilidh*s. During these merrymaking events, Celtic Christians would gather to play the common musical instruments of their culture, to sing the songs that had been passed down, and to share the stories that connected them to their ancestors, to creation, to God, and to each other. The oppressors understood that to destroy the song is to destroy the soul.

That is why each one of us must keep singing our song, and keep learning from the songs of others. We can make beautiful music—together and apart.

Even in a different key.

20

DON'T LEAVE ME HANGING

The Theological Significance of Athletic Supporters

I have fought the good fight. I have finished the race. I have kept the
faith. . . . I am a fool for Christ.

—THE APOSTLE PAUL (WHO SPENT THE FIRST PART OF HIS
LIFE PLAYING FOR THE WRONG TEAM WHILE PERSECUTING THE RIGHT TEAM,
BUT MADE UP FOR IT IN EXTRA INNINGS)

Let me root, root, root for the home team, if they don't win it's a shame.

—"TAKE ME OUT TO THE BALLGAME"

I have nothing against orange juice. Without it, the Tequila
Sunrise would never have dawned. The mimosa would consist
of way too many tiny bubbles. The Sunday brunch thirst
would remain unquenched without its official mascot. Even by
itself, without transformation by a substantive spirit, orange
juice remains one of my favorite breakfast beverages, ranking
just behind coffee, Coca-Cola, grapefruit juice, and beer.
However, I do not think that it is an appropriate name for a
Major League Baseball stadium.

Minute Maid Park?

Pardon me while I puke on my tofu dog.

Why not just call it Pussy Willow Field? Or Feng Shui Stadium? Or perhaps the soft supple grassy area with occasionally curvaceous earthen mounds where the young mitten-clad men in tight pantaloons roam resplendently toward the territorial demarcation pointy thingy near the peaceful winding pathway formerly known as the warning track?

Houston is one of America's ballsiest cities. Its baseball stadium should not be named for a pasteurized beverage created by diluting a can of frozen fructified concentrate! At least when the stadium was initially named Enron Field, it conjured up images of dead dinosaur products that had to be dug or pumped or bombed out of the ground by a bunch of guys wearing oil-drenched hard hats who called themselves roughnecks, similar to rednecks, except with a helmet. We gullible baseball fans finally discovered the truth about Enron, that they would not have known a commodity from a commode, that they were a corporation partly run by a bunch of narcissistic, Imagineering pretenders. But even after we figured out that Enron was overseen by a group of suit-wearing sloughnecks who cashed in on the largest discovery of fairy dust ever to be pumped down the Never-Never Land pipeline, even post-Enron collapse, the name of the ballpark could simply have been tweaked to become "Screw You Stadium" or "A Sucker Is Born Every Nine Innings Field." At least it would have evoked some sense of passion among the fans, and among those whose 401(k)s, thanks to Enron, knew more about commodes than commodities.

Call me old-fashioned, but I believe sports stadiums should reflect the real values and historic context of a people

and place. Instead of offering naming rights to the highest corporate bidder, stadium names should offer odes to civic pride,
local culture, and even the truth about our hometown selves,
as ugly and unpolished as it might be. In Houston, for example, sports teams and names should own up to their reality.
The Bullshitters or the EPA Chokeholders or the Hard Knock-
ers or the Spicy Tequila Worms or the Barbe-Conquerors or
the Sweaty Astronauts could welcome visiting teams to "You
Have a Problem Stadium."

Then again, Minute Maid Park does reveal certain truths
about the team that plays there: MINUTE—amount of time
in their fifty-year history that the Astros have threatened to
win the World Series. MAID—an appropriate mascot for a
team that frequently gets *swept* by the opposition. PARK—a
place frequented by children at play, and adults who fail to
show up for work. Besides, the five-dollar cups of orange juice
make those nine-dollar cups of beer look like real bargains.

Sports names used to mean something more than marketing schemes and lucrative payouts. They used to reflect the
roots, daily lives, historical realities, common activities, and
predominant trades of those who lived in the city or region,
those tried-and-true subjects who followed *their* teams with an
unwavering, almost pathological, loyalty. Some names speak to
a particular identity and locale. Steelers. Packers. Cowboys.
Broncos. Dolphins. Vikings. Spurs. Knickerbockers. Angels.
Rangers. Rockets. Browns. Padres. I get the connection. Longhorns. Aggies. Buckeyes. Hoosiers. Gators. Nittany Lions.
Fighting Irish. Badgers. Crimson Tide. Trojans. Horned Frogs.
Rainbow Warriors. Banana Slugs. The phallus-shaped mollusk
called the Geoduck and pronounced "Gooey-Duck" (Go Ever-
green State!).

When the Lakers played in Minnesota, the "Land of 10,000 Lakes," the moniker made sense. The team that now plays basketball in Los Angeles, despite the alliterative eloquence of simply co-opting the formerly Nordic name, should be called something that makes sense in Southern California: the Tans, the Velvet Ropes, the Plastic Surgery Scalpels, the Road Rage, the Casting Couch Covers, or even the Laid-Back Beaches.

When the Jazz played basketball in New Orleans, they were, indeed, the Jazz. When they moved to Salt Lake City, they should have considered their milieu and become something completely different, such as the Latter-Day Leopards, the Respectable Rattlers, the Joseph Smith & Wessons, the Tabernacle Archconservative Crocodile Choir, or the Terrifying Temple Squares. Salt Lake City is a lovely metropolis, but, as Duke Ellington once said about the music that made New Orleans famous, "It don't mean a thing if it ain't got that swing!"

The unfortunate reality in modern sports is much like the unfortunate reality in modern spirituality. We have forgotten who we are and from whence we came. We have lost the deep connection to tradition and history, to people and place, to culture and context. Such motivators as covenant, commitment, and constancy have given way to the team with the largest market share or the coolest logos and the religious approach that is hipper than thou, or watered down enough to appeal to the greatest number of "fans." We have forgotten what it means to be a community of the faithful, to pledge allegiance to a team regardless of the standings or the statistics. Anyone can jump on the late-inning bandwagon of the latest winner. It takes integrity and fortitude, grit and guts, not to mention heart and soul, to root root root, and root yet again for the home team, especially when the home team sucks.

The true athletic supporter, like the true follower of Jesus, will not leave you hanging. They will not abandon you when you falter. They will not cast stones when you sin. They will not bail at the first sign of failure. They will not head for the exits even if defeat seems imminent. Such devout and devoted fans understand that sometimes the last can be first and the first can be last, and that there are values that far outlast any one-season wonder. Shifting allegiances, like fantasy leagues, teach us little about the game that matters—the one played on the field, in our lives, our hearts, and our souls.

I admit that winning is a lot more fun than losing. I desperately want my teams to win and will do everything in my power to support them in that quest, even if it means wearing burnt-orange underwear and ridiculous Styrofoam horns on my head, or quoting the same Bible to affirm that some have used to oppress, or wearing a favorite cross that is often used as a weapon of opposition more than an expression of love. I realize that my unwavering support makes no difference in the outcome of the game. It is still important that the outcome of the game makes no difference in my unwavering support! There is an old spiritual that expresses this sentiment more beautifully than the most fervent college cheer:

Done made my vow to the Lord,
And I never will turn back.
I will go, I shall go
To see what the end will be.

Sometimes I'm up, sometimes I'm down,
But still my soul is heavenly bound,
See what the end will be.

When I was a mourner just like you [this verse is dedi-
   cated to all Chicago Cubs fans]
I prayed and prayed till I came through.
See what the end will be.

Done made my vow to the Lord.
And I never will turn back.
Oh, I will go, I shall go
To see what the end will be.

In other words, sports fans, there is a lot to be said for
staying true to the end, to remaining faithful and in the stadium until the very last out is certain. As Yogi Berra said, "It
ain't over till it's over." For the true fan, it's never over. "Wait
till next year" is not just an excuse for mediocrity. It means
win, lose, or draw, I'm all in. I'll be back next season, and next
Sunday. Despite the predictions of any prognosticator, my
faith sustains me to see what the end will be, and even to
return when I know what the end has typically been.

During my seminary days in Chicago, I learned more
about faith at Wrigley Field than in the divinity school library.
I learned that if you want to understand more about the old-
fashioned virtues of loyalty, fidelity, and commitment, ask any
real Chicago Cubs fan. I am talking about the old-school fans,
the ones who have no problem admitting out loud, "Any team
can have a bad century now and then." I speak of the fan who
has never referred to his favorite team as "the Cubbies" or "the
Cubbie Bears." They are called the Cubs by these diehards, and
they know that these animals are offspring of bears. The real
fan knows that, although they may be cute to the nonfan, they
are capable of eating you. I am not talking about the obnox-

ious "Ernie-come-lately" pretenders who got hooked by watching the North Side team play on WGN. They are like so many make-believe Atlanta Braves "fans" who wouldn't know a grit if it bit 'em on the ass. These slaves to cable television lack any real passion for their hometowns and are to baseball what the McRib is to barbecue—an abomination not worth discussing.

No, I'm talking about real Chicago Cubs fans, not near North Side hipsters who like to be seen after the game drinking whatever brewski is cool that week, in whatever Wrigleyville bar is hip that month. I speak of the fan who drinks Old Style because it tastes like beer and eats hot dogs because there is nothing better and who sits in the bleachers because it's cheap, not because it's trendy. I am talking about the fan who not only does not dread the length of a doubleheader, but still gets there early and stays late, the one who gets goose bumps when someone says, "Let's play two," and who knows that the Ernie who said it was never paired with Bert on *Sesame Street*. This is the fan who fervently believes that Harry Caray was Buddha incarnate and that "Take Me Out to the Ballgame" should be sung with the same devotion as "The Star-Spangled Banner" and "Real Men of Genius."

I refer here to the fans who threw back home run balls hit by opposing players long before every other stadium encouraged its fans to do so. You don't have to encourage real Cubs fans to do anything, and certainly you don't have to induce cheering by stating obvious directions on the scoreboard, such as "Noise" and "Louder." These are the folks who are absolutely annoyed by "the Wave" because it makes no contextual sense and interrupts their ability to see, much less follow, the game—that is, the one played on the field, not in the club-level concourse. These are the fans who show up, stay to the end, cheer as loud when they're behind as when they're ahead, and cheer even louder when there is no hope at all. The true Chicago Cubs fan understands "Done made my vow. And I never will turn back. I'll see what the end will be," because they'll still be there in the ninth inning. It would be sacrilege to leave early.

True saviors, like true supporters, tend to get this unlikely pairing of persistence and paradox. True saviors, like true supporters, don't throw in the towel when the team gets behind, or lay down the cross when it gets too heavy to carry. They are true to the end, regardless of what anyone may prematurely assume about ultimate outcomes. Just ask Jesus. Considering that he was the number-one draft pick, I would guess at some point he thought the road to the playoffs would lead through Yankee Stadium rather than the Via Dolorosa, and that Game Seven of the World Series would be played anywhere other than Calvary's Field. But, given the odds, he still insisted on a no-trade clause and continued to pay more attention to angels than agents. I am pretty sure he wondered on more than one occasion why he hadn't been assigned to a winner, but he kept on the jersey he'd always known and showed his true colors to the end. He stepped up to the plate one last time, even when all of his so-called fans had given up and gone home. He stayed the course and endured the most painful loss of all. It sounds like something Yogi Berra would have said. He lost so that we could win. An apparent defeat led to ultimate victory.

I believe the Bible says, "It's not whether you win or lose, it's how you play the game." Even if the Bible does not say that (which it doesn't), it's still true that sportsmanship, both on and off the field, is as important as fidelity. I learned this important truth after a long career as that obnoxious guy who feels he has to challenge the visiting fans at every turn. This attitude is to sports what fundamentalism is to religion. It serves no purpose whatsoever, makes the experience unpleasant for everyone, and really misses the point of it all, of sports *and* religion.

The archrival is not necessarily the Antichrist. And those who disagree with us spiritually may be "right" or even "righteous" on occasion. I had my own conversion experience at Busch Stadium in St. Louis one year when the Astros and the Cardinals were battling for the National League pennant. I traveled to see Game Six in St. Louis with a private investigator whom I met at a sports bar where we were celebrating an unlikely Astros victory following Game Five in Houston. Such occasions cause one to bond immediately with fellow fans and engage in absolutely ridiculous and unpredictable behavior— that I still do not regret to this day—such as traveling all the way to Missouri with someone who claims to be a private investigator . . . or a priest.

We packed our Texas flag and our Astros flag and even unfurled them in the outfield of Busch Stadium. I couldn't believe the reception we got, surrounded by all those red faces and red jerseys. They treated us with dignity and respect and kindness. They cheered just as loudly for their beloved Cardinals as they ever had, but not at our expense. They didn't cheer against the Astros, and they didn't try to make life miserable for us. They simply cheered for their team and welcomed us as an opponent worthy of respect. I vowed from that day forward to change my ways when opposing fans were in my hometown ballpark, that I would treat them with the same dignity and respect that I was afforded.

The next year, I attended another playoff game in Houston, when the Astros and Cardinals were, yet again, battling it out for National League supremacy. I spotted a couple of guys with Cardinals jerseys wandering around near the stadium, looking as if they were lost, if not afraid. I spoke to them and welcomed them to Houston. I asked them if they knew where the bars were to get a pregame beer. They told me that they had been yelled at and had a couple of beer bottles thrown at them, so they weren't really sure what they would do. I invited them to join me at the watering hole across the street and bought them each a peace-offering beverage that makes people buds—and wiser. Since Anheuser-Busch was based in St. Louis and had a giant brewery in Houston, I figured we shared significant kinship in this beverage, kind of like the common cup at Communion—and it was the least I could do to be a good sport. I intend to behave with such grace, even while rooting loudly for the home team, for the rest of my days. I have now seen the lite, and it is not just for beer.

Not everyone has gotten that memo. A few years ago, my sister-in-law Maelene, who is pretty much the sweetest person on the entire planet, accompanied her family to see the University of Texas Longhorns play the Ohio State Buckeyes at Ohio State. My sister-in-law is a petite woman without a mean bone in her body. At the time of this incident she was in her late fifties. She was walking through the stadium parking lot at Ohio State, just before the game started, returning to a nearby hotel because she ended up without a ticket to the game. She is nice that way. It was a popular game, and they simply weren't able to secure an extra ticket. She wasn't about to take a ticket from her husband or her son, who both bleed orange. So here, a middle-aged, nonthreatening woman is walking to her hotel wearing a Texas sweatshirt when an Ohio State fan runs up behind her and shoves her to the ground. I would like to use this opportunity to say to that Ohio State Buckeye fan publicly—you are a loser, a disgrace to your team, your state, and to competitive sports in general. In sports, as in faith, we don't build ourselves up by tearing anyone else down, or inflicting harm on those whose loyalties lie elsewhere.

Such cruel fanatics are, unfortunately, as much a part of organized sports as they are of organized religion, and it hurts both games. The more enlightened fans and faithful can live with paradox. They can admit that losing is not the worst thing that can happen. Do not judge an entire team or religion by its fanatics, those who would shove others to the ground to make themselves feel better.

In fact, one should pretty much never pay attention to the fundamentalists of any religious or sports tradition. They take themselves far too seriously for anyone else to take serious their claims. The fundamentalists of religions, regardless of which religion we speak, are not the true fans. They are more like the idiots who start stadium stampedes, the haters who hurl epithets, if not beer bottles, at those who disagree. They yell "Kill the umpire" and just might should the umpire fail to call every ball and strike the way they see it, which in their minds is the *only* way to see it. These poor sports are the ones who think the box scores and the statistics tell the *whole* story and reveal all truth, but will argue ad nauseam should the box scores add up differently than the way they counted on. Don't listen to these people, and don't buy them beer.

If you want to understand a team or a tradition, listen to the poets, the cheerleaders who stay positive and go deeper. In the Muslim tradition, much maligned in recent years because of the actions of a few extremist fundamentalists, the Sufi mystics understood, unlike al-Qaeda or the Christian Crusaders, that ultimate victory does not necessarily entail annihilating the enemy. They believed that spiritual insight can coexist with pathos and paradox, maybe even shift our own understanding and engender a new appreciation for defeat. An ancient Sufi proverb reads: "When the heart weeps for what is lost, the spirit laughs for what is found." With true faith, often you must lose in order to find, and when you focus too intently on finding and keeping, you end up losing and weeping. Such an intense "win at all costs" focus reveals that you are the one who is actually lost. What finally matters is not so much the standings as where you stand, with whom, and for how long.

In the Christian faith, we occasionally, although not often enough, ask our people to take vows. Vow taking is a lost art form that should be reclaimed. Noncommittal seems to be the name of the game for the majority of the spiritually inclined in the modern age. Like baseball stadiums and organ music, it's time to appreciate retro. God makes promises. People promise back. God promises to be there for us. And we promise to show up for him. God promises to give us grace. We promise to be graceful and grace-filled. God promises to love and forgive us. We promise to love and forgive others. Both parties mean what they say and agree to do everything in their power to uphold their promise and keep their commitment. Works for me.

In the service of Holy Baptism in the Book of Common Prayer, there are two sets of vows taken by the candidate or by those who are taking vows on the candidate's behalf. One, that he or she will not play for or support the opposition, will not back or cheer for the "other" team, at any time. And the other team is not the Cardinals or even the Yankees. Nope, it's not even Jerry Jones! The enemy is every evil force in this world that is opposed to the loving, reconciling purposes of God. This game is not unlike blackjack—we're not playing against the other players. We're only trying to beat the dealer, the dealer of injustice, inhumanity, hatred, and every other sinful behavior that serves none and makes life miserable for all. Vow taking is not for the faint of heart. With this first set of vows, we agree that even if we find ourselves a visiting fan in a hostile environment, we will oppose evil at every turn, fanatically. We will literally "hate" what is evil, pray and cheer against it, and work to defeat it. But that's only half the vows. It's never enough to be "against" without being "for."

The second set of vows asks us to clearly align ourselves with a particular team. We covenant with Christ to be faithful, present, and vocal. We commit to show up at games, support the team in every way we can, admit our true colors and team loyalty, and even encourage others to get behind our new number one. Vows are always taken in the context of community, because true spirituality is always a team sport. Devotion to a single star player, even if it's the self, is not to be confused with enlightenment.

I learned this important lesson from former Houston Astros pitcher and manager Larry Dierker. I have always admired Larry Dierker. He is smart, and he is talented. He is kind and gracious. Once, when he was on the island of Kauai, he agreed to come and speak at a church fund-raiser for no cost. Dierker knows the game of baseball and is uncommon in his ability to articulate intelligently what he thinks is going on, or should be going on. He is also deep enough to admit that there will always be a certain "mystery" component to every game decision. Call it gut, instinct, luck, or the movement of the Holy Spirit—it's part of the way you have to play the game.

Years ago when Barry Bonds was about to set the single-season home run record, Bonds and the San Francisco Giants came to Houston to play the Astros in the Astrodome. The Dome was a cavernous stadium with an impressive old-school scoreboard that captured the essence of the local culture. When an Astro hit a home run, the scoreboard, equipped with tens of thousands of colored lightbulbs running the length of a football field, would light up in a brilliant display. A giant cowboy would fire a gun, rockets would blast off, a bull would charge, both the Texas and U.S. flags would unfurl, and the baseball would bust through the roof of the Dome and enter an orbit in outer space. The worst thing the city of Houston has ever done was not to preserve that scoreboard. That's like Paris selling the Eiffel Tower for scrap iron.

The scoreboard would stay silent and dark if an opposing player hit a home run, even if it was Barry Bonds, and even if he was chasing a record. At the time Bonds and the Giants came to town, the Astros were still very much in contention for the pennant; it was late in the season, and a victory by the home team would have mattered. The Dome was sold out that night, and it became clear early on that most of the "fans" were there, not to root for the 'Stros, but to see a single individual pursue a home run record.

Dierker did not get that memo. He understood that his job as manager was to win ball games and do everything in his power to support his team in that endeavor. Sensing he served a greater purpose—the Astros' quest to beat the

Giants—he called for Bonds to be intentionally walked. Judging from the unrighteous indignation indicated by the howls of protests and derision from the "fans," you would have thought that Dierker had gone to the mound to burn an effigy of Nolan Ryan. The "hometown" crowd was incensed and outraged and was not going to stand for such team loyalty in the face of one man's pursuit of history. I have heard a lot of taunting at ball games in my life, but I have never heard one manager put up with so much verbal abuse for doing what he thought was the right thing. I was there that night, and I admit that when one is part of such a crowd, one begins to feel pressured by a mob mentality. One can understand in such scenarios how that crowd in Jerusalem shifted so quickly from shouts of "Hosanna in the Highest" to equally fervent shouts of "Crucify, crucify him!"

It did not help Dierker's cause that the team he managed played ineptly and anemically that night, but he still was baffled by the fans' behavior. He finally caved in to the catcalls and boos and, late in the game, allowed his pitcher to pitch to Bonds, who promptly availed himself of the opportunity and hit one out of the park. Most fans stood and cheered. The scoreboard was silent, and it all left a rather empty feeling in my stomach and a distinct distaste in my mouth.

After the game, Dierker expressed his justifiable frustration with the hometown fans. He indicated that he understood his job was to do everything in his power to win the game, and that his primary priority and concern was for the team that he managed, not the opposing individual who was out to achieve singular acclaim.

A few years later, I happened to be in San Francisco at the hometown-fan-filled Giants ballpark when Bonds hit 715 to pass Babe Ruth. It was the right place and right time, and I stood and cheered. It seemed "meet and right so to do," as one ancient Communion prayer puts it. He was not on my team. But I found myself in a different context. It was a hometown moment for a hometown hero. And it's always okay to "root, root, root for the home team."

I still feel some of Dierker's pain. In that "hometown" moment he must have felt like the children of Israel in bondage in Babylon, with the opposition telling them to share a familiar song and wondering how to "sing the Lord's song in a foreign land." For Dierker, in that familiar place at that difficult time, home field advantage was turned into the bitterest of ironies. I think I feel even more strongly about such things now, years removed, whether we speak of sports or spirituality. One person's pursuit of pious attainment does not outweigh our collective responsibility for the good of the team. It is "our team," after all.

Loyalty is sometimes costly. I began to understand this at age six. I wrote to my favorite football team at the time, the Green Bay Packers, and told them that I was their biggest fan and to please send me photos of Bart Starr, Ray Nitschke, and Willie Davis, as well as a team photo and "anything else you think I should have." They wrote me back, thanking me for my unwavering support, and included a price list for all of the items I had requested. Who knew that even the most fervent fan would have to *pay* to support his team? I sent them my dime for each photo. The team photo I received of the Green Bay Packers still sits on my shelf where I display all those things I value and that have earned my loyalty over the years. Such treasures are worth every penny I ever paid for them.

When Barry Bonds hit that home run in the Astrodome against my team, I will bet you that the person who caught that ball not only did not throw it back onto the field, but never even thought of doing such a crazy thing. I suppose anyone who would throw such a lucrative catch back would have to be a real fool. Yes, a real fool.

Or maybe a real fan.

21

MY WILI

I didn't come here and I ain't leavin'.

—WILLIE NELSON

Now we're gonna be face-to-face.
And I'll lay right down in my favorite place.

—STOOGES, "I WANNA BE YOUR DOG"

A wise person once said that until one has loved an animal, a part of one's soul remains unawakened. I have loved three animals over the course of my life. Each of them has awakened the parts of me that are most soulful, most connected to my Creator, and most connecting to all creation. Beneath the ornery ornamentation of my colorful language, I am essentially an orthodox theologian and I have come to think of them as my "Trinity of Terriers."

The first member of the terrier trinity, the Source, the Father, the Original, was Sam Houston. An eighty-two-pound Airedale born in Fort Worth, Sam almost lost his life, and did lose his ears, in a house fire when he was a puppy. Sam was rescued in dramatic fashion by the neighbors, guys who, though not overtly religious, knew and lived out the traditional religious meaning of the word *neighbor*, risking their own lives for the sake of a so-called lower species. The fiery flames may have claimed a couple of furry appendages, but they did not claim Sam's sense of humor, sense of purpose, and sense of basic trust. He still felt that even when bad things happen, life can be good and meaningful and filled with treats.

I used to read the Bible to Sam just before bedtime to remind him of God's faithfulness. He was particularly fond of what he called "the Twenty-Third Psalami." Sometimes his spiritual insights were as well developed as his sense of humor. For example, he succinctly summarized that all of our spiritual inquiry, religious curiosity, and existential reasoning could be summarized with one simple question: *Are you gonna eat that?*

Naming my number-one dog Sam Houston seemed a logical choice for this fifth-generation Texan. I grew up breathing petrochemical fumes in his namesake city, scents no dog would sniff, waffling over the refinery land surrounding the site of the Battle of San Jacinto, where his namesake hero caught Santa Ana in his underwear with his furry appendages wrapped around a lovely lass they called "the Yellow Rose of Texas." While we may yet "Remember the Alamo!" we should also fondly recall the Yellow Rose. If not for her sultry charms, I might have named my first dog Pancho Villa.

The second member of the terrier trinity, the Son, the Rambunctious Reconciler, the "One Who Tended to Get in Trouble and Probably Should Have Been Crucified on More Than One Occasion Had I Not Come to His Rescue," was the smaller, stronger, scholar-athlete Airedale of the family—Andrew "Jack" Jackson. Jack was born in the great state of

Oklahoma. You would think his theme song would have been Merle Haggard's "Okie from Muskogee." Not Jack. He consistently opted for a trio of tunes by Jewish country-western singer and sometimes Texas gubernatorial candidate Kinky Friedman: "I'm Proud to Be an Asshole from El Paso," "Waitress, Waitress, Won't You Sit on My Face," and "Get Your Biscuits in the Oven and Your Buns in the Bed."

Like Sam Houston, Andrew "Jack" Jackson was also appropriately named. Jack's human mother, Rachel, had deep roots in the state of Tennessee. She was not only related to Andrew Jackson; she was named for Jackson's wife, Rachel. If you know your American history, you will remember that Sam Houston and Andrew Jackson were good friends. In American canine history, Sam Houston and Andrew "Jack" Jackson were *best* friends. So, naming my first and second dogs made a lot of contextual, historical, spiritual, and sociological sense.

When I moved to Kauai the day after Valentine's Day in 2006, I left my love back in Texas. Jennifer was a gem. She was highly motivated, brilliant, and successful. She possessed an unusual combination of business acumen, joyful affect, and a deep faith. She was a committed Christian who read her Bible daily and prayed, out loud, with fervor and feeling. By age thirty, she was named chief financial officer of a London-based energy company, and founded and directed a nonprofit development center for at-risk urban youth. She played the viola and drank her single-malt Scotch neat.

What I brought to the table was equally as impressive: a significant Pez collection, an oblivious social awkwardness around all nonanimals, and a really big pension, one of the very few perks of the priesthood. Jennifer eventually fell in love with and married a NASA engineer who was twenty-two years younger than I, and who read his Bible daily and prayed out loud with fervor and feeling. Well, let me just say that I am not the least bit jealous. And let me add that while this guy may work for NASA, he is certainly no rocket scientist. Okay, well, maybe he is a rocket scientist, but he would certainly not know a "Bunny Pez" if it bit him on the behind. And I will not even mention the highly sought-after "Lamb Pez," which I doubt he has ever even heard of, much less seen, and certainly not possessed.

Anyway, when I got to Kauai, I was lonely. I'm sure my social isolation remains incomprehensible to the reader.

My good friends, former mainland veterinarian Dr. Valerie McDaniel and her husband, Mack, came to visit me shortly after my arrival on Kauai. While it is not on the normal tourist trail (Elvis never sang there, Mitzi Gaynor never filmed there, and the *Jurassic Park* dinosaurs never roamed there), the Kauai Humane Society is worth a visit. Their facilities are among the finest in the world. Among the local critters, it is known as a "Five Paw Resort." Often, adopted animals on the island will reminisce about their days at the society, wondering aloud, "When are you taking me back to the Four Seasons for my spa treatment?"

Just before our arrival at the Humane Society, I mistakenly admitted to Mack and Val that, while touring the facility, we just might possibly keep our eyes open for any special creature that might be looking for a human partner in crime. There were several absolutely adorable puppies that we stopped to pet, but puppies are to adoption what spirituality is to religion—too easy and too cute. So we wandered out back to where the big dogs stayed. I immediately saw, printed on the chain-link fence of one enclosure, a word that is very dangerous for me. The word was *Airedale*.

"Mack and Val, come quickly!" I shouted. "Unbelievably, there is a real, live actual Airedale over here! It's a sign from God and a true miracle!"

The critter heard my excited shouts and made a bark-line straight toward me. As fast as anything on four legs could run did this beast bolt from his inner sanctum. His appearance was unexpectedly unexceptional and also unexpectedly endearing—one ear awkwardly flopped on top of his head, giant tongue hanging out the side of his mouth drooling on the pavement, goofy grin on his face, long black tail wagging faster than a vintage Aloha Airlines plane propeller. He had the most joyful, expectant, hopeful, grateful, life-affirming eyes you have ever seen. He turned and pressed his entire body sideways through the small openings in the chain-link fence so that we could pet him. There was only one problem. This hound looked about as much like an Airedale as I look like Mariah Carey. I later discovered that, on Kauai, any creature in possession of facial hair, of any sort, is called an Airedale. If you have whiskers, you are an Airedale. Here, Tom Selleck is an Airedale. Geraldo Rivera is an Airedale. Wolf Blitzer is an Airedale. And Jesus is the King of Terriers!

This guy was less the King of Terriers, and more the court jester of mutts. A poi dog, as we call bunches of unidentifiable anything in Hawaii, he was black and skinny with the world's longest tail, which wagged with the force of a lethal weapon; a big white spot on his chest; thin ears; short hair; and a long snout. I remember thinking, "This one better have an extraordinary personality, because he sure isn't gonna get by on his looks!" This is a dog that would never be found at Westminster—the show, or the abbey.

Despite his lack of looks, we took the "Airedale" outside to a grassy area to play with him. He immediately ignored the more expensive fluff toy and proceeded to derive great joy from completely destroying a plastic bottle. A sucker for cheap dates, I was almost in love. Then Valerie gave him an impromptu exam right on the spot. She pronounced him physically healthy, but more important, psychologically sound. Whatever he has been through, she said, he's got a great attitude and is just glad to be alive. This one is rare, she said. He's a keeper.

So I kept him. I took Sir Goofy the Airedale Impersonator home with me the very next day.

Immediately, I had a real dilemma. As you might imagine, dogs' names are very important to me. I wondered what I could possibly name my new beast that might combine my long-standing roots in Texas with my new Hawaii home. My first inclination was to name him Mai Tail, but only serious drinkers would get it, or to combine all of my interests into a single name and call him Coconut Brah. I kept thinking. I also prayed, out loud, with fervor and feeling. I suddenly realized that the port of entry for my new island home was named Nawiliwili Harbor. I also recognized that my favorite watering hole and dive bar on the entire island was the Nawiliwili Tavern. In fact, the Nawiliwili Tavern was owned by one of my St. Michael's parishioners. Given my deep roots and these hopeful new realities, I named my new dog *Nawiliwili Nelson*.

As the third member of the terrier trinity, Wili has lived into his name. A feisty spirit, he is often as elusive as the wind. There may be a fiery unpredictability in his movement, but it is his presence that warms the heart, if not the skin, of everyone within licking distance. He still likes to press his entire body against mine, a move that works all the better now that there is no chain-link barrier. He is quite the comforter and consoler after every bad day.

Unlike his namesake, Wili doesn't smoke a lot of dope, but he does like to drink beer, and he has certainly had his moments of living out his Trinitarian calling—less as a holy terrier and more as a holy terror. Early on, he chewed up my most expensive pair of sunglasses, which I proceeded to wear anyway for several years even though they sported visible tooth marks, just to see if I might set a new fashion trend. I did not. He also has an unusual habit of eating the faces off his chew toys, leaving their torsos, appendages, and other extremities completely intact. I believe that this frightening tendency may, in fact, be Wili's cry for a deeper intimacy in his relationships. Although it could be that he just likes the way faces taste. I know I do.

Early on, Wili's theme song seemed to be "On the Road Again." All the Humane Society could tell me about his past is that they found him wandering along the side of the road. Apparently, Wili just could not wait to get on the road again. If given the opportunity to go on tour and Wili saw any kind of opening—a door, a fence, an office window, the space between my legs, the space between your legs—he would bolt and be out on the road again faster than you can say, "Hello. My name is No No Bad Dog. What's yours?"

Upon Wili's very first visit to St. Michael and All Angels Church, he seemed to sprout wings and take off in a most un-angelic manner. He somehow managed to escape the rector's study after finding no copies of the Victoria's Poodle catalog. As soon as someone cracked the door leading to the reception-ist's office, he was out of it faster than a fundamentalist at an art opening. He ran like a flash of black lightning, past the columbarium that contains no niches (a liturgical innovation I have yet to understand), past the outdoor baptismal font, and under the giant plastic tomato on the children's playground. He did not stop at the beautiful koa wood door featuring St. Michael slaying the dragon, nor did he dart into the church's bathrooms, appropriately named Adam and Eve. He ran straight for the corner of Umi and Hardy Streets, one of the busiest intersections in town, made a sharp left at the former county jail, and headed onto the campus of the Wilcox Elementary School.

The entire time, I was running frantically after him, screaming "Wili!" at the top of my lungs, a word that my dog, who grew up in Hawaii, confused with the Hawaiian word *wiki,* which means "faster." Countless cars came to a screeching halt to avoid flattening my new best friend onto the pavement. Wili appeared to be having the time of his life, playing his new favorite game, "Keep Away from Bill."

I was terrified twofold: (1) that Wili would live out a favorite song of another Texas troubadour, Robert Earl Keen, and keep traveling the road that goes on forever, and enjoying the party that never ends, and I would never see him again; and (2) that I would soon be making a sharp right toward the new county jail, charged with a variety of civic and criminal infractions including, but not limited to, criminal trespass, leash law violations, disruption of school property, endangering the lives of minors, and a general inability to maintain control of a mutt. I could already envision the *Garden Island* headlines the next day: "Priest Loses Control of Wili," "Priest's Wili Discovered at Local School," and "Episcopal Dog Liable and Liberal." Even back in Austin, I could imagine these headlines: "Whiskey River Take My Bone!" and "Mamas Don't Let Your Canines Grow Up to Be Cowboys!"

For a brief moment, I thought I had him cornered in the Wilcox courtyard, just outside the cafetorium, within eyesight and earshot of the principal's office. Then, like a Southern Baptist spotted by his pastor at a liquor store, he vanished into thin air. I was frantic. Even though I knew I was disrupting the school day, I continued to cry out after him, "Wili! Wili! Where are you?"

Then, in the distance, I heard a soft, rational, calm, reassuring female voice. It was coming from inside the first-grade classroom: "He's in here."

I ran into the classroom with great fear and trepidation, expecting to find a frightened mass of chaos with children crying and running for their lives. I expected to encounter overturned desks, dismembered textbooks, chewed-up sack lunches, and one very upset teacher who would be dialing 911 with one hand and holding off a ferocious wild animal with her uplifted and outstretched teacher's chair in the other. It was going to be ugly, unpleasant, and humiliating. If Wili had not already eaten several of the children, the teacher had probably paddled him into a pulp of unrepentant fur.

Instead, I ran inside and found an entire classroom of happy, smiling, welcoming, entertained children who were petting Wili as he paraded his way gently among their desks. The wise teacher stood there with a look of complete serenity on her face, arms folded across her chest like teachers do when they are somewhat displeased but mostly amused and certainly in control.

"I am so sorry," I howled penitently. I apologized profusely to the entire class, and I grabbed my delinquent dog like he was a sinner in the hands of an angry God and began to drag him back to church, the same way most of us get there.

"Come back and see us, Wili," the teacher called out after him. The children chimed in unison as we made our way out of the first-grade classroom: "Byyyyyyyye Wiliiiiiiiiiii!"

—

I am so glad that there are schools and churches and humane societies and hospitals and bars. I am so glad that human beings have such a strong tendency to go to the effort of organizing ourselves around the things we value. We create an institution that attempts to preserve the meaning of the value that we so value, which often entails creating some necessary hierarchy, administration, facilities, teachers, priests, bishops, and hall monitors. We create within these organizations very important features like expectations, guidelines, a canon of learning, and even boundaries. We install doors that can be safely closed to protect those inside and can also be flung wide open to allow those in need to enter. Good and important works can be perpetuated and improved upon when we go to the trouble to get ourselves organized, educated, and structured.

Wili has never argued that obedience school is too restrictive for a truly enlightened canine, or that organized animal welfare is a futile attempt to provide structure for freedom-loving sentient beings. For that might mean barking up the wrong spiritual tree. I think Wili knows that the institution is not the enemy and that the organization is not the inherent evil. I am often perplexed by those who expend

energy arguing against the human tendency to institutional-
ize or organize those things that are truly important. Such
folks often elevate personal spirituality as the preferred path
to enlightenment and well-being over religious institutions.
They often tell us that they are "spiritual but not religious." I
hear that more and more these days. I suspect this sometimes
means that they simply don't want to go to the effort that the
valuable things often call upon us human beings to undertake. Wili and I believe in institutions, and we are so grateful
for them. Our lives, as well as our souls, often depend on
them.

Perhaps if I were more "spiritual," I would have let Wili
run free that day and not attempted to confine him to a particular space, saying, "Flee, o animal spirit, be free as the wind.
Let only your olfactory senses and the Great Canine Consciousness be your guide as you soulfully search for fulfillment
and bliss. And should you be run over by a car, well then, the
Cosmos and your own internal and eternal longing must have
conspired to dictate such an outcome."

I am not very spiritual. I am much more religious, and the
religious person that I am would much prefer shouting the following to the fleeing dog: "Get your furry black ass back in
this church before I come after you like the Hound of Heaven
and pull your tail so hard you will believe in a literal hell!" The
second option may indeed be the more profound encapsula-
tion of timeless truth, and it might actually save someone's ass
in the process.

Spirituality is highly overrated. Religion is highly underrated. The differences between the two can be expressed in a
multitude of metaphors. Spirituality shows up at the
Humane Society when it feels like it and pets a puppy be-

cause it is soft, uttering the ancient esoteric, but truly spiritual, expression "gootchie gootchie gooh." Religion goes to the back of the dog pound and adopts a damn dog who proceeds to live in your home, shed on your bed, chew up your underwear, pee on your grass, and poop on your rug, while uttering the equally religious expression "SON OF A BITCH! IF I DIDN'T LOVE YOU I WOULD KILL YOU RIGHT NOW!"

Spirituality floats just above planet Earth. Religion sniffs the dirt and marks some territory. Spirituality can be "visualized" all by yourself. Religion is what you have been through with a group of folks you'd not normally even associate with. Spirituality protects its own soul, and covers its own ass. Religion lays down its life for its friends, and sometimes even mere acquaintances. Spirituality says, "OOOOHHHMMMMM." Religion says, "OH! MY! GOD!" Spirituality focuses on the prenup. Religion is in for the long haul. Spirituality lusts after the latest feel-good fad. Religion learns to love what is sometimes most unlovable. Spirituality is the lightest of beers. Religion is Chimay, brewed by monks in a real monastery. Yep, the best beer in the world is a product of a religious institution. Thank God the monks are not just "spiritual" or else my thirst would be eternally unquenched.

The difference between spirituality and religion is not unlike the difference between the typical attitude of a cat and a dog toward the Master. A dog understands the reality to go something like this: Hey! These people I live with feed me, love me, and provide me with a nice, warm, dry house. They pet me, give me treats and toys, scratch me, and take good care of me. They must be God! A cat understands the reality to go something like this: Hmm. These people I live with feed me, love me, and provide me with a nice, warm, dry house. They pet me, give me treats and toys, scratch me, and take good care of me. I must be God!

Religion has sometimes done great harm to the world. In the name of religion, groups of people have been oppressed. Wars have been fought. The institution has at times been preserved whether it was in the best interest of humanity or not. Oftentimes, such evil has been perpetuated by fundamentalist strains of religion. Fundamentalism often looks out for its own interests and fails to see the big picture.

On the other side of the equation, religion has sometimes brought great benefit and blessing to the world. Hospitals have been built. The creative pursuit of beauty has been fostered and funded. Injustices have been overturned. Hungry people have been fed. I wonder how history might have been written if the Reverend Martin Luther King Jr. had been a spiritual guru who wrote self-help books, as opposed to a Baptist preacher with walking shoes, deep convictions, a backbone, and a really big mouth. True, there were religious leaders who were shockingly silent or even worked against the civil rights movement. I would argue that those folks were not religious, and they were not leaders.

I understand that truth is large, and there is more than one pathway to God. And yes, I know that religion sometimes comes across as restrictive, oppressive, unreasonable, detached, dysfunctional, and capable of more harm than good. Well, so can our mothers, and I still believe in moms! And I still observe Mother's Day as a major feast day worthy of celebration.

I know the church is full of hypocrites, so come on in.

There's always room for one more! And yes, the pews are, in fact, filled each Sunday with folks who completely fail to live up to the high standards they espouse. In the words of Willie Nelson, let the one who is without sin be the first to get stoned!

Wili and I give thanks that the folks at the Kauai Humane Society believe strongly in institutional animal welfare. We are grateful that they have gone to the trouble of organizing themselves around the care of animals, rather than simply allowing the animals to find their own way in the world, fend for themselves, and pursue their own paths. Wili and I are also glad that there are schools and churches, teachers and clergy, students and worshippers. We are glad that such places have doors that can be shut and even locked to keep us safe and out of harm's way and provide us with a time and place apart to rest and be renewed. We are also glad that these doors have hinges and can be flung wide open, allowing anyone to wander in and find a welcoming embrace, an understanding authority who may have some wisdom to share, and even a home away from home. Let us not wage war on doors just because they are sometimes closed. Remember, as the old spiritual adage suggests, or is it a religious adage: When God closes one door, it may be time to kick the son of a bitch in.

Being opposed to institutional religion because it is an organized form of spiritual expression makes about as much sense as refusing to go to a bar because one does not believe in organized drinking. Some things simply taste better when shared: beer, bread, wine, to name just three. Some things make more sense when we explore them together, like religion and spirituality, to name just two. Some animals just live a richer, fuller, more meaningful life, when shared with a human—Nawiliwili Nelson, to name just one.

Gandhi, who taught King a lot about true religion, even though his differed considerably from King's, once said, "Where there is fear, there is no religion."

If that is true, then, what are you afraid of?

22

ALL THAT GLITTERS
IS SOMETIMES GOLD

I don't usually wear diamonds in the afternoon,
but this is a special occasion!

—LIBERACE, EASTER SUNDAY 1979, GRAND

OPENING OF THE LIBERACE MUSEUM, LAS VEGAS

Bright light city gonna set my soul, gonna set my soul on fire.

—ELVIS PRESLEY, "VIVA LAS VEGAS"

*T*hroughout history the spiritual quest has led the soul-searching seeker into the desert—literally and metaphorically. The wilderness offers the sensory-overloaded traveler a place of isolated otherness, where respite and renewal may recharge the battery of the soul. There also, the sensually deprived automaton may finally escape the clutches of robotic routine and plunge fully into an oasis of refreshment.

The desert sun can reignite the embers of a spirit that has been doused and become dormant. The arid and discomforting conditions may test, tempt, try, temper, and transform the

willing and the reluctant. Being incognito in the middle of nowhere encourages the unearthing of long-buried treasure and
the reawakening of darkened dreams, approaching their grand-
est scale.

The wasteland lays bare the full frontal frontier of the
human soul, leading to an honest-to-God evaluation of what
one is made of, other than dust, what one truly desires at the
deepest, most private place, and what one is willing to risk to
obtain ultimate salvation and eventual liberation. Reality's
limits are tested as the skeptic dismisses the light as an illusory,
unobtainable, dissipating mirage, while the seer beholds the
revelation of a holy city, a place where full participation in life's
primary quest—to live—might be actualized.

Out there, the lifting of the veil can reveal an elusively no-
madic and newfound beauty, or it can plunge the curious into
a spiraling abyss of bad choices. But the seeker has not come
this far to leave anything hidden or covered, anything unexplored or unwagered. In the desert, not taking a chance would
be the biggest gamble of all. No risk. No revelation. Everything is left to chance. Nothing is left on the table. What is
given there stays there. What happens there remains within
one's soul for all eternity.

At least that has been *my* experience of Las Vegas.

Not long after moving to the middle of the Pacific Ocean,
I was pleased to discover that Las Vegas is the number-one va-
cation destination for those of us who call Hawaii home. I
must be living in the right place, because the "ninth island" of
Las Vegas has been my home away from home for most of my
ordained years. Ironically, or perhaps not, it is the place where
I have learned many of my most profound spiritual lessons.
Once my blackjack dealer, upon discovering I was a priest,

asked me if I knew the difference between a prayer that is prayed in a casino and a prayer that is prayed in a church. In a casino, he said, one really means it! True. The stakes are often not nearly high enough in church, are they? Maybe we should raise the minimum bet around the altar, just to keep it interesting.

During my first midlife crisis, at age thirty, after partaking of a few margaritas with my friends Kevin Thornton and Fred Williams at Z Tejas Southwestern Grill in Austin, Texas, I wondered aloud if anyone at the table had ever been to Las Vegas. Survey said, "No." I then wondered aloud if anyone at the table would like to go to Las Vegas. Survey said, "Yes." As impulsive people without real jobs are prone to do, we left the next morning and drove straight through.

We were forced to share a small bed and a floor at the Imperial Palace, a property so unimperial and nonpalatial that the lack of a roll-away was the least of our concerns. We wandered from casino to casino, playing mostly slots that we mostly lost. On the way out of town, we saw, dazzling in the desert sun, a welcoming oasis called the Z Tejas Southwestern Grill. Hoping it was not just a mirage mirroring our disappearing funds, we took such a vision as a sign that our journey, although not materially productive, must have had some sort of spiritual significance.

After partaking of a few more margaritas, our survey said that perhaps in our losing large quantities of that highly overrated commodity called cash, our life's more underrated priorities would somehow be brought to light. We would then be able to see previously unimagined possibilities which would lead us toward our true spiritual destinies—or at least second jobs. Then again, it is also possible that the Spirit stops at the threshold called stupid, and that tequila shots speak louder than testimonial shouts, regardless of how hard we pound on our self-justifying pulpits.

Whatever the case, the desert did its number on me and I keep going back for more enlightenment.

Over the years in Las Vegas—not to be confused with "Vegas," a heretical half name uttered only by those who never venture beyond the Strip—I have experienced insights that outnumber the spokes on a roulette wheel, valuable lessons that have taken me as much into the black as into the red. My time in Las Vegas has encouraged both confession and absolution, revealed both haze and light, and produced both regret and resurrection. In Las Vegas I have fallen in love, and I have fallen in lust. Sometimes I have simply fallen. I have lost big, and I have won big. Okay, truthfully I have lost really big, and I have won sort of big. Okay, truthfully, I have had my ass handed to me on a playing card, a joker I believe, and I have sometimes earned enough to pay for my cab fare back to McCarran Airport.

It was in Las Vegas that Robin Leach told me that I didn't look like a priest, that Hugh Hefner's publicist told me that he liked my theology, and that the most attractive cocktail waitress I have ever seen told me that I would have to move because I was blocking access to her station. It was in Las Vegas that I was kissed by Wayne Newton, since my date was kissed by Wayne Newton and I later kissed her. So I have now been exposed to the germs of the 1.3 million people Wayne Newton has kissed during his shows over the last three hundred years. I am not complaining. His kissing was far better than his singing. They held the show that night for thirty minutes so that a late-arriving Michael Jackson and his entourage could be seated right behind us. If only a tardy Wayne Newton had been seated right behind us for a Michael Jackson show, I would have gladly joined in the chorus of "Danke Schoen!"

Over the years in Las Vegas, I have stayed in every hotel at least once, including the Motel 6. The glittering Motel 6 sign just off the Strip may be the most overlooked landmark in the neon city. Besides, my trip based at the Motel 6 turned out to be among the most memorable. I drove with a former girlfriend all the way from Austin just before New Year's. We had a flat tire in Arizona just before one of those DO NOT PICK UP HITCHHIKERS! PRISON AREA! signs. We did not see that sign because we had a flat tire. Fortunately for us, our cell phones had died, and my former girlfriend did not own a tire jack. Our gambling started early on that trip with much higher stakes. The good news is that should I ever be incarcerated in Arizona, I now know people who know people.

On New Year's Eve, we mistakenly ventured out of the Bellagio, where we were drinking free cocktails and mingling with the beautiful. My former girlfriend wanted to be out on the Strip "where the real action was." We discovered we had left the real action when we waded into a sea of drunken frat boys, only to find the Bellagio doors had been locked behind us. Baptized by a frothy foam originating from God knows where, while the ocean of bodies shoved us from every direction, we fought our way through the mayhem to find asylum at a run-down casino resembling, well, an asylum. Surrounded by suds and steroids and sports jerseys of teams that had not won since Sinatra ruled the town, I can honestly say it was the worst New Year's Eve of my life. The good news is that now when I read the biblical accounts of hell, I have an experience from which to draw insight and imagery.

While "7" may be the eternal number in the spiritual tradition and in slot history, I have never been so glad to see a "6" in all my life. The next morning, New Year's Day, my former girlfriend atoned for her sins by driving all the way across town to fetch me two dozen, right out of the oven, melt in your mouth, Krispy Kreme doughnuts. I devoured them while watching Ricky Williams and the Texas Longhorns devour their Fiesta Bowl opponent. Who knew that a New Year's Day spent in my room at an off-strip budget motel eating fried dough while focused on a mostly meaningless football game on a tiny television screen would be among the most decadent experiences in all my years of traveling to Sin City?

That's Las Vegas, baby. It gives you what *it* wants in the way *you* least suspect. All I can tell you is that my morning at the Motel 6 was rich and beautiful and satisfying and in some ways better than the Bellagio.

Occasionally I will travel to Las Vegas for the sole purpose of preaching. When I am in Las Vegas to perform my priestly duties, the odds are excellent that I am the only one on the plane, at the blackjack table, at the swim-up bar, in the buffet line, at the Neon Boneyard, or even the Viva Las Vegas Wedding Chapel who is there to preach.

If you want to see people at your blackjack table start to guard their chips a little more carefully, just tell them that you are Father Miller and you are in Las Vegas to say Mass. Then multiply the number of times you hear "right, and I'm a nun," times the number of sermons you will preach that week, and you have your table limit for the entire trip.

One summer I traveled to Las Vegas to speak at Grace in the Desert Episcopal Church, perhaps the best-named church west of the Mississippi. It went well. I shared some insights from my first book, *The Gospel According to Sam: Animal Stories for the Soul*. I typically title this lecture "A Conversation with DOG," and it seems to resonate particularly well with those who have (1) a dog and (2) a sense of humor. That night was no exception. Sam was well received. Afterward, a very distinguished gentleman who spoke with the unmistakably refined British accent of a cultured and educated Anglican revealed his identity as a producer at the local National Public Radio station in Las Vegas. He said that should I ever return to Las Vegas, they would like to interview me on NPR.

The following summer I was back in Las Vegas to preach, this time at Christ Church, downtown, whose bell tower is overshadowed by the nearby Stratosphere. The image offers a pretty clear indication of the values and priorities of the place. The NPR interview was set for a Friday morning. While my buddy Everett McKinley drank tropical beverages and entertained the towel girls by the pool, I was hunched over a desk in the hotel room, poring laboriously over my meticulously prepared notes, rehearsing and reviewing a host of well-organized, insightful anecdotes and profoundly entertaining sound bites capturing the depth and breadth of my dog Sam.

I was excited about the radio interview. People have often commented that I have a great face for radio, and I had a feeling this could be my breakthrough moment in connecting with a broader audience. As I entered the studio, I felt I was well prepared to impart my vast knowledge to the world of NPR listeners. Finally, I had a chance to really shine in the desert.

How do you spell M-I-R-A-G-E?

I should have known I was in trouble when the interviewer, a well-known radio host who dominated the more erudite airwaves each morning, asked me if I was the Bill Mueller who was the American League batting champion in 2003 and who led the Boston Red Sox to a 2004 World Series title? Was I the Bill Mueller who was the only player in Major League history to hit a grand slam from opposite sides of the plate in the same game? Survey said that I was not that guy.

The interview went downhill from there. I wanted to talk about my dog. He wanted to talk about my facial hair. I wanted to share the many ways in which divine truth is revealed in all creation, particularly those critters utilizing the revelatory devices of tail and tongue. He wanted to discuss the intricacies of health-care reform, a topic about which I know less than my dog.

While I will not say that it was the worst radio interview in the history of broadcast journalism, it was close. All the knowledge I had laboriously outlined and painstakingly prepared, all of those carefully crafted gems of wit and wisdom— all went for naught. I felt like I had memorized and played basic strategy perfectly, only to lose my entire savings at a single table in a single session.

As I left the radio station, I passed Carlos Santana's drummer, who was next in line to be interviewed. I wondered if he would be asked questions about sacramental theologies and canine revelation. His hair seemed much more interesting than mine, but I wondered if it would go unnoticed. I was feeling a lot more surreal than supernatural, and I was tempted to ask him to apply a drumstick to the side of my head. Perhaps it would knock some sense back into me.

I finally recognized that I had overlooked two very important realities as I had prepared my interview material: (1) it was not my show, and (2) I was not the one who got to ask the questions.

It seems like God had something similar to say to Job way back when. Job and his friends had come up with all the answers before the questions had even been posed. They had prepared, pontificated, and piously assumed that they had all the material memorized and mastered regarding why some win and why some lose. When the interview actually started, the One who had all of those answers offered only more questions. These, too, were questions that Job had not anticipated and was unprepared to answer.

Like God speaking from a whirlwind, the dust storm that is Las Vegas frequently reminds people that they are not really in control. One can memorize basic strategy, play the odds, stay disciplined, and even stay sober. One can prepare, peruse, and plot till the sun comes up and the lights fade into the desert landscape, but one cannot dictate how the cards are dealt, nor explain how or why. Out in the desert, I don't run the show, ask the questions, call the shots, or manage the slots. Realizations that instill true self-awareness can be more liberating than a bachelor's weekend in Las Vegas.

—

The truth is not always pretty, but, if Las Vegas had no dark side, the light would be underappreciated. My most frightening experience in Las Vegas occurred late one night in the deep, dark recesses of the original Caesar's Palace casino. If I'm gonna gamble (which I am), I'd rather gamble there than anywhere. That low crystal ceiling dome just reeks of Rat Pack chic. The blackjack dealers there are not models.

They are blackjack dealers. What a concept. Blackjack dealers who know how to deal cards, how to make conversation, and how to advise you on basic strategy should you choose to play it by the book. A gin and tonic and a single-malt Scotch simply taste better way back there in the back of Caesar's, about as far from the mall and all of the nouveau biche as one can get.

One night, I got up from the table and I began to wander among the maze of discreetly tucked-away slot machines. Out of nowhere a very drunk man, who had apparently lost a very large amount of money, nearly body-blocked me, thrusting a very large horseshoe-shaped diamond ring in my face. He slurred a shockingly penitent plea right at me, wondering if I would buy his ring because he had lost all his money and needed to get home. Judging from the size of the ring and the size of the many diamonds that adorned it, this was a man of some means. How meaningless such means were in that moment.

I am usually cool, calm, and collected when confronted with painfully bleak human dilemmas, and I typically respond with compassionate composure. This man's predicament scared the chips out of me. The appropriate ethical response completely eluded me. I wanted no part in even beginning to explore the available options, all of which seemed so wrong at so many levels. I cashed out my chips and ran toward the mall as fast as humanly possible. Sobriety never looked so spiritually significant as in that moment. The glittering reality he placed in front of my face contained not even a glimmer of light. I escaped into the night, where the neon light revealed that the cheap rhinestone might be a far better value than the costly diamond.

This thought brings me to the most illuminating, most life-affirming attraction and religious pilgrimage site in the city. No, I do not speak of the Girls of Glitter Gulch, although several friends claim to have had religious experiences while there. I speak of the greatest monument to the greatest artist in the greatest city in the desert in all the world. I speak of the Liberace Museum.

Wladziu Valentino Liberace grew up in Milwaukee, home of the Milwaukee Brewers, the best-named baseball team east of the Mississippi, in a devoutly religious and musically inclined household. His father, who played in John Philip Sousa's band, once said that music in the house was more important than food. Being in Milwaukee, he would never have said such a thing about beer.

When Liberace was a budding young musician, he met his idol and mentor, the acclaimed Polish pianist Ignacy Jan Paderewski, backstage at the Pabst Theatre, the best-named theater east of the Mississippi and home to truly blue-ribbon entertainment. Liberace's theme song turned out to be the "Beer Barrel Polka," composed by a Czech musician. The theme contained the best drinking song lyrics ever composed on either side of the Mississippi: "Roll out the barrel! We'll have a barrel of fun!" I'll drink to that.

Liberace was the ultimate Las Vegas ambassador. He understood that art did not have to make a profound or discordant statement, or any statement at all, in order to be good, beautiful, powerful, or true. He personified the notion that one could be both artist and entertainer, believing that to be both at once sometimes meant playing serious classical music "with the boring parts left out." I'll drink to that, too. For a while he adopted the Vegas-esque stage name "Walter Buster-keys." Liberace was, like Las Vegas, a combination of hidden secrets and outright flamboyance, the optimism that hopes for a better deal and the pragmatism that plays the hand that's dealt.

His life, at first glance, seemed to be one of superficial excess, but that is to deny his deep sense of stewardship. He said that the many acquisitions of his life had been placed in his care to look after and share with the world. When he saw a broken chair, an unwanted dog, or a forgotten antique, each cried out to him to be cared for and saved. His religious convictions did not waver throughout his life. Even factoring in record-setting performances from Radio City Music Hall to Soldier Field (what I would give to tell people that I heard Liberace at Soldier Field), Liberace considered meeting the pope the highlight of his life. The photo capturing his encounter with His Eminence hangs on the wall of the museum and states, in tender words that you just *know* he composed, "His Holiness John Paul II lovingly imparts his Apostolic Blessing to Lee Liberace."

As our museum guide said of Liberace's predilection for pianos, "he liked big ones and small ones," so could the same be said of most of the realms of his life. His loves were many and varied, traditional and queer, manly and effeminate, overt and private, ranging from costumes to cars, religion to rhinestones, hillbilly boys (as his mother called them) hidden in closets to papal blessings piously displayed. While wandering the museum Liberace, the artifacts seem at once contradictory and harmonious, unknown and (wink-wink) known all too well, unpretentious and gaudy, over the top and absolutely understated.

He loved to tell his critics that they made him cry—all the

way to the bank. Yet he used much of his fortune to further the careers of aspiring artists through the Liberace Foundation for the Performing and Creative Arts. He inspires me. If I ever get married in Las Vegas, I plan to have my rehearsal dinner, bachelor party, and reception right there at the Liberace Museum Showroom. Perhaps we'll even throw in the sacred ceremony as well. My bride and I could arrive in his rhinestone-encrusted Cabriolet, while adorned with matching sequined hot pants. The bishop could wear just what a bishop normally wears, which is flamboyant enough, if you ask me.

Toward the end of the reception I would raise a toast not only to the master musician but to the man who really made him what and who he was. That is, Liberace's glazier, the formidably and appropriately named John Hancock (wink-wink). A glazier is to glass what Liberace is to ivories. A great glazier is not only a construction professional, but a true artist who knows everything there is to know about this crystalline sand that once littered a desert or a beach and now provides illumination both within and without. Mere windows were child's play for Liberace's glazier. If Liberace were Dustin Hoffman in *The Graduate* that "one word" he would have heard would not have been *plastics*. It would have been *rhinestones*. Hancock covered more automobiles with rhinestones than any glazier in human history. In fact, Hancock covered more of everything with rhinestones than any other glazier in human history.

One of Hancock's monumental creations in the Liberace Museum is the Rhinestone Roadster, adorned with enough sparkle to match the Ice Blue costume and Rhinestone Baldwin Grand piano that Liberace wore and played for his 1986 Radio City Music Hall finale. The roadster comes complete with Chevy 350 engine *and* a rhinestone toolbox should it need repair. Another stellar example is the 1970 Volkswagen Beetle that looks like a Rolls-Royce. Hancock covered the whole vehicle with etched mirrored tiles. And I must also mention the gold-flecked auto complete with silver candelabras attached to the sides, added so that when Liberace picked up his laundry like a regular guy, everyone would know that this was no regular guy picking up his laundry. I am not sure which sacred relic in the museum imparts more spiritual wisdom—the family Bible opened to the book of Proverbs or the rhinestone-covered construction hard hat. Both reveal beautiful truth.

The museum's contradictory and complementary uniqueness is highlighted by its location in a common Las Vegas strip mall on East Tropicana Boulevard, far off the tourist trail. What a surprise it is, upon entering the common-looking strip center, to find before you the most uncommon collection on the planet.

The unanticipated exhilaration the pilgrim encounters reminds me of the time my father took me to the Houston Livestock Show and Rodeo to see a performance by Gomer Pyle. I loved Gomer Pyle. His unsophisticated southern humor and artless antics made me laugh out loud. Sure enough, after the bronco riding, steer roping, and calf scramble had all ended, the lights dimmed in the cavernous Astrodome, and out onto the dirt floor marched my hero Gomer Pyle. After we all joined in a hearty chorus of "Gaaawleeeee," "Shazaaaaaaam," and "Surprise, surprise, surprise," the surprise was on us unsuspecting costumed cowboys with dime-store holsters and rhinestone shirts. Some sophisticated dude had body-snatched Gomer Pyle right there in the Astrodome! I thought it was a demon, but the lady next to me said it was his "Inner Jim

Nabors" shining through. This eerie creature began to belt out operatic overtures on par with Luciano Pavarotti. I exited the rodeo that night a more cognizant, if somewhat confused, cowboy, asking my nine-year-old self, "What the hell was that?" Gomer Pyle is Jim Nabors, and Jim Nabors is Gomer Pyle. Suddenly the Holy Trinity was not nearly so far-fetched, and, for a brief moment, religion made all the sense in the world.

At the Liberace Museum, after one wanders the temple grounds, one finally draws near to the Holiest of Holies. For there is one objet d'art that is the Holy Grail, the Blarney Stone, and the *Mona Lisa* of the entire collection, all rolled into one dazzling display. It is the world's largest rhinestone, 115,000 karats of pure lead glass lovingly crafted and gratefully bestowed upon our man Walter by the Swarovski Gem Company from Vienna, home of the small but delicious sausage that is also composed entirely of sand. Upon first sight of that glistening, glittering, explosion of pure light, I wanted to bow, genuflect, touch, kiss, laugh, weep, worship, and whisper witty innuendo all at the same time. I do not know that I have ever in my entire life experienced within myself such a synthesis of sheer joy, skeptical awe, and bemused bewilderment.

A man from the East Coast lurked near the rhinestone. He came from a place where they do not name their theaters after brewers of beer or their museums after flamboyant entertainers. He scowled and remarked, with a lack of insight I have previously only witnessed in an atheist confronted by the creation most revelatory of God's existence, the platypus, "I don't think so. This is all just a little too gaudy for me."

He may as well have admitted that he was not in possession of his own soul. The word *gaudy* is generally understood to be adapted from older French, English, and Latin words that mostly refer to something shiny, bright, playful, joyful, and even illuminating. Even after all these years, the word still functions in certain British collegiate settings as a term meaning "rejoicing," "partying," or "festival." In other words, it could very well refer to a major religious feast day! Such as Easter, for example.

It doesn't get any more over the top or outrageous than the shiniest, brightest, most playful, joyful, and illuminating moment in religious history. It doesn't get any more unbelievable than a Risen Lord laughing his way all the way to the top by way of a tomb. There is still a gaudy glimmer of radiant resurrection light that emanates from deep within me whenever I imagine Liberace standing in the parking lot of that strip center on East Tropicana Boulevard on Easter Sunday of 1979 wearing a checkered pink, yellow, and blue jacket with matching yellow slacks and yellow shirt. He had a giant gold pectoral cross dangling around his neck and his outstretched fingers were adorned with six diamond rings. He welcomed those guests who had come to see the new repository of all that glittered in his life, work, ministry, and play—everything that had joyful meaning to him. He told the amazed throngs, "I don't usually wear diamonds in the afternoon, but this is a special occasion."

Easter often is.

Regarding this gaudiest of days, I am particularly mindful of one early Easter morning when the sun was just beginning to peek over the hills to the east of St. James Episcopal Church in Austin. A long Holy Week would finally culminate in joy made manifest with shiny trumpets, blooming flowers, and radiant, gold-trimmed vestments. Desperately in need of caffeine, I was still fumbling with my keys as I stumbled upon a human figure completely enshrouded in a gold blanket and wedged up against the church's front door. This was not the sight I had anticipated on such a fine Easter morn.

Blond hair, blue eyes, unshaven face, and big smile slowly emerged from the gold blanket. The stranger was squinting toward the still rising sun when he said, "Good morning, Father. Happy Easter to you."

"Oh great," I thought. "This is just what I need on my busiest feast day in the entire liturgical year." I knew exactly how this scenario would play out. Been there. Done that. Too many times. He would regale me with a hard-luck tale of woe and blatantly ask me if I might spare some cash so that he could gamble it away on his hard-luck lifestyle. As he arose and began to gather up his few belongings, I decided I would cut my losses and cut to the chase.

"So, what can I do for you this morning?" I asked directly, as I already started to reach for my wallet, pull out twenty bucks, and be done with it.

"Oh, nothing really," he said, waving his fingers through his golden mane. "What can I do for *you*?" he then wondered.

This was not going according to plan, so I proceeded to try to go ahead and get to where I knew we'd end up anyway.

"I mean, do you *need* anything today? Can I *give* you anything?"

He looked at me with a gaze that I would swear contained some sort of intimate knowledge and unconditional love and responded, "No, not really. Do *you* need anything?"

I gave up and invited him in for a cup of coffee and the use of our restroom. "I sure do appreciate that, Father," he said. "I know this is a real busy and special day for you."

I plugged in the coffeepot and went into the church to make sure all of those extra decorations and over-the-top adornments were in their proper place. It was a very special day, after all. Just a few minutes later, my Altar Guild directress and right-hand woman, Hortense Lawson, appeared on the scene.

"Did you see that guy?" I asked, wondering where he might be hiding himself.

"What guy?" she asked.

I told her about the blond guy sleeping in the gold blanket who was wedged against the door early on Easter morning and that he was probably in the restroom, that is, if he hadn't already robbed us blind while I wasn't paying attention. I was a bit fearful as I ran off to find him. I looked in every room. He was nowhere to be seen. I ran outside and looked down the street. All I saw was the brightest, most blindingly golden sunrise I have ever seen in my entire life. I walked back into the church and uttered that statement I often utter when confronted with something so holy and unreal that I don't even begin to get it: "What the hell was that?"

Mrs. Lawson encouraged me to take some time off after Easter. She said she was a bit worried about me and that perhaps I was overworked and tired. She wondered if I might need to go back to Las Vegas to get some rest and get grounded so that I might stop testing reality and seeing a revelation in every mirage.

So I went back to Las Vegas. I keep going back, and I keep

rediscovering that the old maxim is partly true: All that glitters is not gold.

But sometimes it is.

And other times, it is worth even more.

The Liberace Museum, sadly, closed its doors on October 17, 2010—a visible reminder that all that glitters is often underappreciated.

23

ABOUT THE BEER

Take one down. Pass it around.

—"NINETY-NINE BOTTLES OF BEER ON THE WALL," DRINKING SONG

Blessed are those who hunger and thirst for righteousness,
for they shall be filled.

—MATTHEW 5:6

He is the most interesting man in the monastery. During papal visitations, the pope kisses *his* ring. At the end of his prayers, a voice from heaven frequently responds, "Can I do anything else for you?" Around him, Protestants genuflect, puritans imbibe, fundamentalists appreciate ambiguity, and nuns develop peculiar habits. His dogs are named Poverty, Chastity, and Guess Again. He does not always drink beer, but when he does, he drinks Chimay. And he frequently ends services with this benediction: Stay thirsty for righteousness, my friends. Amen.

His name is Armand Veilleux. He is the abbot of Scourmont Abbey in Belgium, a monastery known more for its beer than its piety. Scourmont Abbey is my mother ship. Some people travel halfway around the world to bend over backward to kiss the Blarney Stone. I travel halfway around the world to bend over frontward, genuflect, and place on my lips the sacramental bottle called Chimay. Knowing that one of the best beers in the world is brewed within the cloister walls of a house of prayer somehow makes everything right with the world. Here the doors are locked at dusk and visitors observe silence along with the rest of the brothers—that is, when they are not engaged in the fervent worship of the Source of *all* creation, including barley and hops.

The Chimay tasting room and restaurant is reserved for tourists. The monastery is reserved for pilgrims. There is a big difference between the two types of travelers. Tourists drink and pray. Pilgrims pray and drink. My hosts, the family of the Reverend Kempton Baldridge, who had just driven halfway across the country to bring me to this holy place, sat outside the restaurant with me and their golden retriever, Max, and enjoyed every sample of beer and cheese it had to offer. I finished off my feast with a giant meatball, stuffed with cheese, wrapped in bacon, and drenched in gravy that incarnated God's love and grace. Just beyond our table, the cows grazed happily on a thick grass sandwich. Max lounged lazily in the brilliant sun, praying for a morsel of meatball, if not a sip of beer. There I had the privilege of conversing with people who are kind, interesting, and interested. I knew at that moment that I was very close to the Kingdom of God.

Just a few feet away and around the corner was Scourmont Abbey, where I hoped not only to pray and drink, but to meet the most interesting man in the monastery. The only person I encountered who spoke any English, a fellow pilgrim and minister from Quebec, told me that waiting to meet with Armand was like waiting for the Second Coming of Christ. I'd best be patient and not get my hopes up. The chances of actually meeting up with him in my lifetime were on par with attending Bible study with Osama bin Laden. Even so, I made myself at home at the monastery. And waited. And prayed. And drank.

There the goodness of creation and the goodness of the religious institution came together in one place, each lending meaning to the other. The celestial chanting of the monks in a language not of my world echoed through the vast, high-vaulted church. In the woods and nearby gardens, saintly statuary greets and accompanies pilgrims who walk and pray. All is conversation between earth and heaven.

This is how I take my church, no sugar and real cream. I like it less as a familiar slap on the back, and more a mysterious elevating force. Worship at the abbey was ensconced in the context of transcendence, yet interspersed with reminders of the immanent. It is to worship with an awareness that God is indeed above and beyond, yet completely close by, occupying our most human moments.

As the monks sang with their lips, I sang with my heart—at a level just above, beyond, and below. In such moments we come to realize that even if you can't quite pronounce or memorize the literal lyrics, you can hum along from the center of your being. The meaning resonates much deeper than the note.

Since I spoke and understood nothing of the language, I was content to be inspired by the charity of gestures, bodily acts that communicate eternal truth. We stood. We sat. We knelt. We bowed. We crossed. We reached. We embraced. We received. We gave. We ate. We drank. We tasted. We saw. We smelled candle wax as ancient as the finest brewer's yeast, with hints of incense and perhaps even malt.

The brothers smiled. I smiled back. Brother Jacques, who reminded me of a rodeo clown in an old French comedy, shook his head as he straightened another brother's uneven stole of the wrong color. He rolled his eyes, smirked, and winked at me, as if to say, Even the professionals are amateurs when it comes to our attempts to honor God.

The dining room was as revelatory as the church, if not more so. Guests are served first and are fed well. Meals are simple and satisfying. Breakfast consists of bread, jam, cheese, fruit, and coffee. Lunch is hearty, with each of the three major food groups represented: meat, potatoes, and gravy. Dinner is healthy, heavy on the soup and vegetables. The food is fine, but it is the beverage selection that sets this dining room apart, conveying the consumer toward the heavenly sphere. With every meal, at every place setting, above and to the right of the fork, there is a beer. That's right, a single bottle of Chimay adorns every placemat. At my first lunch, the dear sister sitting next to me broke her vow of silence only to ask, "Want my beer?"

I broke my vow of silence by responding, "Is the pope German?" (He was at the time!)

My patience, persistence, and prayers eventually paid off. On my final afternoon at the abbey, Brother Jacques told me, through our Canadian translator, that the abbot would meet with me after supper. I asked where I would find him. Brother Jacques looked at me like I had just asked him where I would find the casino, and said, through the now-animated Canadian, "*He* will find you! You just stay right where you are." Of course, one does not approach the most interesting man in the monastery; he finds you, in his time, on his terms, in his way. Reminds me of the One for whom he works.

I had prepared a list of insightful and revealing questions for the abbot: What is the historical relationship between the abbey and the brewery? Has anyone ever substituted Chimay for the wine at Holy Communion? If you had to choose between a vow of celibacy and a life without beer, what would it be? Do French girls ever become nuns? Can you recommend one as my spiritual director? I noticed at lunch today that some of the guests did not drink their beer. Will they be banished to eternal damnation? And finally, may I have another beer?

He found me all right. And he led me beyond two sets of double doors, into his inner sanctum, to a place off-limits to most pilgrims and all tourists. I knew at that moment how those Levitical priests must have felt whenever they entered the Holiest of Holies. I wanted to genuflect. Or kneel. Or buy him a beer.

He asked me to be seated and said he would return momentarily. I was nervous. I felt like an awkward adolescent on a first date, with the hottest girl in school, at a fine French restaurant, where I did not speak the language. When he returned, all of my anxieties melted away. He was carrying a Chimay tray, and on it were two Chimay beers, two Chimay glasses, one Chimay bottle opener, and a bowl of potato chips. Immediately, I knew what he was up to. After all, I own a bar. He was plying me with salty snacks so I would order more beer. Still I played, and drank, along.

He began to tell me the story of Chimay and Scourmont Abbey. As it turned out, the story neither began nor ended as I had anticipated. That is true of most stories about holy people and holy places. He pointed out that in that part of the world beer has been the beverage of choice for centuries. "In Belgium as it is in heaven," I chimed in. He said that there is nothing unusual about drinking beer and serving God, or even about brewing beer and serving God. One man's "weird" is another man's "normal," he proclaimed. Not wanting to be weird, I proceeded to drink my beer.

He told me about a favorite abbot who had preceded him some time ago. He was a man of great spiritual depth with a practical concern for the world. The surrounding area at the time was quite poor, and the majority of the neighbors were considered to be ignorant peasants by some. This particular abbot made it his priority to establish educational programs at the monastery so that the locals would learn all the skills they needed to find God and to find jobs, not necessarily in that order. Then the monastery began to assist the local farmers in establishing farming cooperatives. They proceeded to broaden their concern to become a center for all types of social services. Over time, Scourmont Abbey became a veritable Department of Education, Agriculture, and Health and Human Services, not unlike the ancient Celtic monasteries, which may not have been all things to all people, but were many things to many people. This is how monks roll, how they discern God's will for their ministries. If something needs to be done to help people and no one else is doing it, the monks do it! Works for me. But what about the beer, I wondered.

About fifteen years ago, he said, the monastery realized that, with the brewery, they possessed a huge economic power, producing revenue far in excess of what the monks would ever need to carry out their local ministries. So they made provision for the brewery to be spun off as a nonprofit foundation with the same philosophy concerning the importance of hard work and the value of human relationships. Specifically, the foundation was to focus on the needs of the economically disadvantaged, not only locally, but globally.

I was so moved that I suggested the following slogans:

1. Drink a Beer. Feed a Child

2. Beer Changes Things

3. The More You Sip, the More We Serve

4. Beer—It's Not Just for Breakfast at the Monastery Anymore

5. Tap into Transforming the World

The abbot was mildly amused but pointed out that they already had their slogan, printed on the labels of most of their beer: "Beer brewed with art is drunk with wisdom." You had me at "Beer." A beautiful sentiment. And I was feeling smarter with every sip.

The brewery is still on the grounds of the monastery; he asked if I had even noticed it. I had not. It is in the background, he told me, and that would become his sermonic theme: Beer in the Background. The quality, he bragged, was the same as it ever was, although modern technology is now utilized in the process. He said that sometimes people are disappointed that the monk's mysticism is now infused with action and engineering advances and marketing ploys, but brewing beer is much harder work than anyone realizes.

He paused to take a swallow of Chimay White, not quite in the same category as Chimay Blue, which is aged for up to

fifteen years. (Note: Chimay comes in red, white, and blue—
so not only is drinking Chimay a spiritual experience, it is also
my patriotic duty as an American, as it is for every other citizen whose flag bears those colors.) He admonished me that
this is not a beer to gulp but to enjoy, not a beverage with
which to get drunk, but to savor—that Chimay is not about
the quantity, but about the quality. Then he stopped preachin'
and went to meddlin', calling American beer "cat piss." That's
right. The abbot of Scourmont Abbey called American beer
"cat piss." I was not going to argue, for he alone knew where
our next round might come from.

"Oui, oui," I quickly agreed. If there was one thing I had
learned about these Belgians, it was that you do not doubt
their determination, degustation, and observations about uri-
nation. The best-known statue in all of Belgium is called
"Manekin Pis," and it is precisely what it sounds like. Copen-
hagen has its little mermaid. Brussels has its little boy pissing
in the wind. But I get it. Beer has implications for behavior
that we previously have taken for granted, bodily functions
that should be celebrated if not commemorated.

The abbot was obviously very proud of their product. He
proceeded to tell me a joke about a convention of brewery ex-
ecutives, all gathered at the airport, all waiting for the same
plane. The three representatives, one from Heineken, one from
Carlsberg, and one from Chimay, all meet up and decide to
detour for a preflight beverage at the airport lounge. The
Heineken representative speaks up first, telling the bartender,
"First round is on me—three Heinekens, please!" They each
down a Heineken.

The Carlsberg representative then jumps in: "This round is on
me—three Carlsbergs, please!" They all drink their Carlsbergs.

Finally, the Chimay representative turns to the bartender and says, "This round is on me—three Pepsi-Colas, please!" The two other beer reps are aghast and demand to know what he thinks he is doing by ordering such a lightweight beverage.

"Oh," the Chimay executive explains, "it's still too early to drink *beer!*"

The abbot admits, "This is not very humble, is it?" But as Dizzy Dean once said, "It ain't braggin' if you can do it."

At Chimay they can do it, and they have been doing it for a long time. They've been brewing with the same yeast for fifty years, and their sole water source is a local aquifer that is painstakingly protected for perpetuity. They allow no pesticides to be used on the land above, and they have even dug an extensive moat around the land just in case a truck overturns and there is a fuel spill. "You see," he says, "if something is done with love and care, there will be a good result."

All royalties from the brewery, 100 percent, are given away to charity. In fact, that is one major condition for being labeled a Trappist ale—that a majority of the income generated is given away for the good of others. The second stipulation is that Trappist ale must be brewed on monastery grounds. There are specific conditions and expectations that must be met if you are going to call yourself by a certain name or link yourself with a certain location. As in brewing so it is in religion. You can't just brew any beer and claim that it is Trappist ale any more than you can do anything and claim that you are a Christian. Showing up at the monastery or the church and giving away most of your proceeds to the poor would be a good start for an authentic ale, as well as for a real Christian. He tells me that the other true Trappist ales are Westmalle,

Orval, Rochefort, Westvleteren, Achel, and Le Trappe. I now have my bucket list.

He settled into his chair, becoming increasingly aware that I was not out to steal his trade secrets, confiscate his beer, or try to portray him as something or someone he is not. He asked me about my life, my dog, my writing, my church, and my beer preferences. He told me a joke about a woman on an airplane who lands only to find that her dog is frozen. Something got lost in the translation, but I laughed anyway because I found it quite funny how much airplane humor had worked its way into the abbot's routine. I wondered if perhaps I had finally endeared myself to him, if I was approaching that level of intimacy reached by the "disciple whom Jesus loved," the one who put his head on Jesus's chest at the Last Supper. This apostle was thought to have founded the Celtic approach to Christianity. He was the one who listened for the heartbeat of God. I realized that even if he thought I was Peter, and I had come by way of Rome rather than Dublin, I had arrived. For he asked the question for which I had been waiting all my life: "Would you like to try a Blue?" Twist my stole.

As we slowly drank our Blues, he reiterated that he is not a brewmaster or a CEO; he is an abbot. He affirmed that his primary interests are prayer, study, welcoming guests, worship, outreach, education, and economic assistance. In the end, what he really wants to do is make the world a better place.

"One beer at a time," I offered.

He told me that his secretary spends most of her time helping people get connected and improve their lot in life, whatever their need, such as the Algerian he has hiding in the monastery, even as we speak.

"Shh," he whispered to me, as he held a finger to his lips. In the most shocking revelation thus far, he told me that beer was not a major part of his life, although he certainly liked beer, and if he was entertaining guests he would certainly have one.

"Or two," I said, pointing at his Blue.

He told the story of a former abbot who was a large man and a diabetic and could not even drink beer, but he allowed himself to be photographed with a beer in what became the most viewed photograph in Chimay's history. Ironically, the teetotaling abbot became the poster child for Trappist ale! This is why, he said, he will not allow himself to be photographed with a bottle of beer and why he no longer grants interviews to journalists. "They will focus only on the beer," he proclaimed, as he took another appreciative taste of Chimay Blue. I began to focus only on the beer, since it was worthy of my undivided attention.

"I am a man of the spirit, concerned about spiritual things," he added. He told me that even though church attendance might be dwindling, people are seeking an experience of God more than ever, for their number of seekers on retreat continues to rise. "People are hungry for God," he observed. "And thirsty for beer," I almost added, but refrained. His sermon drew to a close, reiterating that our ultimate quest is not about filling the gut, but satisfying the soul, not about squeezing the most profit from every barrel, but about brewing with great care and love, doing our very best, and giving the proceeds away to those who are truly in need. It is not about sitting on our asses and getting drunk. It is about getting off our asses and making a difference, utilizing whatever gifts and resources we have been given and giving back. It is about taking one down and passing it around. In the end, it is about sharing what God has entrusted to us.

I recognized toward the end of our time together, a time measured by only two beers (in American time, that would have been a case), that I had come to love and appreciate this man—his laugh, his sense of humor, his kindness, his depth, his wisdom. I appreciated his perspective, his priorities, his motivation, and his willingness to stand up, walk to the other room, and get me another beer. I thanked him profusely for his time, his story, his ministry, his beer.

"Just remember," he concluded, with words that bordered on blasphemy yet rang so true that I will recall them for the rest of my days, "it's not about the beer."

It's not about the beer.

—

George MacLeod would probably agree with Armand Veilleux. After all, he was the second most interesting man in a monastery a few thousand miles and one religious tradition away. MacLeod was a Scottish Presbyterian minister, soldier, pacifist, ecumenist, humanist, statesman, and thorn in the side of the religious establishment, as well as the nonreligious establishment. He was founder of the religious community that rebuilt the old Celtic abbey on the sacred island of Iona. MacLeod was a passionate advocate for the connection between faith and action, believing that any spirituality worth its salt moved way beyond the realm of the theoretical, mystical, or even theological and planted itself firmly on the highways and byways of life, in the details, busyness, and ongoing activities of the world. MacLeod would probably have argued that one can learn far more about the soul by serving in a soup kitchen than by retreating to an ashram, that the prayers prayed at a monastery would be answered only by engaging the hard work of transforming the stuff of creation into something that people can see, experience, or taste, and that true religion always does some good for the world outside the walls, with the proceeds profiting all.

Like James in the New Testament, who preceded him, MacLeod believed that "faith without works is dead," and like Martin Luther King Jr., who followed him, that life's ultimate question is simply this: "What are you doing for others?" Mac-Leod also maintained that just because organized religion was a mess, that was no reason to abandon it, just as, though people are a mess, it is no reason to abandon them. Despite the imperfections of the institution, one should keep showing up, darkening the door with our shadows as well as our light, to say one's prayers, to eat and drink and be reminded of our collective call and identity, to continue to join forces in such a community that he called "a chaos of uncalculating love."

MacLeod believed that true spirituality is to drink deeply from the well of real life in the real world, to sink one's teeth into the matters that matter for most people; he stated un-equivocally that "painstaking service to humankind's most ma-terial needs is the essence of Christian spirituality." He loved to tell the story of the little boy who stood on a street just outside and threw a rock through the stained-glass window of the Church of the Incarnation. The rock nicked the letter *e* out of the opening shout from a hymn of praise in the stained glass, changing "Glory to God in the Highest!" to "Glory to God in the High st." It was there on the High Street, and on *all* the busy streets of Glasgow, that MacLeod would proclaim that

God is most glorified. It is "outside the camp" even "outside holiness, out to where soldiers gamble, and thieves curse" where faith is ultimately found, fashioned, developed, and deepened.

The beauty of MacLeod's theology is that he engaged in advocating social change and social service all while maintaining the most delightful sense of humor, a necessary quality for anyone who desires to change the world and maintain one's sanity at the same time. If one is truly serious about spirituality, one understands the serious pitfalls of spiritual solemnity. The true agent of change recognizes that it is only when we laugh, and cause others to do the same, that we get a good whiff of spirit and that we inhale the immanent presence of our joy-inducing God.

Although his heavenly humor was certainly not in the same league or at the same altitude as that which originated at Scourmont Abbey, MacLeod could hold his own in the realm of holy hilarity. He frequently asked his fellow clergy why Presbyterian pastors preach longer sermons than those of any other ministers, offering that they don't; it just "seems that way." In 1998, when MacLeod was in his nineties, he visited the newly built MacLeod Centre for International Reconciliation, on the island of Iona. It is said that when he entered the great room, he stood still and began to recite the Lord's Prayer. Suddenly, all those gathered bowed their heads respectfully and reverently. MacLeod abruptly stopped praying and admonished the much-too-pious assembly: "I was just testing the acoustics!"

MacLeod was also known, just before radio broadcasts of his sermons from Iona, to place raw fish on the monastery grounds to attract seagulls. Just as MacLeod began his profound observations from the holy island, the sound of seagulls serenading would convey the deep sense of presence of the spirit through the natural world. You just know that Mac-Leod's inner prankster enjoyed every moment of that overhead squawking, another element of his belief that God enlists our most creative and active efforts to achieve God's purposes in the world. And that often, such collaboration yields a smile, if not a chuckle.

Someday I hope that I might enter such a pantheon of interesting people, such men as dare to take the matter of their lives and do something that matters in the lives of others. Men who brew the finest beer and give away the proceeds and dare to proclaim that it's not even about the beer. Men who link prayer and action, who envision and even create communities that "love kindness, do justice, and walk humbly with their God."

If I am ever to become a truly interesting man, it will not be because of what I tear down, but because of what I build up. It will not be because of what I believe, but because of what I do. It will not be because of how many beers that I drink, but because of how many beers that I share.

Take one down.

Pass it around.

Stay thirsty for righteousness, my friends.

24

THIS PRIEST WALKS INTO A BAR

The search for meaning is the search for the lost chord.

—P. J. CURTIS, IRISH RHYTHM-AND-BLUES AUTHORITY

I want a drink of that water that the man turned into wine.

—JOHNNY BUSH

*S*o, this priest walks into a bar. Although it may be funny, it is no joke. I own a bar and live music venue called Padre's in the tiny West Texas desert town of Marfa, in the middle of nowhere. It is important to remember that, in humanity's ongoing search for meaning, one man's nowhere is another man's somewhere. One person's vast, barren nothingness is another person's limitless, inspiring somethingness. One man's dust is another man's gold. Add in cool, high desert weather, big starry skies, and the best sunsets that side of Hawaii, and you have described my home away from home—Marfa, Texas.

Marfa originally gained fame as a movie and modern art Mecca. Elizabeth Taylor, James Dean, and Rock Hudson all bunked at the historic Hotel Paisano while filming the classic

Giant. More recently *No Country for Old Men* and *There Will Be Blood* found the austere setting to be cinematically conducive. Several decades earlier, the godfather of minimalist art, Donald Judd, moved to Marfa and turned an old cavalry fort into minimalism's happy place, Chinati, named after the mountains in the distance toward Mexico. His former house and studio, the Block, is within a beer bottle's toss of Padre's.

Marfa embraces an interesting assortment of humanity—a mostly Mexican and Mexican-American population, with a few cowboys, ranchers, hipsters, hikers, bikers, writers, artists, retirees, and little old ladies thrown in for good measure. It is not uncommon to be standing in line at the Dairy Queen waiting for a Peanut Buster Parfait (further proof that God loves us), sandwiched between a black-clad German art critic and a dude wearing real spurs on his boots, not to make a fashion statement, but because he needs them to do his day job. Marfa may be the smallest town in America with its own National Public Radio station, and certainly the only NPR town whose high school football team is called the Shorthorns. Although that may be funny, if you know your cattle, you will know that is no joke, either.

Padre's is housed in a one-hundred-year-old adobe building that was formerly a feed store, carriage house, and, for almost seventy years, the Memorial Funeral Home of Marfa. It is one of those buildings that look like a sacred space, regardless of what sobering activities have taken place inside. The place greatly resembles a Spanish mission, with white stucco exterior, a trinity of indented arches adorned with black wrought-iron bars, and a red-tile roof. We had already bought the building and named our new establishment when we were stunned to discover that, years before, there was a beer brewed in California called Padres Beer, whose advertising emblem was a Spanish mission. We tracked down a vintage can and saw emblazoned upon it a dead ringer for our building—another sign that God moves in mysterious ways.

The first building we tried to buy in Marfa was the former Lighthouse Baptist Church. According to our Realtor, the good pastor and people of the Lighthouse Baptist Church had decided to pack up and move because there were too many sinners moving into Marfa—you know, people whose sexual orientations, political affiliations, and religious associations were suspect. She also revealed that there were rumors of a sex tape involving some of the good Christian people of the congregation. As the Bible says, "Let he who claims to be without sin cast the first Internet posting of pornography, blame it on someone else, and get the hell out of Dodge." So, the Baptists moved on to higher and drier ground. Fortunately, we got outbid on the building—a blessing since the place had all the soul of a double-wide trailer covered in concrete blocks, or of a sound track to a certain type of video, popular on the Internet, even among Baptists.

Thank God we eventually discovered the adobe gem, which as a former funeral home had more soul than we could say Rosary over. The layout was perfectly suited to use as a live music venue and bar. The chapel became the performance space, adorned with the original pews. The bad news was that the building was structurally unsound, requiring the hiring of an engineer, the erection of a solid steel structure that was attached to the stripped-down adobe skeleton, and the unanticipated investment of a significant amount of financial capital. The good news was that this new design allowed us to raise the roof by fifteen feet and add clerestory windows that gave the main room the transcendent feel of a cathedral, appropriate for what we hoped would become the Mother Church of Texas Music—St. Waylon and Willie's.

We added antique chandeliers from a Spanish church, a red velvet curtain that had adorned the stage of the Alpine (Texas) Middle School Auditorium, stunning tiled arches to hold a variety of spirits, a one-of-a-kind bar built out of the original hundred-year-old hardwood floor, and a black matador with red cape keeping watch from the top shelf—a longtime friend who had kept vigil in my parents' living room since childhood. We fashioned the dining tables out of old shuffleboard tops and unearthed a bunch of vintage jukeboxes and pinball machines to turn the back room garage into a true Texas icehouse. Finishing touches included stained-glass benches for the courtyard that were designed by the same artist who created the Moore Window at Trinity Church Chapel, a giant metal sculpture from Mexico featuring a guitar playing señor, "Padre Pedro," and an original Kinky Friedman for Governor poster that he had signed "To Bill: They Ain't Makin' Jews Like Jesus Anymore!" The final product was a watering hole that felt like it had been hosting full-immersion baptisms since John the Baptist was a boy.

Sometimes people ask me, "Why do you own a bar?" In the words of the aforementioned Kinky Friedman, *"Why the hell not!"*

As I get older, I find myself quoting Kinky with increasing frequency. In fact, some have suggested that perhaps I am to the priesthood what Kinky is to politics. His campaign slogans included "How Hard Can It Be?" and "No Cow Left Behind." He was the only candidate in the race who supported *both* public prayer in schools *and* gay marriage. Kinky got 16 percent of the vote, which is about 15 percent more than I would get should I ever run for bishop.

Padre's began as the creative yen of a mostly untalented, wannabe musician who also wanted to be able to drink for free. However, when I now calculate all that I have personally invested in the Padre's project, I figure every Shiner Bock I down costs me approximately a grand. At this rate, Padre's will be out of money long before I run out of beer.

I suppose I should have known that I was destined for weirdness in my clerical life when my buddies took me out to celebrate on the eve of my ordination—to a Village People concert! Why the hell not? It was, in retrospect, an appropriate and prophetic celebration since Padre's has become a gathering place for cowboys, Indians, cops, bikers, contractors, and the Border Patrol, not to mention every other character not covered by the Village People. Most of them like to dance and drink, and all of them like to party.

Occasionally, someone will criticize my dual citizenship and calling, as priest and bartender, churchman and bar owner. I happen to have an unusual combination of interests. I like music, beer, Marfa, Hawaii, God, Christians, sinners, sermons, stories, humor, truth, mystery, Holy Communion, and cheeseburgers. I have no qualms following what I perceive to be my call, even if it goes in more than one direction. Our respective journeys are not dictated by how well traveled or well mapped they might be. If our paths intersect or parallel, let us give thanks, learn from each other, and meet up at the next rest stop. If not, keep on moving in the direction in which you are guided.

There is an old spiritual that speaks to this truth, "I'm on My Way": "If you don't go, don't hinder me. If you don't go, don't hinder me. If you don't go, don't hinder me. I'm on my way, great God, I'm on my way!" Such an odyssey could be called individuation, self-actualization, bliss, meaning, or vocation, but in the end, it's just that thing that I do. And God is probably pleased, but at the least entertained.

Passion and purpose should not be confused with externally imposed expectations. Nor should they be supplanted by happiness and success, two deeply misunderstood and highly overrated pursuits. I am sometimes reminded of the story of the father of gospel music in America, Thomas A. Dorsey. Dorsey started out playing the blues in Ma Rainey's band before he finally found his true calling at the Pilgrim Baptist Church in Chicago. But not everyone appreciated his efforts to synthesize the syncopated rhythms of jazz and blues with the staid strains of standard hymns. The result of his call? As Dorsey said, "I have been thrown out of some of the finest churches in America!"

His greatest loss, and the real turning point of his life, came when his wife and newborn died during childbirth. Dorsey, stunned by such a turn of events, sat down at his piano and wrote one of the world's most profound hymns, "Take My Hand, Precious Lord," singing, "Lead me on. Let me stand."

Success and happiness? Not really.

Passion and purpose? Absolutely.

Thomas Dorsey played the music he heard and moved to the beat that he felt was God's. So, even in his bitterest and most disappointing moment, God took his hand, led him on, and let him stand.

—

One of the nicest things ever said about my writing ability fell far short of a ringing endorsement. Nonetheless, I'll take it. One Sunday after church, a gentleman, who spoke with a distinguished and distinctive British accent, admitted that he had just finished my first book, *The Gospel According to Sam*. The sentiment of Sam's gospel could be contained within a favorite statement by, who else, Kinky Friedman: "Money may buy you a fine dog, but only love can make him wag his tail!" This rather sophisticated academic had found something of value in Sam, and a modicum of talent in the one who had written it. He said to me, "Yes. You'll be reading along and, without warning or expectation, there are these *sudden bursts of literary merit.*"

Sudden bursts of literary merit! What a way to write. What a way to live. The honest-to-God truth is that I am highly inconsistent. I usually fall far short of what I could do or be or write, and I live out most of my days with unremarkable unremarkability. But if, by the grace of God, there are sudden bursts of brilliance or imagination or inspiration or insight, I wag my tail in appreciation.

I will celebrate all sudden bursts of literary merit. Sudden bursts of spiritual merit. Sudden bursts of creative merit. Sudden bursts of moral merit. Sudden bursts of Christian merit. Passion and purpose, direction from above, may not happen every day and every hour, but I'll take it when I can get it. And when I get it, I will give thanks!

Beyond such sudden bursts of passion and purpose, beyond our own self-actualization or individuation and the unique appropriation of our particular gifts, to live out the life to which God calls us is to invest in something beyond ourselves. It's not just about realizing my dreams, finding myself, or discerning my purpose. It's about taking a chance for the benefit of the world, about risking my hard-earned capital and investing in something that is way beyond what's in it for me.

Faith is sometimes flying by the seat of our pants, the giving of our last dime, or the utilization of wings we never knew we had. Led by God, we leap. Inspired by God, we invest. We squander all of our material and spiritual capital, not really knowing if there will ever be a return on our investment. But we pay the price anyway and believe that it might be worth it.

We did not invest so much money, love, time, sweat, stress, imagination, and hard work into Padre's just to turn a profit (which we haven't), or because we thought we might someday be famous or even appreciated (the jury is out on both counts). We engaged in this undertaking because we thought it was an interesting idea that might make a positive difference. We believe in the power of music, the renewing capacities of good food and strong drink, and the possibility of bringing people from all walks together in one place to celebrate life and create community.

One of our investors is a ninety-two-year-old widow who was the former chair of the Trinity Church Altar Guild. She invests in all sorts of things to make the world a better place. In fact, she is one of the most generous human beings I have ever known. Every time a kid in my church needs to go to camp, or we need to feed another hungry person, or raise any money for any cause, she sends us a check. She once told me that one of the things remaining on her bucket list was to invest in a bar. This is a woman who knows her single-malt Scotch as well as her multi-interest soul. She has heard the music and decided to sing along. Not only that, but she's willing to fork over the cover, and even pay the band!

She reminds me how important it is to dig deep to pay the price for the things that matter in this life, that the bottom line of what we think we have is not the bottom line of what we can do. One of our priorities at Padre's is to pay for what matters to us, whether we can afford it or not. Every summer I write a personal check to the Marfa Youth Baseball Association to support the Padre's Rock-N-Rollers—even when we're down to our last dime. Some things are worth more than a balanced checkbook.

One of the great tragedies of American society has been how little we value the artists who dwell among us, particularly those who play the music that speaks to the soul. As an owner of Padre's, whenever I am in town, I am given the following responsibilities: clean the toilets, weed the flower beds, pick up cigarette butts from the back patio, and work the door. The most depressing among those tasks? Work the door. It is at the door that I discover what cheapskates inhabit God's good earth. Every time I try to take the cover charges for a band and I have to deal with the thousand excuses as to why people don't want to pay, I want to put a dollar in one of those vintage jukeboxes and play Hank Williams's classic "There's a Tear in My Beer."

I have seen multitudes of people walk away and drive to the local convenience store and drink their six-pack in a parking lot rather than fork over three bucks to support a hardworking five-piece band. We rarely break even on live music at Padre's and we sometimes lose our financial assets, not to mention our asses, in support of a band we believe in, and believe people ought to hear. If there is anything that can save us, it is music. Here are the three commandments that may lead to our society's salvation and will, at the very least, keep our souls from shriveling up and blowing away:

1. Thou shalt always pay the cover, and do so cheerfully.

2. Thou shalt always tip the band, and buy their CD if one is available.

3. Thou shalt always support live music and those establishments that dare to feature it.

Count the cost. The music is worth it. And it's important to God.

Who knew that the bar business would teach me some of the most important spiritual lessons of my faith? Follow your heart. Pursue your God-given dream with passion and purpose, whether or not it makes you happy or successful. Listen for the music. Feel the deeper beat. Pay the cover. Invest in eternity, or at least in someone who went to the trouble to learn to play the accordion and who possesses the ability to motivate all of us to get up and dance.

Remember that it is not about you alone. The quest for meaning is not just about your personal vision. It is about learning to love one another, learning how to come together and work together and dance together and drink together, all for the cause of a common goal. Collaboration and reconciliation are values that withstand the test of time. The Bible and Beatles agree: We all get by with a little help from our friends. Even the Apostle Paul understood that it takes a team to transform the world, telling those dysfunctional partyers, known as the Church in Corinth, "I planted, Apollos watered; but God gave the increase." Someone has to plant. Someone has to water. Someone has to weed. Someone has to fertilize. And someone has to harvest. It takes a village of visionaries, investors, contractors, staff, and customers to raise up the best bar in Texas. And even so, success is never guaranteed.

Our stewardship of Padre's has never stopped at the front door of 225 West El Paso Street. We've tried to be good neighbors to everyone within shouting distance, even the local Catholic church. Before we applied for our liquor license, I was given the task of visiting with the nun who lives across the street from Padre's. I had been warned that Sister Rosa was "one tough hombre," not a description you hear every day about a nun. After making my peace with the parish priest, who was very kind and welcoming but told me he was "against the beer," which I interpreted as meaning he was "for the tequila," I said my prayers and knocked on the nunnery door.

Now, I know my nuns. I was taught to drink by my adopted Catholic family across the street. Growing up with them and going to all kinds of Catholic functions, I partied with all sorts of nuns. I drank my first beer playing bingo with nuns. I remember that I won seven dollars and a sausage—thanks to nuns. I have bowled with nuns. I have even danced with nuns. One of my favorite nuns taught me the Texas two-step. She was not only a nun, but a dance instructor. When I lived in Austin, a nun served as my spiritual director. She encouraged me to listen to the music, walk to a different beat, and drink quality beer. I even heard from her not long ago when her foundation for spiritual development was having a silent auction. She requested a Padre's gift certificate, which we happily supplied!

Sister Rosa did not request a Padre's gift certificate. I don't think she dances, and I know she doesn't drink. In fact, as far as I could tell, her standard response to every life-affirming activity is "Nun of the above." What I had heard was true—she was one tough hombre. Although she did not strike me with a ruler, I felt her judgmental criticisms land on me with the force of a sledgehammer. She questioned my values, my motives, my identity, and my drinking habits. Let's just say that I failed in "Operation Fun with Nun," and after meeting with the sister, I needed a drink. But in the end, the church did not formally oppose our liquor license, perhaps because they knew that their parishioners would be among our most frequent customers. God bless the Roman Catholic Church.

What I told Sister Rosa was the truth—we wanted to be a positive force in the community, to bring people together, to make a difference for good. We've tried to be true to that identity—supporting nonprofits in town, sponsoring a local soccer team, providing a place for fund-raisers for local charities, keeping our prices low on Lone Star every happy hour. And even if profit and providence don't align, that's okay.

At Padre's, we believe that all patrons are created equal. We do not believe in velvet ropes and reserved tables. We encourage our patrons, should they ever encounter such exclusive tendencies, to take their business elsewhere, like to Padre's. Padre's is one of the few places in the Big Bend region that draw every demographic, where divisions, at least for the first set, cease. It was a bold vision, and by the grace of God, and the goodwill of our investors and customers, it has mostly come to pass.

Padre's Grand Opening Weekend was an occasion to witness firsthand two of the great pillars of our faith: reconciliation and resurrection. It was a moment when my favorite prayer from the Easter Vigil seemed to come to pass right before my eyes:

> *O God of unchangeable power and eternal light: Let the whole world see and know that things which were cast down are being raised up, and things which had grown old are being made new, and that all things are being brought to their perfection by him through whom all things were made.*

All kinds of people came together to sing a new tune in a harmony that had heretofore been unheard. All kinds of music and beverages reaffirmed the diversity of God's good world. There was a resurrected space, new life for what had been a place to contemplate death. There was even a new voice from a great singer who had been without one for many years.

Texas legend Johnny Bush was the first performer to officially grace the Padre's stage. His story was really our story, a story about resilience and resurrection. Decades ago, Johnny Bush was one of the hottest names in country music. He had a rich, velvety voice combined with a superb vocal range that combined to create a stage and recording persona the people dubbed "the Country Caruso." At some point he lost his voice and his ability to share his gift. Johnny Bush had been silenced. Recently, thanks to advances in medical technology, Johnny Bush had found his voice and he could sing once more.

That magical Friday night, Johnny Bush took the Padre's stage and sang all his classic hits, including his own composition that had become Willie Nelson's theme song, the tune with which Willie begins virtually every concert, "Whiskey River." His voice was strong and solid and old and new at the same time, sharing such gems as "Tequila and Teardrops," "You Gave Me a Mountain," and "Undo the Right." He even added to his standard set list some favorites he had chosen just for the occasion, such as Willie Nelson's "Family Bible" and my personal favorite, "I Want a Drink of That Water That Jesus Turned into Wine." Johnny Bush had written that tune with his brother, a Baptist preacher. That night, the Baptists and the Catholics came together, to be reconciled and to celebrate resurrection, on the dance floor, and at the bar. I wish that happened more often.

The weekend's musical selection reflected the rich diversity of the region. On Saturday night, a local conjunto band, Grupo Exito, shook the adobe walls with an entire set sung in Spanish. On Sunday night, one of the best R&B and soul bands around shook more than a few booties. Element was composed mostly of guys from Chicago who now lived in Lubbock. Don't laugh. Lubbock has given the music world some true legends. Ever heard of Buddy Holly?

The highlight of the weekend was the blessing service and gospel show at high noon on Sunday. The place was packed with well-wishers, including a dozen souls who traveled all the way from Hawaii for the occasion. The blessing of Padre's was certainly not the first religious service conducted in a bar, but it may have been the first religious service presided over by a priest who owned the bar!

On that bright sunny Sunday, with beams of light breaking through the clerestory windows and shining down upon us all, I welcomed folks by quoting from the seventeenth-century journal of a Spanish explorer, who wrote of this region, "It contains steep places, dry places, few watering holes, and great distances. For this reason it cannot be inhabited nor populated by rational Christians." Here's to ironic, if not irrational, Christians who set out to make a dry place wetter, by adding one very important watering hole to the vast landscape!

The service began with a blessing prayer from the bishop of Texas, whose image was projected on the adobe walls. The service continued with prayers for the souls of the departed who had been buried from that place, offered by our contractor and his wife, a couple I had married years prior in Austin. Our gospel vocalists sang a "Requiem" in their memory. One of our founding partners read a passage from the Prophet Isaiah that speaks of a God who swallows up death and wipes away tears, who prepares a feast of rich food and well-matured wines for all people. His wife led us in a portion of Psalm 30, calling on the congregation to sing praises to the Lord, the One who has turned our morning into dancing, and clothed us with joy.

A member of St. Paul's Church in Marfa read a grace adapted from the Irish saint Brigit of Kildare:

> I should like a great lake of finest ale
> For the King of kings.
> I should like a table of the choicest food
> For the family of heaven.
> Let the ale be made from the fruits of faith,
> And the food be forgiving love.
> God bless our food.
> God bless our drink.
> All homes,
> All place, O God, embrace.

Not to be outdone, her husband, a recent Marfa transplant from the Smithsonian Institution, a man who still possessed his wonderful Fort Worth drawl, added a Celtic blessing from eighth-century Ireland giving thanks for music and mead.

The unofficial but dearly beloved poet laureate of Marfa even read a poem we had commissioned for the occasion. The poem was about a special woman he met when he had first moved to Marfa. She had shown great kindness to him and welcomed him to his new home with open arms. Her name was Miss Addy, and she gifted him with a small expression of her love, a crocheted wall hanging that read simply WELCOME. Years later, Miss Addy died, and the poet had attended her Rosary right there in the space that would become Padre's. Miss Addy had been a faithful member of the local Catholic church, and he felt that she would have welcomed us to Marfa with the same graciousness she had extended to him. He wrote:

I met Miss Addy
near a decade ago
The checkout line
at the Dollar Store
Her load was so big
and she so small
And she had a little
dog. So I insisted on
driving her home
She gave me a token
of her thanks. And I
became one of her
many friends. She

died in that time
and we prayed her
Rosary in the place.
Time hurries on and
someone comes along
and things that were
growing old are being
made new. Miss Addy
would say, It is good
What has been done
in the resurrection of
this dying place. She
would say Thank You
and Welcome to this
new home. A place of
song and dance and joy.
Take her token. Hang
it on yonder wall.

Welcome to Padre's.

The framed poem, along with Miss Addy's handmade WEL-COME hanging, now adorns the front entrance of Padre's. Al-though it is the first thing our patrons should see, I fear that most walk right past it, as they do with so much of God's most inspiring work and words—without seeing or appreciating them at all.

Our former manager and founding partner got the last word. He emerged from the kitchen wearing his John Wayne bandanna, work boots, and apron. With the fiery zeal of a fervent preacher, he exhorted the faithful with Psalm 150 to praise the Lord with the trumpet, lute, harp, tambourine, dance, and loud, crashing cymbals. Remember what the Bible says next time you think the music is too loud!

So we still praise God at Padre's, with every note and every toast. It is a sacred space where we celebrate and contemplate the musical and spiritual reality that a chord is composed of more than one note. And a song is composed of more than one chord. The solo show has its place, but it takes a band to fill the dance floor and to raise the roof.

Make a joyful noise unto the Lord.

But don't forget to tip the band.

—

Life and love go on. Let the music play.

—JOHNNY CASH

ACKNOWLEDGMENTS

Some names in this book were changed to keep everyone guessing. The following, however, are real.

Thank you to:

My dogs who have kept me reasonably sane over the years: Sam, Jack, and Wili.

My faith communities who have partied, prayed, and persevered like there is a tomorrow: the Youth Group of St. John the Divine, Houston (1986–1991), St. James Episcopal Church, Austin (1991–1999), Trinity Church, Houston (1999–2006), St. Michael and All Angels Episcopal Church, Lihue, Kauai (2006–present).

My editors Eileen O'Brien, Lauren Summerville, Amy Juhala, and Beth Adams at Howard Books, for reminding me that I am a priest and that priests can't say that.

My agent, Lee Gessner, who believed in me and my message.

Max Lewis for being a bold thirteen-year-old musician who rode his bike to Padre's one spring afternoon and asked to play a set, and for introducing me to his wonderful parents, Vince and Michelle, who have opened doors I never imagined I would walk through.

My family, for reminding me that God knows my name, especially Bill, Evelyn, Tom, Maelene, Chris, Jenni, Preston, Bailey, Rosemary, Hank, Freck, and Betty.

My good friends, with whom I am honored to share a beer, especially Bill, Rachel, Monica, Chuck, Jimmy, Miles, King, Margaret, Pat, Dana, Blake, Ryan, Jimmy, James, Lina, Jim, David, Matt, Randy, Mack, Everett, Todd, Ben, Jeff, Amy, Kevin P., Ken, Michael, Renaella, Kevin T., Fred, Steve, Bart, Jack, and Carolyn.

God, for creating beer.

Jesus, for including wine in the Lord's supper.

The Holy Spirit, for making life so interesting and enjoyable.

—WILLIAM B. MILLER, KAUAI, HAWAII, DECEMBER 10, 2013,

THE FEAST DAY OF THOMAS MERTON

"BE ANYTHING YOU LIKE, BE MADMEN, DRUNKS, AND BASTARDS OF EVERY SHAPE AND FORM, BUT AT

ALL COSTS AVOID ONE THING: SUCCESS."

—THOMAS MERTON